THE DEUTERONOMIC SCHOOL

Society of Biblical Literature

Studies in Biblical Literature

Edited by
Dennis T. Olson

Number 2

THE DEUTERONOMIC SCHOOL
History, Social Setting, and Literature

THE DEUTERONOMIC SCHOOL
History, Social Setting, and Literature

Raymond F. Person, Jr.

Society of Biblical Literature
Atlanta

THE DEUTERONOMIC SCHOOL
History, Social Setting, and Literature

Library of Congress Cataloging-in-Publication Data

Person, Raymond F.
  The Deuteronomic school: history, social setting, and literature /
Raymond F. Person, Jr.
      p. cm. — (Studies in biblical literature ; 2)
Includes bibliographical references and index.
  ISBN 1-58983-024-5
  1. Bible. O.T. Deuteronomy—Criticism, interpretation, etc. 2. Bible. O.T. Deuteronomy—Criticism, Redaction. 3. Bible. O.T. Deuteronomy—Language, style. I. Title. II. Studies in biblical literature (Society of Biblical Literature) ; 2.
  BS1275.52 .P47 2002
  222'.066—dc21

                                2002006307

            07 06 05 04 03 02   5 4 3 2 1

Portions of chapter 2 and chapter 3 are revisions of portions of Raymond F. Person, Jr. *Second Zechariah and the Deuteronomic School* (JSOTSup 167; Sheffield: Sheffield Academic Press, 1993). Permission granted by Sheffield Academic Press.

Printed in the United States of America
on acid-free paper

TABLE OF CONTENTS

ACKNOWLEDGEMENTS

My research concerning Deuteronomic literature began as a student at Phillips Theological Seminary, studying especially the Deuteronomic redaction of Jeremiah with Leo G. Perdue. I continued my work on Deuteronomic literature in my doctoral program at Duke University, publishing my first article on Kings based on a seminar paper I wrote for Melvin Peters' Septuagint seminar[1] and writing my dissertation on the what I understand to be Deuteronomic prose in Zechariah 9–14 under the supervision of Eric Meyers.[2] I have learned much from these teachers and thank them for their continuing support and friendship.

I have profited from conversations with other colleagues in Hebrew Bible. I want to thank Dennis Olson of Princeton Theological Seminary who as editor of SBLMS has both challenged and encouraged me on this project. I also want to thank Steven McKenzie of Rhodes College for his careful reading of the manuscript and helpful remarks and David Janzen of Bluffton College for our stimulating conversations, especially concerning my use of Ezra.

---

[1]Raymond F. Person, Jr. "II Kings 24,18–25,30 and Jeremiah 52: A Text-Critical Case Study in the Redaction History of the Deuteronomistic History," *ZAW* 105 (1993): 174–205.

[2]Published as Raymond F. Person, Jr., *Second Zechariah and the Deuteronomic School* (JSOTSup 167; Sheffield: Sheffield Academic Press, 1993).

Various individuals at my home institution, Ohio Northern University, have provided financial, technical, and emotional support that has enabled this project to reach completion. I want to thank Vice President Anne Lippert and Dean Byron Hawbecker for awarding me Summer Faculty Development Grants, which have provided me with needed funds for research trips to Duke University in the summer of 2000 and University of California at Santa Barbara in the summer of 2001. I have also been assisted by Ohio Northern students; Seth Auman, Amy Barlak, and Abby Marvin have assisted me with some of the research and April Leiffer has capably been my copy editor. It is a pleasure to work with such good students, who help make me a better teacher.

And last, but not least, I want to thank many friends and my family for their continuing support of my research and teaching. Jason McCurry and Dan Hall provided me with a comfortable place to stay complete with good Southern hospitality during my research trip to Duke University in the summer of 2000. Chris Thomas, Jonathan Wilson, and Randy Garr entertained me when I spent time in Santa Barbara in the summer of 2001. And Elizabeth Kelly, the love of my life, has endured many, many conversations about my research and teaching, usually with good cheer. I want to dedicate this book to Elizabeth from whom I draw tremendous strength in my life and work.

INTRODUCTION

Research on the Deuteronomic History (Deuteronomy through Kings) is clearly in a state of flux. Not only are the standard redactional models being challenged, but scholars are asking some of the most basic questions. For example, Richard Coggins has asked "What Does 'Deuteronomistic' Mean?"; Rainer Albertz has asked "Who Were the Deuteronomists?"; Norbert Lohfink has asked "Was There a Deuteronomistic Movement?"; and Ernst Knauf has asked "Does 'Deuteronomistic Historiography' (DtrH) Exist?"[1] Many of these questions have arisen because some scholars have perceived a "danger of 'pan-Deuteronomism.'"[2] This volume seeks to address these and other issues directly.

---

[1] Richard Coggins, "What Does 'Deuteronomistic' Mean?" in *Words Remembered, Text Renewed: Essays in Honour of John F. A. Sawyer* (eds. Jon Davies, Graham Harvey, and Wilfred G. E. Watson; JSOTSup 195; Sheffield: Sheffield Academic Press, 1995), 135–48; Rainer Albertz, "Wer waren die Deuteronomisten? Das historische Rätsel einer literarischen Hypothese," *EvT* 57 (1997): 319–38; Norbert Lohfink, "Was There a Deuteronomistic Movement?" in *Those Elusive Deuteronomists: The Phenomenon of Pan-Deuteronomism* (ed. L. S. Schearing and S. L. McKenzie; JSOTSup 268; Sheffield: Sheffield Academic Press, 1999), 36–66; Ernst Axel Knauf, "Does 'Deuteronomistic Historiography' (DtrH) Exist?" in *Israel Constructs Its History: Deuteronomistic Historiography in Recent Research* (ed. A. de Pury, T. Römer, and J.-D. Macchi; JSOTSup 306; Sheffield: Sheffield Academic Press, 2000), 388–98.

[2] Coggins, "What Does 'Deuteronomistic' Mean?" 135.

1

REDACTION HISTORY OF THE DEUTERONOMIC HISTORY[3]

In 1943 Martin Noth set the stage for later discussion of the redaction history of what he called the Deuteronomistic History.[4] Noth argued that Deuteronomy–Kings was the unified work of an exilic historian, the Deuteronomistic Historian. This historian used earlier sources to create a narrative beginning with Moses in Egypt (Deuteronomy) and ending with the exile (Kings). Noth's thesis of the unity of Deuteronomy–Kings was widely assumed and until recently went generally unquestioned.

Although Noth's thesis of the unity of the Deuteronomistic History was widely accepted, in the 1970s two different schools of thought developed that created a consensus that behind the Deuteronomistic History are various sources and that the Deuteronomistic History has undergone at least two redactions.[5] However, these two schools of thought continue to disagree about the details. The main two schools are the Harvard school (Frank Moore Cross and mainly Americans) who argue that the Deuteronomistic History underwent both a preexilic and an exilic redaction and the Göttingen school (Rudolph Smend, Walter Dietrich, and mainly Europeans) who argue that the Deuteronomistic History underwent three redactions, each by a redactor with a different perspective—that is, a history

---

[3]The discussion below is necessarily brief, omitting the significant influence of earlier scholars on Noth. For an excellent discussion of this history, see Römer and de Pury, "Deuteronomistic Historiography (DH): History of Research and Debated Issues" and the essays in Steven L. McKenzie and M. Patrick Graham, eds., *The History of Israel's Traditions: The Heritage of Martin Noth* (JSOTSup 182; Sheffield: Sheffield Academic Press, 1994).

[4]Martin Noth, *Überlieferungsgeschichtliche Studien* (Tübingen: Niemeyer, 1943). English translation of the section concerning the Deuteronomistic History: Martin Noth, *The Deuteronomistic History* (JSOTSup 15; Sheffield: Sheffield Academic Press, 1981).

[5]A few scholars continue to argue that the Deuteronomic History is the product of only one individual: Hans Detlef Hoffmann, *Reform und Reformen* (ATANT 66; Zurich: Theologischer Verlag, 1980); Burke O. Long, *I Kings with an Introduction to Historical Literature* (FOTL 9; Grand Rapids: Eerdmans, 1984); Robert Polzin, *David and the Deuteronomist: A Literary Study of the Deuteronomic History* (Bloomington: Indiana University Press, 1993).

writer (DtrG), a prophetic redactor (DtrP), and a nomistic redactor (DtrN).[6] Even within these two schools there is some diversity. In the Harvard school, for example, there is disagreement about when to locate the preexilic redaction. Cross located the first redaction during the reign of Josiah, but other suggestions include during the reign of Hezekiah or Zedekiah.[7] In the Göttingen school, there is disagreement concerning the extent of the different redactional levels, the dating of the levels, and even how many layers. For example, Smend early on proposed dividing DtrN further (DtrN$_1$, DtrN$_2$) and Spiekermann has six different layers.[8]

The growing diversity within these two schools sometimes presents difficulties categorizing specific redactional studies. For example, if Spiekerman has six different redactional layers, can his study still be understood within the Göttingen school or should it be understood as being in a category by itself? Further complicating the categorization of some specific redactional studies is that some recent studies have tried to combine the strengths of both schools and, therefore, do not fit easily into either school. Nevertheless, even many of these recent studies, in the words of

---

[6]Harvard school: Frank Moore Cross, "The Themes of the Book of Kings and the Structure of the Deuteronomistic History," in *Canaanite Myth and Hebrew Epic* (Cambridge: Harvard University Press, 1973), 274–89; Baruch Halpern, *The First Historians* (San Francisco: Harper & Row, 1988); Richard D. Nelson, *The Double Redaction of the Deuteronomistic History* (JSOTSup 18; Sheffield: JSOT Press, 1981); Gary N. Knoppers, *Two Nations under God: The Deuteronomic History of Solomon and the Dual Monarchies* (2 vols.; HSM 52–53; Atlanta: Scholars Press, 1993–1994).

Göttingen school: Rudolph Smend, *Die Entstehung des Alten Testaments* (Stuttgart: W. Kohlhammer, 1981), 110–25; Walter Dietrich, *David, Saul und die Propheten* (BWANT 7.2; Stuttgart: W. Kohlhammer, 1987); Ernst Würthwein, *Studien zum deuteronomistischen Geschichtswerk* (BZAW 227; Berlin: Walter de Gruyter, 1994).

[7]For example, A. D. H. Mayes argues for a Hezekianic date (*The Story of Israel between Settlement and Exile: A Redactional Study of the Deuteronomic History* [London: SCM Publishing, 1983], 133–38) and Ronald Clements argues for a Zedekianic date ("The Isaiah Narrative of 2 Kings 20:12–19 and the Date of the Deuteronomistic History," in *Isac Leo Seeligman Volumn: Essays on the Bible and the Ancient World* [vol. 3; eds. A. Rofé and Y. Zakovitch; Jerusalem: E. Rubinstein's Publishing House, 1983], 209–20).

[8]Rudolph Smend, "Das Gesetz und die Völker. Ein Betrag zur deuteronomistischen Redaktionsgeschichte," in *Probleme biblischer Theologie* (ed. H. W. Wolff; Munich: Chr. Kaiser Verlag, 1971), 494–509; Hermann Spieckermann, *Juda unter Assur in der Sargonidzeit* (FRLANT 129; Göttingen: Vandenhoeck und Ruprecht, 1982).

William M. Schniedewind, "do little more than refine the traditional debate."[9]

If scholarship on the redaction of the Deuteronomic History is going to move forward, the problem of why so many well-qualified scholars using very similar methods have produced such tremendously different results must be addressed. The problem lies in the inability of redaction criticism to distinguish one Deuteronomic redactor from another Deuteronomic redactor, since all Deuteronomic redactors use similar Deuteronomic language and themes! Of course, there have been efforts to discern significant differences in themes so that one Deuteronomic redactor might be distinguished from another—for example, election versus explanation of exile; pro-monarchical versus anti-monarchical; historiographical versus prophetic versus nomistic. However, even though these different themes are evident in various sections of the Deuteronomic History, these different themes become the presuppositions that the various critics assume as they apply redaction criticism and, therefore, these themes provide no objective control for their redactional arguments and produce a tremendous diversity of results.[10]

Chapter 1 below proposes a solution to this problem by the use of text criticism to provide some controls upon the redactional study of the Deuteronomic History.

WHAT DOES "DEUTERONOMIC"/"DEUTERONOMISTIC" MEAN?

Both terms obviously relate to the book of Deuteronomy. Before Noth "Deuteronomic" (*deuteronomisch*) was generally used to refer to the

---

[9]William M. Schniedewind, "The Problem with Kings: Recent Study of the Deuteronomistic History," *Religious Studies Review* 22 (1996): 25. Schniedewind's comment appears in his review of the following works: Iain Provan, *Hezekiah and the Book of Kings* (BZAW 172; Berlin: Walter de Gruyter, 1988); Mark A. O'Brien, *The Deuteronomistic History Hypothesis: A Reassessment* (OBO 92; Freiburg: Universitäts-verlag Freiburg, 1989); Steven L. McKenzie, *The Trouble with Kings* (VTSup 42; Leiden: E. J. Brill, 1991); Knoppers, *Two Nations under God*; and Würthwein, *Studien zum deuteronomistischen Geschichtswerk*.

[10]For a similar critique of redaction critical studies of Kings, see James Richard Linville, *Israel in the Book of Kings: The Past as a Project of Social Identity* (JSOTSup 272; Sheffield: Sheffield Academic Press, 1998), 46–58.

proposed Pentateuchal source D. Since Noth discerned both a D source and later redactional material in the book of Deuteronomy, he coined the term "Deuteronomistic" (*deuteronomistisch*) to refer to the later redactional material. Therefore, in Noth's terminology "Deuteronomic" referred to proto-Deuteronomy (*Urdeuteronomium*)—that is, Deut 4:44–30:20—and "Deuteronomistic" referred to the later additions in Deuteronomy and the literary unity of Deuteronomy–Kings, all of which were the product of Noth's "Deuteronomistic Historian," who was heavily influenced by the legal material in proto-Deuteronomy.

Noth's terminology related to a variety of assumptions that are no longer shared by the majority of scholars, most significantly the assumption that the Deuteronomic History was the product of one exilic redactor. Because there are now several different revisions to Noth's thesis concerning the Deuteronomic History, there are various understandings of what "Deuteronomistic" means.[11] For example, the Harvard school has two Deuteronomists (Dtr[1] and Dtr[2]) and the Göttingen school has three (DtrG, DtrP, DtrN). In addition, in a 1942 article J. Philip Hyatt suggested that the book of Jeremiah was edited by a "Deuteronomic" redactor.[12] Hyatt's thesis has found numerous supporters who have extended Hyatt's work, so that "Deuteronomic" (Hyatt's own term) and "Deuteronomistic" now also refer to most of the prose sections in the book of Jeremiah.[13] Since Hyatt's work others have argued for "Deuteronomic"/"Deuteronomistic" redactions of other prophetic books, especially in the Book of the Twelve.[14] In short,

---

[11]This state is criticized by various scholars, most notably Coggins, "What Does 'Deuteronomistic' Mean?" and Lohfink, "Was There a Deuteronomistic Movement?"

[12]Reprinted as J. Philip Hyatt, "Jeremiah and Deuteronomy," in *A Prophet to the Nations: Essays in Jeremiah Studies* (ed. L. G. Perdue and B. W. Kovacs; Winona Lake: Eisenbrauns, 1984), 113–27.

[13]For example, Ernest W. Nicholson, *Preaching to the Exiles: A Study of the Prose Tradition in the Book of Jeremiah* (New York: Schocken Books, 1970); William McKane, *A Critical and Exegetical Commentary on Jeremiah* (vol. 1; ICC; Edinburgh: T. & T.Clark, 1986); Robert P. Carroll, *Jeremiah: A Commentary* (OTL; Philadelphia: Westminster, 1986); Ronald E. Clements, *Jeremiah* (IBC; Atlanta: John Knox, 1988).

[14]Werner H. Schmidt, "Die deuteronomistische Redaktion des Amosbuches. Zu den theologischen Unterschieden zwischen dem Propheten Wort und seinem Sammler," *ZAW* 77 (1965): 168–93; Hans W. Wolff, *Hosea* (Hermeneia; Phildealphia: Fortress Press, 1974), xxix–xxxii; James Nogalski, *Literary Precursors to the Book of the Twelve* (BZAW

"Deuteronomic" and "Deuteronomistic" now mean various things and are sometimes used interchangably.

This lack of consensus concerning terminology has led some scholars to call for abandoning the term "Deuteronomistic" altogether.[15] Others prefer to keep the term, but want the term to refer to a narrower range of meanings.[16] Whether one chooses to coin some new term to refer to the individual(s) behind the Deuteronomic History (or sections of the Deuteronomic History) or chooses to continue to use "Deuteronomic" and/or "Deuteronomistic," it is especially clear that one must define one's terms well to enable readers to fully understand one's work.

I have chosen to abandon the distinction between "Deuteronomic" and "Deuteronomistic" for the following reasons. First, as stated above, these terms are already used interchangeably. For example, the group of individuals that redacted the Deuteronomic History and Jeremiah are labeled "the Deuteronomic School" by Weinfeld and "the Deuteronomistic school" by Lohfink.[17] Second, Noth's original distinction between "Deuteronomic" and "Deuteronomistic" was based upon his conclusion that the relationship between an early form of Deuteronomy and the Deuteronomic History was unidirectional, moving from proto-Deuteronomy to the Deuteronomistic Historian. This unidirectional influence is problematic, if the redaction

---

217; Berlin: Walter de Gruyter, 1993); Person, *Second Zechariah and the Deuteronomic School*. Although in the first six chapters of this volume I limit all of my comments upon the Deuteronomic History and Jeremiah, this should not be interpreted as a rejection of other arguments for Deuteronomic redaction of other prophetic books. In fact, I remained convinced of my argument for the Deuteronomic redaction of Zechariah 9–14 (see Chapter 7 below). However, I have chosen to focus primarily upon the Deuteronomic History and secondarily upon Jeremiah as the two major works generally accepted as Deuteronomic.

[15]For example, A. Graeme Auld, "The Deuteronomists and the Former Prophets, Or What Makes the Former Prophets Deuteronomistic?" in *Those Elusive Deuteronomists: The Phenomenon of Pan-Deuteronomism* (ed. L. S. Schearing and S. L. McKenzie; JSOTSup 268; Sheffield: Sheffield Academic Press, 1999), 116–26.

[16]This appears to be the position of most of the essayists in Linda S. Schearing and Steven L. McKenzie, ed. *Those Elusive Deuteronomists: The Phenomenon of Pan-Deuteronomism* (JSOTSup 268; Sheffield: Sheffield Academic Press, 1999).

[17]Moshe Weinfeld, *Deuteronomy and the Deuteronomic School* (Oxford: The Clarendon Press, 1972); Lohfink, "Was There a Deuteronomistic Movement?" 63.

history of the Deuteronomic History spanned a long period of time and occurred more gradually than generally imagined (see Chapters 1 and 4 below). Rather, it is more likely that various Deuteronomic texts influenced each other at different times, so that one cannot establish which text is the primary text and which is secondary. Hence, the distinction between "Deuteronomic" and "Deuteronomistic" is no longer significantly meaningful.

Since I abandon the distinction between the terms "Deuteronomic" and "Deuteronomistic," I have chosen to consistently use the term "Deuteronomic" to refer to the Deuteronomic History and Jeremiah as well as the individuals responsible for this literature. I will use the term "Deuteronomistic" only when summarizing the thought of other scholars who use the designation in their own work.

WHAT DOES "SCHOOL" MEAN?

The word "school" can refer to a place of instruction or a group of individuals connected by a common ideology and/or method. When I use the phrase "Deuteronomic school," I am drawing from both of these meanings and more. In this work "Deuteronomic school" denotes a scribal guild that was active in the Babylonian exile and Persian period and had its origins in the bureaucracy of the monarchy. The members of this school, the Deuteronomic scribes/redactors, were trained in this school and may have been involved in the instruction of others.[18] They preserved and reinterpreted earlier material (for example, early forms of Deuteronomy, "the Book of the Annals of the Kings of Judah," Jeremianic poetry) within their particular theological and literary tradition. Thus, the Deuteronomic school had a common ideology that was expressed in a common language, even though changes in ideology certainly occurred over time as social conditions changed.

---

[18]Eric W. Heaton associates the Deuteronomic school with what he understands to be a broad tradition of schools in ancient Israel that educated many common people (*The School Tradition of the Old Testament* [Oxford: Clarendon Press, 1994], 106–14). Although I agree with him that the Deuteronomic school was involved in instruction, I seriously doubt that instruction was as widespread as Heaton argues.

WHAT DOES "DEUTERONOMIC REDACTOR" MEAN?

As will be argued below in Chapters 3 and 4, the Deuteronomic school was probably organized hierarchically. The lower ranking scribes would have been limited primarily to administrative duties and the mere copying of authoritative texts. The higher ranking scribes would have had more freedom to produce new texts and new redactions of authoritative texts. The higher ranking scribes would be considered "Deuteronomic redactors." However, as will be evident in Chapters 3 and 4, drawing a clear line between scribe and redactor or between composition and transmission of literature remains a very difficult task.

THE RELATIONSHIP AMONG THE BOOKS OF THE DEUTERONOMIC HISTORY

As noted above in the discussion of the terms "Deuteronomic" and "Deuteronomistic," Martin Noth understood proto-Deuteronomy as the Deuteronomistic Historian's theological basis for the structure of the Deuteronomic History. Similarly, Hyatt understood Deuteronomy as the theological basis for the Deuteronomic redaction of Jeremiah. Such assumptions about the priority of Deuteronomy continues in many discussions of the redaction of Deuteronomic literature, even if not explicitly expressed. However, a few scholars are now questioning the direction of influence. For example, A. Graeme Auld suggests that the direction runs "from the story of Kings, through Samuel, and on to Deuteronomy."[19] As suggested above, I will argue that such unidirectional understandings of literary influence (whether by Noth in one direction or Auld in another) ought to be rejected, because of the complexity of the redaction history of Deuteronomic literature (see Chapters 1 and 4 below). Clearly various texts influenced each other over a long period of time, so that today we cannot say, for example, that a particular occurrence of the Deuteronomic phrase "to put his [the Lord's] name there" (Deut 12:5, 21; 14:24; 1 Kgs 9:3; 11:36; 14:21; 2 Kgs 21:4, 7) was the first use of the phrase and then the others are copied from the first. Although we might

---

[19]Auld, "The Deuteronomists and the Former Prophets, Or What Makes the Former Prophets Deuteronomistic?" 123.

imagine that this must have been the case since all of these phrases were not written simultaneously, our methods do not allow us to make precise judgments about the priority of any one occurrence. Likewise all of the books in the Deuteronomic History (whatever their ancient divisions were) were not written simultaneously. However, once the books were written and redacted over the course of many years, distinguishing what was written first from what was written later probably had little, if any, significance for the Deuteronomic school. Moreover, even if it did have significance, our methods are inadequate to tease out which book was written first.

Noth also argued that the Deuteronomistic Historian systematically edited his sources into a unified work, the Deuteronomistic History. Although the scholarly consensus now proposes two or more redactions of the Deuteronomic History, the systematic character of the redaction continues to be assumed. For example, the Harvard school's Dtr[1] and Dtr[2] as well as the Göttingen school's DtrG, DtrP, and DtrN are all understood to have updated the entirety of the Deuteronomic History. Since it is highly improbable that the entirety of the Deuteronomic History would have been preserved on one scroll (or any other medium of written text in antiquity), it is possible that Deuteronomic redactional activity in any given period was limited to one or more of the scrolls containing sections of the Deuteronomic History. Therefore, it may have been that a particular redactor updated Samuel and Kings (or whatever the ancient divisions were) but not Deuteronomy, then another redactor later updated Deuteronomy. Again our methods do not provide us with the ability to decide accurately such issues behind the complexity of the redaction history of the Deuteronomic History, so we must allow the possibility of both systematic and more limited Deuteronomic redactions of the Deuteronomic History.

THE RELATIONSHIP BETWEEN THE DEUTERONOMIC HISTORY AND JEREMIAH

J. Philip Hyatt first proposed in 1942 that some form of Jeremiah was edited by a Deuteronomic redactor.[20] His understanding of the redaction of Jeremiah followed the then generally accepted view of the four

---

[20]"Jeremiah and Deuteronomy," 121–26.

"sources" of Jeremiah: Jeremianic poetry ("source A"), Baruch's biography ("source B"), Deuteronomic prose sermons ("source C"), and miscellaneous poetry and prose ("source D").[21] His innovation was that he understood the evidence for the source of Deuteronomic prose sermons ("source C") to imply not simply a source, but a Deuteronomic redaction. Thus, his overall view of Jeremiah is as follows: A Deuteronomic redactor used Jeremianic poetry ("source A") and Baruch's biography ("source B") as sources which he reinterpreted with the addition of his own material, the prose sermons (formerly, "source C"); therefore, the Deuteronomic redaction of Jer, according to Hyatt, is limited to Jer 1–45. In the postexilic period, another redactor ("post-D[euteronomic]") added non-Jeremianic material ("source D").

Hyatt's most developed presentation was his 1951 article, "The Deuteronomic Edition of Jeremiah,"[22] where he provided a list of Deuteronomic phraseology in the prose sermons of Jeremiah. He then discussed each literary unit in Jeremiah wherein he found evidence of Deuteronomic redaction and concluded with a list of what he considered to be post-Deuteronomic additions because of their postexilic date—that is, after the presumed time of the Deuteronomic school.

Although his thesis continues to attract some dissenters,[23] Hyatt's work has influenced numerous Jeremiah scholars, most notably Winfried Thiel, Ernest Nicholson, Emanuel Tov, William McKane, Robert Carroll, and Ronald Clements.

Building upon the work of Hyatt and Herrmann,[24] Winfried Thiel wrote a dissertation intitled "Die deuteronomistische Redaktion des Büches

---

[21]Sigmund Mowinckel, *Zur Komposition des Buches Jeremia* (Kristiania: Jacob Dybwad, 1914).

[22]See also the brief discussion in Hyatt's introduction to his commentary, "The Book of Jeremiah" in *Interpreter's Bible* (ed. G. A. Buttrick; Nashville: Abingdon Press, 1956), 5: 788–90.

[23]Most notably, John Bright, *Jeremiah* (AB 21; Garden City: Doubleday, 1965); William L. Holladay, *Jeremiah* (2 vols,; Hermeneia; Philadelphia: Fortress, 1986/1989); Helga Weippert, *Die Prosareden des Jeremiasbuches* (BZAW 132; Berlin: Walter de Gruyter, 1973).

[24]Siegfried Herrmann, *Die prophetischen Heilserwartungen im Alten Testament* (BZAW 5.5; Stuttgart: W. Kohlhammer, 1965).

Jeremia" (1970).[25] His understanding of the Deuteronomic redaction of Jeremiah is quite similar to that of Hyatt in two ways: (1) His argument is also basically a redefinition of "source C" into a Deuteronomic redaction. (2) Like Hyatt, he also limits Deuteronomic redaction to Jer 1–45 to which post-Deuteronomic material was added.

In *Preaching to the Exiles* (1970), Ernest Nicholson accepted Hyatt's thesis of the Deuteronomic redaction of Jeremiah but developed it further with regard to the so-called Baruch's biography ("source B").[26] He argued that this "biographical" material was primarily theological in purpose, thereby diminishing the distinction previously made between the "theological" prose sermons ("source C") and the "biographical" narratives ("source B"). He also noted Deuteronomic phraseology in these "biographies." Therefore, Nicholson concluded that the distinction between these so-called "sources" should be rejected and that the "biographical" material, like the prose sermons, was from the hand of a Deuteronomic redactor. Nicholson's reformulation of Hyatt's original thesis—that is, the Deuteronomic redactor(s) of Jeremiah produced both the "biographical narratives" and the "prose sermons"—has found wide acceptance. For example, this is accepted by Robert Carroll, Ronald Clements, and Walter Brueggeman in their recent commentaries.[27]

Emanuel Tov's work on Jeremiah[28] is best known for his development of the thesis that LXX-Jeremiah preserves an earlier redaction

---

[25]His dissertation has been published in two volumes: Winfried Thiel, *Die deuteronomische Redaktion von Jeremia 1–25* (WMANT 41; Neukirchen: Neukirchener Verlag,1973) and *Die deuteronomische Redaktion von Jeremia 26–45* (WMANT 52; Neukirchen: Neukirchener Verlag, 1981). Only the second volume underwent significant revision from his dissertation.

[26]*Preaching*, 34–37. See also, Ernest W. Nicholson, *The Book of the Prophet Jeremiah. Chapters 1–25* (CBC; Cambridge: Cambridge University Press, 1973), 10–16.

[27]Robert Carroll, *Jeremiah*, 38–50; Clements, *Jeremiah*, 10–12; Walter Brueggeman, *A Commentary on Jeremiah: Exile and Homecoming* (Grand Rapids: Eerdemans, 1998). See also, Thomas C. Römer, "How Did Jeremiah Become a Convert to Deuteronomistic Ideology?" in *Those Elusive Deuteronomists: The Phenomenon of Pan-Deuteronomism* (ed. L. S. Schearing and S. L. McKenzie; JSOTSup 268; Sheffield: Sheffield Academic Press, 1999), 189–99.

[28]In three very similar articles, Emanuel Tov presents his argument. These three articles are, in order of their publication: "L'incidence de la critique textuelle sur la critique

of Jeremiah than does MT-Jeremiah. However, he not only accepted the thesis of the Deuteronomic redaction of Jeremiah but went on to revise it in relationship to his text-critical work, concluding that both MT-Jeremiah and LXX-Jeremiah were products of Deuteronomic redaction and that at least MT-Jeremiah was postexilic.[29]

Combining the widely accepted reformulation of Hyatt's original thesis by Nicholson with Tov's observation that both LXX-Jeremiah and MT-Jeremiah are Deuteronomic, I understand the present book of Jeremiah as Deuteronomic literature. This does not deny the possibility of some later additions. However, much of what has been considered post-Deuteronomic in Jeremiah was identified as such based upon the erroneous assumption that the Deuteronomic redaction of Jeremiah was limited to the exilic period. The text critical studies of Tov and many others clearly demonstrate that the Deuteronomic redaction of Jeremiah continued into the postexilic period.[30]

The Deuteronomic redaction of Jeremiah, however, raises an interesting question: Why is Jeremiah not mentioned in the Deuteronomic History? Noth explained the general lack of references to the Latter Prophets in the Deuteronomic History as the consequence of the Deuteronomistic Historian not being aware of these works.[31] However, if the Deuteronomic school produced both the Deuteronomic History and Jeremiah, obviously another explanation must be given.

Noth's explanation has generally been rejected and replaced with the argument that the Deuteronomic school had a "supplementary" collection of the Latter Prophets and, therefore, avoided unnecessary duplication.[32]

---

littéraire dans le livre de Jérémie," *RB* 79 (1972): 189–99; "Some Aspects of the Textual and Literary History of the Book of Jeremiah," in *Le livre de Jérémie* (ed. P.-M. Bogaert; BETL 54; Leuven: Leuven University, 1981), 15–67; and "The Literary History of the Book of Jeremiah in the Light of its Textual History," in *Empirical Models for Biblical Criticism* (ed. J. H. Tigay; Philadelphia: University of Pennsylvania Press, 1984), 211–37. For further discussion of the relationship of LXX-Jer and MT-Jer, see below Chapter 2.

[29]"L'incidence," 199. See also "Aspects," 164; and "Literary History," 232.

[30]See further, Person, *Second Zechariah and the Deuteronomic School*, 62–78.

[31] Noth, *Deuteronomistic History*, 86.

[32]For example, Joseph Blenkinsopp, *Prophecy and Canon* (Notre Dame: University of Notre Dame Press, 1977), 98, 102; Ronald E. Clements, *Prophecy and*

Although I am in basic agreement with this understanding, I prefer to avoid the language of "supplementarity," because it necessarily implies that one genre is primary and the other secondary. Rather, I prefer to describe the relationship between the Deuteronomic History and Jeremiah (and any other prophetic books redacted by the Deuteronomic school) as *complementary*. Just as I am not convinced that the relationship between Deuteronomy and Joshua–Kings is based only on Deuteronomy as the primary text which influences the secondary texts of Joshua–Kings, I am not convinced that the Deuteronomic History should be understood only as the primary text that Jeremiah (and other prophetic books) "supplements."

In short, the Deuteronomic school produced a substantial variety of literary forms. First, the Deuteronomic school utilized various genres within the different books it redacted. For example, Moshe Weinfeld has discussed the forms of different orations (valedictory address, prophetic oration, liturgical oration, military oration) in the Deuteronomic History as well as the relationship between Deuteronomy and the forms of vassal treaties and law codes.[33] Second, the books that the Deuteronomic school redacted can themselves be distinguished according to their overall form and content: law (Deuteronomy), historiography (Joshua–Kings), and prophecy (Jeremiah). Therefore, no one literary form can be called the primary literary form of the Deuteronomic school, because the Deuteronomic school was responsible for the production of various literary genres.

THE SO-CALLED PROBLEM OF "PAN-DEUTERONOMISM"

A survey of recent literature reveals a variety of arguments for Deuteronomic redaction in the Tetrateuch and other prophetic books. This has led to warnings of "pan-Deuteronomism," the perceived tendency to associate the Deuteronomic school with all of the Hebrew Bible.[34] Richard

---

Tradition (Atlanta: John Knox, 1975), 47–48. For an excellent review of scholarship on this issue, see Christopher T. Begg, "A Bible Mystery: The Absence of Jeremiah in the Deuteronomistic History," *IBS* 7 (1985): 139–64.

[33] Weinfeld, *Deuteronomy and the Deuteronomic School*, 8.

[34] See Schearing and McKenzie, *Those Elusive Deuteronomists*. This collection of essays contains the most important articles that state this warning, most significantly

Coggins first issued this warning and asserted that "the Deuteronomists have sometimes been praised or blamed for virtually every significant development within ancient Israel's religious practice."[35] For excellent reasons, "pan-Deuteronomism" has been rejected, but a closer look at these arguments against "pan-Deuteronomism" is necessary.

"Pan-Deuteronomism" refers to the collection of various arguments for Deuteronomic redaction in or of diverse books outside of the Deuteronomic History and Jeremiah, despite the tremendous diversity of these various arguments. In fact, the critics of "pan-Deuteronomism" refer to no single scholar or group of scholars with closely related arguments who argue for "pan-Deuteronomism." That is, "pan-Deuteronomism" is a stick figure that some scholars have set up to knock down that does not really exist in the books and articles that they critique. Coggins himself seems to be aware of this, when he wrote: "In what follows a number of references will be made to recent authors and contemporary usage; it should be understood that these are intended as illustrative, rather than as offering negative judgments upon the books and articles referred to."[36] However, these references are understood by Coggins to illustrate "pan-Deuteronomism," which he clearly rejects, and the lack of consensus on what "Deuteronomistic" means, which he clearly criticizes. Such criticism is especially unfair when applied to many of the individual scholars who Coggins uses as his illustrations.

Since Coggins and others refer to my book *Second Zechariah and the Deuteronomic School* to illustrate the danger of "pan-Deuteronomism," I will use myself as an example of how the label "pan-Deuteronomism" is a misnomer when applied to many, if not all, of the works that are referred to as examples of this phenomenon. In *Second Zechariah and the Deuteronomic School*, I argue that the prose in Zechariah 9–14 is Deuteronomic prose, analogous to the prose in Jeremiah. Since I am the first to make this argument, I have argued for expanding the corpus of

---

Schearing, "Introduction"; Coggins, "What Does 'Deuteronomistic' Mean?"; and Lohfink, "Was There a Deuteronomistic Movement?"

[35] Coggins, "Prophecy—True and False," in *Of Prophets' Visions and the Wisdom of Sages* (Sheffield: JSOT Press, 1993), 85.

[36] Coggins, "What Does 'Deuteronomistic' Mean?" 23.

Deuteronomic literature. However, such an expansion does not constitute "pan-Deuteronomism." In fact, in the section on the Deuteronomic school's canon in the postexilic period I explicitly discuss the difficulty of including Joel, Jonah, Haggai, and Malachi in the Deuteronomic school's canon and specifically argue that Jonah should be excluded from a Deuteronomic canon, since it satirizes the Deuteronomic understanding of prophecy.[37] Nowhere have I suggested that any of the Writings are Deuteronomic. Therefore, identifying my work as an example of "pan-Deuteronomism" is unfounded and such would be the case with many, if not all, of the other scholars who have been accused of promoting "pan-Deuteronomism."

This is not to say that many of the issues Coggins and others raise when they express their concern of "pan-Deuteronomism" should be ignored. I too am aware that there is tremendous diversity in what the terms "Deuteronomic," "Deuteronomistic," and related phrases mean and that scholars must state clearly what such terms mean in their writings. I am also critical of some specific arguments for the Deuteronomic redaction of individual books. In fact, Schearing and McKenzie's volume on "pan-Deuteronomism" includes an excellent essay by Ehud Ben Zvi, convincingly arguing against the Deuteronomic redaction of Micah, Zephaniah, and Obadiah.[38] However, whether it is intended or not, grouping various arguments for Deuteronomic redaction together under the label "pan-Deuteronomism" could justify dismissing these arguments without the type of careful analysis exhibited by Ben Zvi.

In short, "pan-Deuteronomism" should be rejected not only because it does not adequately describe the literature of ancient Israel, but because its rhetorical force may also unjustifiably lead some scholars to dismiss arguments made by those accused erroneously of promoting the idea of "pan-Deuteronomism."

---

[37] Person, *Second Zechariah and the Deuteronomic School*, 174.

[38] Ehud Ben Zvi, "A Deuteronomistic Redaction in/among 'The Twelve'? A Contribution from the Standpoint of the Books of Micah, Zephaniah, and Obadiah." in *Those Elusive Deuteronomists: The Phenomenon of Pan-Deuteronomism* (ed. L. S. Schearing and S. L. McKenzie; JSOTSup 268; Sheffield: Sheffield Academic Press, 1999), 232–61.

Below I give my proposal for a way out of the confusion that exists when discussing the Deuteronomic school and its literature, especially the redaction history of the Deuteronomic History. The following proposal advances the discussion by approaching the problem from four different perspectives that have not been taken seriously in most discussions of the Deuteronomic History: (1) the need for text critical controls on redactional arguments in the Deuteronomic History and Jeremiah (Chapter 1), (2) the postexilic setting of some Deuteronomic redactional activity (Chapter 2), (3) evidence from analogous scribal schools in the ancient Near East (Chapter 3), and (4) the predominantly oral culture in which the Deuteronomic school worked and its effects on their scribal activities (Chapter 4). When combined, the arguments in these chapters strongly suggest that redactional changes in the Deuteronomic History and Jeremiah occurred gradually over a long period of time, were the product of various individuals within the Deuteronomic school, and continued into the postexilic period. The Deuteronomic school probably returned to Jerusalem from the Babylonian exile under Zerubbabel and supported the rebuilding of the Jerusalem Temple and the reinstitution of the temple cult with its scribal skills. That is, the Deuteronomic scribes redacted earlier texts and created new texts during this period. Chapters 5 and 6 contain reinterpretations of selected passages from the Deuteronomic History and Jeremiah, reading them to understand what meaning these texts may have had for the Deuteronomic school in the postexilic period. Then Chapter 7 discusses the Deuteronomic school's relationship to some other postexilic literature, specifically the books of Haggai, Zechariah, Chronicles, Ezra, and Nehemiah.

CHAPTER 1

REDACTION CRITICISM AND DEUTERONOMIC LITERATURE

WHAT IS DEUTERONOMIC LANGUAGE?

In order for redaction critical methods to succeed, the literature being studied must contain redactional layers that each have a distinct language. That is, if the piece of literature has passed through numerous individuals or schools, each of which edited the text using their own distinctive language, then the characteristics of their language—for example, unique vocabulary and phraseology, dialectical variety—provides the redaction critic with the details necessary to assign different phrases to the various sources and redactional layers with some degree of accuracy.

As noted above in the Introduction, Deuteronomic literature presents a difficult problem for the redaction critic. Scholars in both the Harvard and Göttingen schools (as well as many of those who do not fit easily into either school) argue for multiple Deuteronomic redactions of the Deuteronomic History. Some scholars of Jeremiah argue for multiple Deuteronomic redactions of Jeremiah. The problem with all of these arguments is the difficulty in distinguishing one Deuteronomic redactional layer from others, since all Deuteronomic redactors use Deuteronomic language.

This problematic situation has led some scholars to question the utility of linguistic arguments based on Deuteronomic language altogether. For example, in "The Deuteronomist and the Writings," James Crenshaw rejects arguments for any connection between "the Deuteronomist" and "Deuteronomistic redactors," on the one hand, and the authors of the books in the Writings, on the other. He writes, "The strongest argument [for Deuteronomistic influence], linguistic parallels, loses force when one considers the paucity of written material from ancient Israel that remains. We simply do not know what literature was available to ancient authors, for we cannot assume that all of it survived as the biblical canon."[1] Linguistic arguments would certainly have more "force" if we knew much more about the literature of ancient Israel (much of which is forever lost); Crenshaw's statement, however, goes too far. In fact, Crenshaw himself does not fully agree with all of the implications of his statement. One of the implications would be to give up completely on the higher critical methods, especially source criticism and redaction criticism. That is, we do not have enough literary material available to adequately establish what linguistic features were common in ancient Israel in order to discern what might be distinctive about a particular individual's or group's language. Yet in the same article Crenshaw writes, "The distinction between Deuteronomic and Deuteronomistic should be retained, the former pointing to an original source and the latter to subsequent works in the same vein."[2] How would one distinguish between what is "Deuteronomic" and what is "Deuteronomistic," if not on some linguistic basis? Arguments for "Deuteronomistic" redaction, including Noth's original thesis for the Deuteronomic History based on Deuteronomy, depend on an understanding of what Deuteronomic language is.

This logical necessity for some form of Deuteronomic language seems to be recognized by most scholars, including some who have

---

[1] James L. Crenshaw, "The Deuteronomist and the Writings," in *Those Elusive Deuteronomists: The Phenomenon of Pan-Deuteronomism* (ed. L. S. Schearing and S. L. McKenzie; JSOTSup 268; Sheffield: Sheffield Academic Press, 1999), 146.

[2] Crenshaw, "The Deuteronomist and the Writings," 146.

criticized "pan-Deuteronomism" such as Robert Wilson and Ehud Ben Zvi. Wilson writes, "the use of linguistic criteria remains the most reliable way of identifying the hand of the Deuteronomists."[3] Ben Zvi writes, "Aside from citations or closely related texts, the best possible evidence for some form of relationship between the prophetic books discussed here [Micah, Zephaniah, and Obadiah] and a deuteronomistic group of writers that is predicated on a particular language would be the presence of 'classical deuteronomistic phraseology.'"[4] What is this "classical deuteronomistic phraseology" that Ben Zvi refers to? There is general agreement, even by critics of the idea of Deuteronomic language, that the most thorough discussion of Deuteronomic phraseology is found in Moshe Weinfeld's appendix to his *Deuteronomy and the Deuteronomic School*.[5] Weinfeld himself acknowledged the logical necessity of understanding Deuteronomic language, when he wrote the following concerning the importance of this appendix:[6]

> the Appendix on Deuteronomic Phraseology ... [is] a vital part of the work, since style is the only objective criterion for determining whether a biblical passage is Deuteronomic or not.

Weinfeld may have overstated the importance of Deuteronomic language, because no interpretive method is completely "objective."[7] However, as Ben

---

[3]Robert R. Wilson, "Who Was the Deuteronomist?" in *Those Elusive Deuteronomists: The Phenomenon of Pan-Deuteronomism* (ed. L. S. Schearing and S. L. McKenzie; JSOTSup 268; Sheffield: Sheffield Academic Press, 1999), 79.

[4]Ben Zvi, "A Deuteronomistic Redaction in/among 'The Twelve'?" 240–41.

[5]Weinfeld, *Deuteronomy and the Deuteronomic School*, 320–65.

The following refer to Weinfeld's list: Ben Zvi, "A Deuteronomistic Redaction in/among 'The Twelve'?" 241; Linville, *Israel in the Book of Kings*, 62–63; Lohfink, "Was There a Deuteronomistic Movement?" 41–42; Wilson, "Who Was the Deuteronomist?" 79; Kugler, "The Deuteronomists and the Latter Prophets," in *Those Elusive Deuteronomists: The Phenomenon of Pan-Deuteronomism* (ed. L. S. Schearing and S. L. McKenzie; JSOTSup 268; Sheffield: Sheffield Academic Press, 1999), 129; Crenshaw, "The Deuteronomist and the Writings," 148.

[6]Weinfeld, *Deuteronomy and the Deuteronomic School*, vii.

[7]Crenshaw is correct in pointing out that Weinfeld's creation of his list and others using Weinfeld's list for determining the "Deuteronomistic" character of other texts are

Zvi concludes, "There is probably no more comprehensive inventory ...
than the one compiled by M. Weinfeld."[8]

Weinfeld understands that Deuteronomic language naturally grew
out of earlier sources. He wrote:[9]

> The main characteristic of deuteronomic phraseology is not the employment
> of new idioms and expressions, because many of these could be found in the
> earlier sources and especially in the Elohistic source. ... What constitutes the
> novelty of the deuteronomic style therefore is not new idioms and new
> expressions, but a specific jargon reflecting the religious upheaval of this time.
> The deuteronomic phraseology revolves around a few basic theological tenets
> such as: 1. The struggle against idolatry. 2. The centralization of the cult. 3.
> Exodus, covenant, and election. 4. The monotheistic creed. 5. Observance of
> the law and loyalty to the covenant. 6. Inheritance of the land. 7. Retribution
> and material motivation. 8. Fulfillment of prophecy. 9. The election of the
> David dynasty.

He structured his appendix on the basis of these theological themes as a way
to organize his analysis and presentation of Deuteronomic phraseology. This
connection between Deuteronomic phraseology and Deuteronomic theology
was crucial for Weinfeld. He wrote:[10]

> What makes a phrase deuteronomic is not its mere occurrence in
> Deuteronomy, but its meaning within the framework of deuteronomic
> theology.

He then provided a fairly lengthy list of phrases that occur often in
Deuteronomy (for example, "you must not show pity" and "foreign gods")
that should not be considered specifically Deuteronomic. In other words,
these phrases are simply common Hebrew phrases that one would expect to
occur in the literary context in which they are found in Deuteronomy.
Concerning these common phrases found in Deuteronomy, he concluded:[11]

---

circular and subjective ("The Deuteronomist and the Writings," 148 n. 12). However, this
charge can be made against all interpretive methods.

[8]Ben Zvi, "A Deuteronomistic Redaction in/among 'The Twelve'?" 241.

[9]Weinfeld, *Deuteronomy and the Deuteronomic School*, 1.

[10]Weinfeld, *Deuteronomy and the Deuteronomic School*, 1–2.

[11]Weinfeld, *Deuteronomy and the Deuteronomic School*, 3.

> In no case can the occurrence of such phrases in a text be used as evidence of deuteronomic origin. Only those recurrent phrases that express the essence of the theology of Deuteronomy can be considered "deuteronomic."

Despite this limiting condition, Weinfeld provides an extensive list in his appendix (45 pages!) of phrases that meet his criteria of Deuteronomic phraseology.

To sum, Deuteronomic literature presents source and redaction critics with the difficult tasks of discerning different Deuteronomic redactional layers. Moreover the methods of source criticism and redactional criticism necessarily depend upon linguistic criteria. Therefore, unless we are willing to abandon source criticism and redaction criticism altogether, we must have some basic understanding of what Deuteronomic language is. For this purpose, there is a scholarly consensus that Weinfeld's appendix of Deuteronomic phraseology is the most extensive, comprehensive, and careful compilation on the topic of Deuteronomic language. As such, it will be used as the basis for the work below where issues of Deuteronomic language are concerned.

THE NEED FOR TEXT CRITICAL CONTROLS

The consensus that Deuteronomic literature underwent multiple redactions requires the ability to distinguish the work of one redactor from another. However, since Deuteronomic redactors share certain typical Deuteronomic phrases, redaction criticism cannot adequately distinguish one Deuteronomic redactor from another on the basis of linguistic evidence. This is the most pressing problem facing the study of the redaction history of Deuteronomic literature.

The solution to this problem lies in the contributions text criticism can make to the redactional study of the Deuteronomic History as demonstrated in the work of A. Graeme Auld, Alexander Rofé, Emanuel Tov, Julio Trebolle, others, and myself.[12] These scholars make many (if not

---

[12] A. Graeme Auld, "Reading Joshua after Kings," in *Words Remembered, Texts Renewed: Essays in Honor of John F. A. Sawyer* (eds. J. Davies, G. Harvey, and W.G. E. Watson; JSOTSup 195; Sheffield: Sheffield Academic Press, 1995), 167–81; A. Graeme Auld, "Judges 1 and History: A Reconsideration," *VT* 25 (1975): 261–85; A. Graeme Auld, "The 'Levitical Cities': Text and History," *ZAW* 91 (1979): 194–206; A. Graeme

all) of their redactional arguments based strictly upon text critical variants; therefore, they use text critical observations as a control upon their redactional arguments. These studies further demonstrate the problems noted above inherent in the redaction criticism of the Deuteronomic History by refuting the prevailing views—that is, the Harvard and Göttingen

---

Auld, "Textual and Literary Studies in the Book of Joshua," *ZAW* 90 (1978): 412–17; Raymond F. Person, Jr., *The Kings–Isaiah and Kings–Jeremiah Recensions* (BZAW 252; Berlin: Walter de Gruyter, 1997); Stephen Pisano, "2 Samuel 5–8 and the Deuteronomist: Textual Criticism or Literary Criticism?" in *Israel Constructs its History: Deuteronomistic Historiography in Recent Research* (eds., A. de Pury, T. Römer, and J.-D. Macchi; JSOT Sup 306; Sheffield: Sheffield Academic Press, 2000), 258–83; Alexander Rofé, "The End of the Book of Joshua according to the Septuagint," *Henoch* 4 (1982): 17–32; Alexander Rofé, "The History of the Cities of Refuge in Biblical Law," in *Studies in the Bible* (ed. S. Japhet; ScrHie 31; Jerusalem: Magnes Press, 1986), 205–39; Alexander Rofé, "Joshua 20: Historico-Literary Criticism Illustrated," in *Empirical Models for Biblical Criticism* (ed. J. Tigay; Philadelphia: University of Pennsylvania Press, 1985), 131–47; Alexander Rofé, "The Monotheistic Argumentation in Deuteronomy 4.32–40: Contents, Composition, and Text," *VT* 35 (1985): 434–45; Adrian Schenker, "Jeroboam and the Division of the Kingdom in the Ancient Septuagint: LXX 3 Kingdoms 12:24a–z, MT 1 Kings 11–12; 14 and the Deuteronomistic History," in *Israel Constructs its History: Deuteronomistic Historiography in Recent Research* (eds., A. de Pury, T. Römer, and J.-D. Macchi; JSOT Sup 306; Sheffield: Sheffield Academic Press, 2000), 214–57; Emanuel Tov, "The Composition of I Samuel 16–18 in the Light of the Septuagint Version," in *Empirical Models for Biblical Criticism* (ed. J. Tigay; Philadelphia: University of Pennsylvania Press, 1985), 97–130; Emanuel Tov, "The Growth of the Book of Joshua in the Light of the Evidence of the LXX Translation," in *Studies in the Bible* (ed., S. Japhet; ScrHie 31; Jerusalem: Magnes Press, 1986), 321–39; Julio C. Trebolle Barrera, "The Story of David and Goliath (1 Sam 17–18): Textual Variants and Literary Composition," *BIOSCS* 23 (1990): 16–30; Julio C. Trebolle Barrera, "Old Latin, Old Greek and Old Hebrew in the Books of Kings (1 Ki. 18:25 and 2 Ki. 20:11)," *Textus* 13 (1986): 85–94; Julio C. Trebolle Barrera, "Redaction, Recension, and Midrash in the Books of Kings," *BIOSCS* 15 (1982): 12–35; Julio C. Trebolle Barrera, "The Text-Critical Use of the Septuagint in the Books of Kings," in *VII Congress of the International Organization for Septuagint and Cognate Studies, Leuven 1989* (ed. C. E. Cox; SBLSCS 31; Atlanta: Scholars Press, 1991), 285–99; Arie van der Kooij, "Zum Verhältnis von Textkritik und Literarkritik: Überlegungen anhand einiger Beispiele," in *Congress Volume* (VTSup; Leiden: E. J. Brill, 1997), 185–202.

schools.[13] For the sake of brevity, I will summarize the work of Alexander Rofé and my own contributions.[14]

Rofé has concluded that "the widely accepted view about ... the last redaction of the Deuteronomistic work in the Exilic period (mid-6th century) now needs to be reconsidered."[15] In a number of articles, Rofé provides evidence that the redaction of the Deuteronomic History continued into the postexilic period. In two articles concerning Joshua 20,[16] he demonstrates that the earlier LXX of Joshua 20 reflects the Priestly code concerning manslaughter and the cities of refuge (Num 35:9–34) and the later, expansive MT reflects not only the Priestly code but also the Deuteronomic code concerning manslaughter and the cities of refuge (Deut 4:41–43; 19:1–13), including a quote from Deut 19:4–6. In another article, Rofé argues that linguistic evidence suggests that the story of David and Goliath in the MT of 1 Samuel 16–18 also comes from the fifth or fourth centuries B.C.E.[17] Therefore, Rofé argues on the basis of text critical, linguistic, and thematic evidence that the redaction of the Deuteronomic History continued into the late fifth or early fourth centuries B.C.E.

In *The Kings–Isaiah and Kings–Jeremiah Recensions*, I provided text critical, linguistic, and thematic evidence for the Deuteronomic redaction of Kings continuing into the postexilic period. Based upon my text critical study of 2 Kings 18–20 (in both the MT and the LXX) and its parallel in Isaiah 36–39 (in the MT, the LXX, and the Isaiah Scroll of Qumran) as well as my text critical study of 2 Kings 24:18–25:30 (in both

---

[13]The one exception is Pisano, "2 Samuel 5–8 and the Deuteronomist." Pisano concludes that in the few cases he studied there is no reason to conclude that the variants to the MT reading of Samuel or the readings in the parallels in Chronicles are either more ancient or more Deuteronomistic. His conclusion therefore does not challenge the prevailing views.

[14]For a discussion of other text critical studies that have a bearing on the redaction history of the Deuteronomic History, see below Chapter 2, pp. 34–50.

[15]Alexander Rofé, "The Vineyard at Naboath: The Origin and Message of the Story," *VT* 38 (188): 103.

[16]Rofé, "Joshua 20" and "History of the Cities of Refuge."

[17]Alexander Rofé, "The Battle of David and Goliath: Folklore, Theology, Eschatology," in *Judaic Perspectives on Ancient Israel* (ed. J. Neusner, B. A. Levine, and E. S. Frerichs; Philadelphia: Fortress Press, 1987), 117–51.

the MT and the LXX) and its parallel in Jeremiah 52 (also in the MT and the LXX), I conclude that the redaction of Kings as represented by the MT continued over a long span of time into the postexilic period. I also conclude that the postexilic redaction was Deuteronomic from the presence of Deuteronomic language in additions in the MT-2 Kings, including the phrase "for the sake of David, my servant" in 20:6.[18] Therefore, although I limited my redactional arguments to text critical evidence, I nevertheless could determine that the Deuteronomic school continued its redactional activity in Kings into the postexilic period.

In sum, the text critically based redactional arguments of Alexander Rofé, myself, and others demonstrate that the prevailing views of the Harvard and Göttingen schools fail methodologically in that they both rely solely on redaction criticism to distinguish one Deuteronomic redactor from another and apply this method only to the generally later, expansive MT of the Deuteronomic History. When text critical evidence is incorporated into redactional arguments, the redaction history of the Deuteronomic History appears to be more complex and gradual, spanning a much longer period of time than previously understood. This general observation will be developed further below in Chapters 2 and 4.

THE REDACTION HISTORY OF THE DEUTERONOMIC HISTORY

The state of the question concerning the redactional history of the Deuteronomic History leaves us with fewer certainties than most redaction critics have been comfortable with in the past. Therefore, because of the limitations of the redactional critical method itself, we must be careful not to state too much. At the same time, some of the conclusions of the Harvard and Göttingen schools remain convincing and valid. When these conclusions are combined with the admittedly limiting influence of text critical arguments for the redaction of the Deuteronomic History we end up with the following scenario.

The literary roots of the Deuteronomic History are clearly in the preexilic period, most likely associated with the administrative bureaucracy

---

[18]Weinfeld's list of Deuteronomic phraseology is based on the MT. This phrase is included as Deuteronomic (Weinfeld, *Deuteronomy and the Deuteronomic School*, 354).

under the monarchy. First, the Deuteronomic History itself refers to certain written sources concerning preexilic events: "the Book of the Acts of Solomon" (1 Kgs 11:42), "the Book of the Annuals of the Kings of Israel" (1 Kgs 14:19; 15:31; 16:5, 14, 20, 27; 22:39; 2 Kgs 1:18; 10:34; 13:8, 12; 14:15, 28; 15:11, 15, 21, 26, 31), and "the Book of the Annuals of the Kings of Judah" (1 Kgs 14:29; 15:7, 23; 22:45; 2 Kgs 8:23; 12:19; 14:18; 15:6, 36; 16:19; 20:20; 21:17, 25; 23:28; 24:5). These references to sources occur at the end of narratives about a particular king and state that additional information about this king can be found in these sources, as the three following examples illustrate:

> Now the rest of the acts of Solomon, all that he did as well as his wisdom, are they not written in the Book of the Acts of Solomon? (1 Kgs 11:42)

> Now the rest of the acts of Jeroboam, how he warred and how he reigned, are written in the Book of the Annuals of the Kings of Israel. (1 Kgs 14:19)

> Now the rest of the acts of Rehoboam, and all that he did, are they not written in the Book of the Annuals of the Kings of Judah. (1 Kgs 14:29)

These references suggest not only that the Deuteronomic school used written sources for the writing of the Deuteronomic History, but also that they continued to preserve some of these written sources after they were used in the composition of the Deuteronomic History. In addition, it is quite likely that the Deuteronomic school used other written sources. Scholars have argued for a variety of other sources behind the Deuteronomic History, including sources for the prophetic stories and the stories of the judges.[19] Although I am convinced that the Deuteronomic school used written sources for its composition of the Deuteronomic History, I am just as skeptical about the ability of source critics to define the limits of the sources for the Deuteronomic History as I am about the ability of redaction critics to discern redactional layers. The compositional and redactional process spanned such a long period of time that it is virtually impossible to delimit adequately what was in the original sources. We can state with some

---

[19]For a review of literature, see Antony F. Campbell and Mark A. O'Brien, *Unfolding the Deuteronomistic History: Origins, Upgrades, Present Text* (Minneapolis: Fortress Press, 2000), 23–34.

degree of certainty what was *not* in a written source, but rather came from the hand of a Deuteronomic redactor—for example, the references to the sources quoted above would not have been included in the sources that they refer to, but would have come from the hand of the redactor(s) who used the source. But we cannot state with any degree of certainly, for example, what in the narrative of Solomon (1 Kgs 1:1–11:43) was in "the Book of the Acts of Solomon."

Some scholars (especially Philip Davies and Niels Lemke) have rejected the idea that references to these written sources are evidence of actual written sources but are rather the author's invention of sources to give legitimacy to his fictive accounts of Israel's history. Specifically, they argue that the Deuteronomic History was written during the Persian or Hellenistic period, inventing "ancient Israel" in order to provide legitimacy to Persian or Hellenistic Judah.[20] This is obviously a possibility that should always be explored for any text that refers to sources which are no longer extant. This possibility, however, should be rejected in this case for the following two reasons. First, the Deuteronomic History recounts historical events for which there is some independent evidence, even though there remain numerous historical inaccuracies in the text. For example, in an article comparing the book of Kings to ancient Near Eastern royal inscriptions, Nadav Na'aman concludes that "the Dtr historian" used written sources that contained some accurate information about the historical events from as early as the late tenth century B.C.E. For example, the campaign of Shishak, king of Egypt, is recounted in 1 Kgs 14:25–28 and, even though it certainly contains some inaccuracies and elaborations, Egyptian sources agree that Shishak's campaign reached the area of Jerusalem and that Judah paid tribute to Egypt.[21] Second, the Deuteronomic History contains

---

[20]Philip R. Davies, *In Search of "Ancient Israel"* (JSOTSup 148; Sheffield: Sheffield Academic Press, 1992); Niels P. Lemke, "The Old Testament: A Hellenistic Book?" *SJOT* 7 (1993): 163–93. See also Thomas M. Bolin, "When the End is the Beginning. The Persian Period and the Origins of the Biblical Tradition," *SJOT* 10 (1996): 3–15.

[21]Nadav Na'aman, "The Contribution of Royal Inscriptions for a Re-Evaluation of the Book of Kings as a Historical Source," *JSOT* 82 (1999): 13–17. Na'aman is concerned with demonstrating that the Deuteronomic redactors had direct access to royal inscriptions. Although I do not completely rule out this possibility, my argument does

linguistic variations, some of which are common to Classical Biblical Hebrew and some of which are common to Late Biblical Hebrew.[22] Such linguistic variation is inconsistent with the idea that the Deuteronomic History was written in the Persian period without the use of earlier sources and is easily explained as a later text using preexilic sources.[23]

The most plausible explanation for the existence of these sources is to trace their origin to the bureaucracy of the monarchy, where scribes would have played an important role in royal and temple administration. Although the extent of the diffusion of education institutions and literacy in preexilic Israel remains widely debated, the existence of professional scribes (especially those in the palace or temple administration) in monarchical Judah is generally affirmed.[24] These scribes probably produced various texts, such as king lists and annuals, none of which exist in their preexilic forms today. It is likely, however, that some of these texts were the sources for the composition of the Deuteronomic History.

The Deuteronomic History's earliest redactional layers may also come from the period of the late monarchy. Scholars in the Harvard school argue that the first redaction of the Deuteronomic History (Dtr[1]) was preexilic, most commonly associated with the reign of Josiah. This edition of the Deuteronomic History was supposedly created to support Josiah's

---

not require such direct access—that is, the Deuteronomic school simply had access to preexilic sources that contained some accurate historical references. It is certainly possible that the Deuteronomic school did not have access to royal inscriptions, but that the authors/redactors of the Deuteronomic school's preexilic sources had. This would be more consistent with the argument of Simon B. Parker ("Did the Authors of the Books of Kings Make Use of Royal inscriptions?" *VT* 50 [2000]: 357–78). Parker argues for the possible existence of royal inscriptions in preexilic Judah, but against the authors of Kings generally using such inscriptions.

[22]Secondary literature contains numerous references to features of Classical Biblical Hebrew found in the Deuteronomic History and this is sometime used in arguments for a preexilic or exilic setting for the composition/redaction of portions of the Deuteronomic History. Features of Late Biblical Hebrew are often overlooked, but will be discussed briefly in Chapter 2 below.

[23]For an excellent critique of Davies' arguments concerning linguistic variation, see Avi Hurwitz, "The Historical Quest for 'Ancient Israel' and the Linguistic Evidence of the Hebrew Bible: Some Methodological Observations," *VT* 47 (1997): 301–15.

[24]See further Chapter 3, pp. 68–71 below.

reform and had a generally optimistic outlook for Judah. Based on the difficulty of discerning the earliest layers of Deuteronomic redactional activity, I cannot assess this thesis well. It is quite possible that scribes in the preexilic period had already begun the task of combining the various sources together to form a more coherent narrative of Israel's history. It is also quite possible that the "finding" of the law book during Josiah's reign (2 Kgs 22:3–20) was accompanied by some new literary production that later led to the Deuteronomic History. But even if this is the case, I prefer to reserve the phrase "Deuteronomic school" for that group of scribes who produced the first complete Deuteronomic History from Moses to the exilic period. Therefore, even though the Deuteronomic school probably had its scribal roots in the professional scribes of the late monarchy and drew upon writings produced by these professional scribes, I prefer to talk about the origin of the Deuteronomic school in the exilic period, when the overall framework of the Deuteronomic History probably first took form. This preference denotes the tremendous change in outlook that the destruction of Jerusalem and the Babylonian exile must have made on the people of Judah, especially those who were taken into exile, including the professional scribes of the royal bureaucracy.[25]

The Babylonian deportations of 597 and 587 B.C.E. included numerous individuals in the bureaucracy of the royal palace and temple in Jerusalem, most likely including scribes. As a guild of at least some of these exiled scribes, the Deuteronomic school collected, preserved, and redacted the preexilic sources that they and others brought to Babylon as well as additional material concerning the period following the destruction of Jerusalem (for example, Jehoiachin's release in 2 Kgs 25:27–30). Most likely the overall shape of the Deuteronomic History—a narrative from Moses in the wilderness to the Babylonian exile—took form during the exilic period.

---

[25]In some sense, this is a return to Noth's original thesis that the Deuteronomic History was produced in the exilic period. For a recent argument reasserting the exilic date for the Deuteronomist, see McKenzie, "The Trouble with Kings," esp. 310–14. However, my position disagrees with both Noth and McKenzie in that they both focus their remarks upon one individual, *the* Deuteronomist, whereas I prefer to speak of a group, the Deuteronomic school.

Some vestiges of the monarchic bureaucracy continued throughout the Babylonian exile for, when the Persians defeated the Babylonians, they began a process of returning exiled populations to their homeland with the support of what remained of the bureaucracies conquered by the Babylonians. It is in this political context that we can speak of the Deuteronomic school's return to Jerusalem. The Deuteronomic school's return most likely occurred under Zerubbabel to provide scribal support for the Persian-supported bureaucracy that was to be restored with the rebuilt temple (see further Chapter 2). In this context, the Deuteronomic scribes continued their redaction of the literature they preserved, including the Deuteronomic History and Jeremiah.

CHAPTER 2

THE DEUTERONOMIC SCHOOL IN
THE PERSIAN PERIOD

CRITIQUE OF PAST ASSUMPTIONS ABOUT THE DEUTERONOMIC SCHOOL

The majority of scholars limit the dating of the Deuteronomic school's final redactional activity to the exilic period. This majority view is based on the groundbreaking work of Martin Noth. Noth dated his "Deuteronomistic Historian" to the exilic period:[1]

> He wrote in the middle of the 6th century BCE when the history of the Israelite people was at an end; for the later history of the post-exilic community was a completely different matter—both its internal and external conditions were different—and it was the Chronicler who first thought of explaining it as a linear continuation of the earlier history of the nation.

Noth's argument for an exilic date of the Deuteronomic History can be summed up in the following way: since the period discussed in the Deuteronomic History ends with the exile and does not include a discussion of the return to Jerusalem, the work of the Deuteronomistic Historian must

---

[1] Noth, *Deuteronomistic History*, 79.

be exilic. Noth's argument has been readily accepted by the majority of scholars who limit Deuteronomic redactional activity to the preexilic and/or exilic periods. This majority comprises two different schools of thought: those who argue for the unity of the Deuteronomic History (that is, only one redaction or one Deuteronomic redaction) and scholars in the Harvard school.

Most interpreters who argue for the unity of the Deuteronomic History—that is, there is only one author/redactor—simply accepted Noth's exilic date for the redaction of the Deuteronomic History. For example, Burke Long defended an exilic date by simply stating that "whatever their theories about the redaction and compositional history, most scholars agree that in its present form the books of Kings (and the Dtr History of which they are a part) originated in the exile."[2] Therefore, those scholars who have maintained the Deuteronomic History's compositional unity have simply accepted Noth's exilic date without providing any additional support.

Scholars in the Harvard school reject Noth's argument for compositional unity of the Deuteronomic History, but this rejection has not affected their acceptance of Noth's exilic dating for the final form of the Deuteronomic History. Cross explained the "failure of … a dominant theme of God's coming restoration," a theme he expected in every exilic text, "by moving the primary Deuteronomistic history from the setting of the Exile."[3] In other words, Cross assumed Noth's exilic dating of the final form of the Deuteronomic History, but found it odd that there was not a strong theme of restoration in this exilic work. Therefore, he argued that if the majority of the Deuteronomic History comes from the Josianic period, one can easily explain this "failure." To this "primary Deuteronomistic history" (Dtr[1]), the narrative of which ended in the Josianic period, an exilic Deuteronomistic redactor (Dtr[2]) "updated the history by adding a chronicle of events subsequent to Josiah's reign."[4] Again, the argument for the exilic redaction of the Deuteronomic History was simply the following:

---

[2]Long, *I Kings*, 32. Similarly Hoffman, *Reform und Reformen*, 316–20; Robert Polzin, *Moses and the Deuteronomist* (New York: Seabury, 1980), 72.

[3]Cross, "Themes and Structure," 289.

[4]Cross, "Themes and Structure," 41.

the redaction process begins where the historical narrative stops and ends shortly thereafter.

In contrast to the Harvard school, the Göttingen school has to some degree challenged the generally held view of an exilic setting for the Deuteronomic History. The Göttingen school argues for three redactions: a history writer (DtrG), a prophetic redactor (DtrP), and a nomistic redactor (DtrN). The first two redactions (DtrG and DtrP) are assumed to be exilic and the final (DtrN) postexilic. Although DtrN is dated to the postexilic period, Noth's exilic dating remains the beginning point for the dating of Deuteronomic redaction activity. Whereas Cross revised Noth's thesis by positing a second *earlier* redaction, the Göttingen school revised Noth's thesis by positing two *later* redactions.[5]

Some scholars, however, have not assumed Noth's exilic date of the Deuteronomic History.[6] In some cases, these scholars did not necessarily challenge the logic of Noth's exilic date; they simply presented their argument for postexilic redaction by the Deuteronomic school. Some of these scholars, however, have directly challenged the Nothian argument. For example, Robert Carroll claimed:[7]

> it should not be assumed that Deuteronomistic circles operated for a brief period and then disappeared; nor should the possibility of a much later (i.e., fifth-century) date for Deuteronomistic activity be ruled out a priori. ... The

---

[5]When Dietrich first proposed three redactions (*Prophetie und Geschichte* [FRLANT 108; Göttingen: Vandenhoeck und Ruprecht, 1972]), he located all three redactions in the exilic period. Smend rejected this dating scheme because of the brevity of the exilic period and dated the last redactor (DtrN) to the postexilic period (*Entstehung*, 110–25). Dietrich then accepted this revision (*David, Saul und die Propheten*, 152). Thus, Noth's argument for an exilic setting for the Deuteronomic History played an even more important role in the dating scheme of the Göttingen school than may be obvious when we look only at the current dating scheme with DtrN in the postexilic period.

[6]A. Graeme Auld, "Prophets through the Looking Glass: Between Writings and Moses," *JSOT* 27 (1983): 15; A. Graeme Auld, "Prophets through the Looking Glass: A Response to Robert Carroll and Hugh Williamson," *JSOT* 27 (1983): 44; Carroll, *Jeremiah*, 65–82; Linville, *Israel in the Book of Kings*, esp. 69–73; Rofé, "Joshua 20," 145; Rofé, "The Vineyard at Naboth," 103; Thomas C. Romer, "Transformations in Deuteronomistic and Biblical Historiography: On 'Book-Finding' and other Literary Strategies," *ZAW* 109 (1997): 10–11; Tov, "Aspects"; Tov, "Literary History."

[7]Carroll, *Jeremiah*, 67.

termination of the history with an episode from c. 560 (II Kings 25.27–30; cf. Jer. 52.31–34) does not necessarily date the history to the mid-sixth century. It may simply represent a positive ending of the story of the kings of Israel and Judah with a detail from the life of the last living Judean king.

In addition A. Graeme Auld sarcastically wrote:[8]

> The fact that Kings ends with the fate of Judah's last king tells us no more about the date of composition (generally believed exilic) than the fact that the Pentateuch ends with the death of Moses.

In sum, Noth's exilic date of the Deuteronomic History was based completely upon the following argument: the narrative of the Deuteronomic History ends in the exilic period; therefore, the Deuteronomic History must be exilic. This argument is an argument for a *terminus a quo* used for a *terminus ante quem* as well. The arguments made by the three major schools of scholars discussed above began with the assumption of Noth's exilic date without further argumentation. However, Noth's exilic date has not gone unchallenged; therefore, a reevaluation of all stages of the redactional history and their settings is necessary.

TEXT CRITICAL EVIDENCE OF POSTEXILIC, DEUTERONOMIC REDACTION

The general view concerning the relationship between text (i.e., "lower") criticism and literary (i.e., "higher") criticism has traditionally been strictly sequential—that is, text criticism establishes *the* text to which one applies literary criticism. This view is exemplified in the following statement by David Noel Freedman:[9]

> In dealing with these portions of the Bible, we distinguish between their literary and textual history. The former is concerned primarily with the creative literary activity by which earlier oral traditions were shaped into a continuous record, the extensive editorial redaction of the different written sources, and the final compilation of the available materials resulting in the

---

[8] Auld, "Response to Carroll and Williamson," 44.
[9] David Noel Freedman, "The Law and the Prophets," In *Congress Volume: Bonn 1962* (VTSup 9; Leiden: E. J. Brill, 1963), 252.

appearance of the completed work. The latter is concerned with the transmission of the text and the process by which it was finally fixed.

However, since the discovery of the Qumran materials, text criticism has become more than simply a tool to establish "the text" for the literary critic. Text criticism has begun to be incorporated even more into the discussion concerning literary history, especially for those texts where the Qumran materials and the ancient versions differ significantly from MT.

In this section, I will begin by summarizing some representative studies of the textual and literary history of the Deuteronomic History in which the author clarified the correspondence between text criticism and literary criticism. Then, I will discuss the implications of these studies on the dating of the final Deuteronomic redaction of the Deuteronomic History.

(1) Rofé, "Monotheistic Argumentation in Deut 4.32–40": Alexander Rofé reconstructed the literary history of Deut 4:1–40 as follows: (a) The earliest source in Deut 4:1–40 is the "short 'sermon'" of Deut 4:32–40, which is best preserved in the Samaritan Pentateuch and the LXX against the MT in Deut 4:33, 36. This "sermon" was not a part of proto-Deuteronomy (4:44–26:19; 28), but was composed by the Deuteronomistic school. (b) Shortly later another Deuteronomistic redactor produced the first version of Deut 4:1–40, incorporating the "sermon" as a pietistic ending to the section. Again, this version is understood by Rofé to be preserved best in the Samaritan Pentateuch and the LXX against the MT. (c) The MT-Deut 4:1–40 is the result of a later Deuteronomistic redactor from the Persian period who drew upon both D and P sources. The original Deut 4:1–40 (SamPent and LXX) portrayed the people in the wilderness as being fearful of the Lord, thereby explaining why Moses alone received the revelation of the law; however, the additions in the MT suggest that all of the people have prophetic status. This elevation of the people to prophetic status has "affinity to midrashic notions,"[10] suggesting its lateness.

(2) Rofé, "Joshua 20":[11] By combining "historico-literary criticism" and text criticism, Alexander Rofé concluded that the textual history behind

---

[10]Rofé, "Monotheistic Argumentation," 435.
[11]Rofé, "Joshua 20."

the present text of Joshua 20:1–7 is as follows: (a) A short version preserved in Codex Vaticanus (LXX^B), which lacks 20:4–5 and differs significantly in 20:6, reflects knowledge of the Priestly code concerning manslaughter and refuge (Num 35:9–34). The language and themes in this short version are closely related to those of this Priestly code. (b) This short version was later redacted with the addition of 20:4–5 (found only in MT) and some re-writing of 20:6. These later revisions reflect knowledge of the Deuteronomic code concerning manslaughter and refuge (Deut 4:41–43; 19:1–13). Therefore, the version found in MT-Joshua is a Deuteronomic redaction of an earlier Priestly tradition.

Having established this textual history, Rofé argued that such an addition, which has knowledge of both D and P, must have been late. Such an observation is confirmed by the fact that LXX-Joshua 20 does not contain the reading, which suggests that the additions were late enough that they had not made their way into the various textual traditions. Rofé suggested that these Deuteronomic additions were probably made sometime in the fourth century.

(3) Tov, "Growth of the Book of Joshua":[12] After carefully examining the variants, Emanuel Tov concluded that the edition reflected in MT-Joshua–Judges expanded a shorter and earlier edition that is reflected in LXX-Joshua–Judges. Therefore, following LXX-Joshua–Judges, Tov argued that the more original text of Joshua–Judges lacked Judg 1:1–3:6. His examination of the pluses in MT-Joshua–Judges led him to conclude that MT-Joshua–Judges is Deuteronomic.

(4) Auld, "Reading Joshua after Kings":[13] Various commentators have suggested that Josh 8:30–9:2 may be a redactional addition, because it does not fit well into its present context in MT. Graeme Auld notes that there is text critical evidence supporting this suggestion in that Josh 8:30–35 appears after Josh 9:1–2 in LXX-Joshua and that a Qumran fragment suggests that Josh 8:30–35 preceded Josh 5:2. Because of the different locations, Auld concludes that Josh 8:30–35 and 9:1–2 are late redactional

---

[12]Tov, "The Growth of the Book of Joshua," 321–39. See also Auld, "Judges 1 [1:1–2:5] and History,"; Rofé, "The End of the Book of Joshua according to the Septuagint."

[13]Auld, "Reading Joshua after Kings."

additions. He reconstructs the history of the text as follows: (a) Josh 8:30–35 was first added before Josh 5:2 as represented in the Qumran fragment. (b) Josh 8:30–35 was later moved to its location in MT and LXX after the campaign at Ai—that is, after 8:29—but elements in 5:1 influenced the addition of 9:1–2, which occurred in different locations in MT (after 8:30–35) and LXX (before 8:30–35). Thus, Josh 9:1–2 like 5:1 described the thoughts and actions of "all the kings."

Auld notes that MT-Josh 8:30–9:2 is generally regarded as a Deuteronomic text, because it recounts Joshua's obedience to Moses' instruction to write the law on stones in Deuteronomy 27. Hence, we have text critical evidence of a late redactional addition betraying a strong Deuteronomic influence.

(5) Tov, "1 Sam 16–18" and Rofé, "Battle of David and Goliath":[14] Emanuel Tov examined the textual difference between MT-1 Samuel 16–18 and LXX-1 Samuel 16–18 and observed that MT-1 Samuel 16–18 is almost twice as long as LXX-1 Samuel 16–18. After showing that the translator of LXX-1 Samuel 16–18 used a literal method for his translation, Tov showed how MT-1 Samuel 16–18 is a conflation of two traditions, one found in LXX-1 Samuel 16–18 and the other which was an independent source used by the redactor of MT-1 Samuel 16–18. Therefore, LXX-1 Samuel 16–18 preserves the earlier stage of the redaction of the Deuteronomic History and MT-1 Samuel 16–18 manifests a later stage of development, which incorporated an independent source.[15]

---

[14]Tov, "The Composition of I Samuel 16–18," 97–130; Rofé, "The Battle of David and Goliath." See also Emanuel Tov, "The Nature of the Difference between MT and LXX," in *The Story of David and Goliath: Textual and Literary Criticism* (ed. D. Barthélemy et al.; OBO 73; Fribourg: Éditions Universitaires Fribourg/Göttingen: Vandenhoeck und Ruprecht, 1986), 19–46.

[15]See also Johan Lust, "The Story of David and Goliath in Hebrew and Greek," in *The Story of David and Goliath: Textual and Literary Criticism* (ed. D. Barthélemy et al.; OBO 73; Fribourg: Éditions Universitaires Fribourg/Göttingen: Vandenhoeck und Ruprecht, 1986), 5–18; P. Kyle McCarter, *I Samuel* (AB 8; Garden City: Doubleday & Company, 1980), 306–07; Hans J. Stoebe, "Die Goliathperikope 1 Sam. 17,1–18,5 und die Text-Form der Septuaginta," *VT* 6 (1956): 397–413; Trebolle, "The Story of David and Goliath (1 Sam 17–18)."

Contra Barthélemy, "Trois niveaux d'analyse," in *The Story of David and Goliath: Textual and Literary Criticism* (ed. D. Barthélemy et al.; OBO 73; Fribourg: Éditions

Alexander Rofé analyzed the David and Goliath story of MT-1 Samuel 16–18 and showed that its linguistic features suggest a postexilic date.[16] Therefore, Rofé placed the MT version of the David and Goliath story within the same period as some of the other later Deuteronomic

---

Universitaires Fribourg/Göttingen: Vandenhoeck und Ruprecht, 1986), 5–18; Simon J. de Vries, "David's Victory over the Philistine as Saga and Legend," *JBL* 92 (1973): 23–26; David W. Gooding, "An Approach to the Literary and Textual Problems in the David-Goliath Story," in *The Story of David and Goliath: Textual and Literary Criticism* (ed. D. Barthélemy et al.; OBO 73; Fribourg: Éditions Universitaires Fribourg/Göttingen: Vandenhoeck und Ruprecht, 1986), 5–18. For the debate between Tov and Lust, on the one hand, and Barthélemy and Gooding, on the other hand, see the papers and responses in D. Barthélemy, et al., eds. *The Story of David and Goliath: Textual and Literary Criticism* (ed. D. Barthélemy et al.; OBO 73; Fribourg: Éditions Universitaires Fribourg/Göttingen: Vandenhoeck und Ruprecht, 1986). Tov and Lust both criticized Barthélemy and Gooding for first using literary criticism and then text criticism and argued that the sequence must be reversed (see especially Lust, "Second Thoughts on David and Goliath," in Barthélemy, *The Story of David and Goliath*, 87–91.)

Barthélemy's and Rofé's criticism of Tov is that, although the Greek translator was relatively literal in his translation, the *Vorlage* of LXX was an abridged Hebrew text. The abridgement of this Hebrew text was to remove contradictions which resulted from the conflation of two stories. Tov responded that Barthélemy's (thus, indirectly, De Vries' and Rofé's) suggestion is based upon an odd coincidence in that some ancient revisor happened to extract the material which once belonged to an independent story, thereby preserving the other independent story. Such a coincidence, according to Tov, is highly unlikely. Therefore, given the general tendency for the expansion of biblical material and the general observation that LXX of Samuel reflects a shorter text than MT of Samuel, Tov maintained his position for the earlier version of LXX and the conflated version of MT.

[16]Rofé's analysis included some examples of late features in material common to LXX and MT; however, most of his linguistic evidence comes from MT additions. This observation alone should have caused him to reexamine his understanding of LXX as preserving an abridgement, but he made no distinction between LXX and MT when discussing the linguistic evidence. His linguistic arguments which are not in LXX are given here in his order: (1) the plene spelling of דָּד in 17:37; (2) the spelling of יְקֹהכֹאשׁ with an שׁ (17:17); (3) Hiph'il infinitive absolute of עֲגָד as a denominative verb (17:16); (4) the idiom זָגַע בְדוּדְךָ (17:28); (5) the use of יִזִּי with an indefinite noun (17:17); (6) the use of regular perfect verbs in the frequentive sense (17:34–35); (7) the temporal clauses in 17:55 and 17:57; (8) his understanding of לֹעֲמֹא ("Battle of David and Goliath," 128–31).

passages in the Deuteronomic History which he has identified, sometime in the fifth or fourth centuries B.C.E.

Combining the work of Tov and Rofé, it appears clear that MT-1 Samuel 16–18 was produced by a postexilic Deuteronomic redactor who combined two independent accounts of the story of David and Goliath.

(6) Schenker, "Jeroboam and the Division of the Kingdom":[17] Building upon previous work by others (especially Trebolle and Talshir[18]), Adrian Schenker has argued that the alternative reading of the tradition concerning Rehoboam and Jeroboam in LXX-1 Kgs 12:24a–z preserves an earlier edition of Kings that the editor of MT-Kings later revised. He also argues that both texts are Deuteronomic on the basis of Deuteronomic phraseology and themes. Therefore, he presents text critical evidence of two different Deuteronomic editions of the tradition concerning Rehoboam and Jeroboam and the division of the kingdom.

(7) Williamson, "Death of Josiah":[19] After noting the Chronicler's conservative use of his source in various places, Hugh Williamson argued that the textual difference between the account of Josiah's death in 2 Kgs 23:28–30 and 2 Chr 35:20–27 suggests that the source the Chronicler used was more similar to LXX-Kings than to MT-Kings. Therefore, his work on

---

[17]Schenker, "Jeroboam and the Division of the Kingdom."

[18]Julio C. Trebolle Barrera, *Salomón y Jeroboán. Historia de la recensión y redacción de 1 Reyes, 2–12, 14* (Salmanca and Jerusalem: Institute Español Biblica Arqueologico/Universidad Pontificia, 1980) and Zipora Talshir, *The Alternative Story of the Division of the Kingdom. 3 Kingdoms 12:24a–z* (Jerusalem Biblical Studies 6; Jerusalem: Simor, 1993). Although Talshir concludes that LXX-Kgs in comparison to MT-Kgs does not preserve the original reading in all of its details, she does conclude that the MT and LXX are independent revisions based upon a common tradition; therefore, her work could also be used to argue for two Deuteronomic, though independent, redactions.

Contra McKenzie, *Trouble with Kings*, pp. 21–40. McKenzie has argued specifically against Trebolle's analysis of LXX-1 Kgs 12:24a–z, arguing that it is based upon the MT and is therefore a later addition.

[19]Hugh G. M. Williamson, "The Death of Josiah and the Continuing Development of the Deuteronomic History," *VT* 32 (1982): 242–48. See Christopher T. Begg's challenge of Williamson's conclusions ("The Death of Josiah in Chronicles: Another View," *VT* 37 [1987]: 1–8.) and Williamson's responses to Begg's criticism ("Reliving the Death of Josiah: A Reply to C. T. Begg," *VT* 37 [1987]: 9–15.).

the Chronicler suggested different levels of redaction of the Deuteronomic History, with the LXX-*Vorlage* representing the earlier redaction.[20]

(8) Person, *The Kings–Isaiah and Kings–Jeremiah Recensions*:[21] Assuming that the redactors of Isaiah and Jeremiah borrowed from the book of Kings, I compared 2 Kings 18–20 (in both the MT and the LXX) and its parallel in Isaiah 36–39 (in the MT, the LXX, and the Isaiah Scroll of Qumran) as well as 2 Kings 24:18–25:30 (in both the MT and the LXX) and its parallel in Jeremiah 52 (also in the MT and the LXX). This text critical comparison led to the following generalizations: (a) MT-Kgs is a later, expansive text and (b) the LXX traditions of the prophetic books generally preserve the earliest text, even though they also have independent redactional revisions (LXX-Isaiah 36–39 and LXX-Jeremiah 52).

These text critical observations also suggest the following about the redaction history of Kings. (a) Both redactions of the book of Kings (LXX and MT) are Deuteronomic, in that Deuteronomic language and themes are found in material they have in common as well as in the MT additions. (b) MT-Kings is a postexilic text, probably from the fifth or fourth century B.C.E. The evidence for this postexilic dating includes the following:

(i) The earliest redaction of this material cannot be before the latest events which it describes—that is, the release of the exiled king Jehoiachin in 561 B.C.E. (2 Kgs 25:27–30 // Jer 52:31–34). The extensive re-working between the two redactions betrays a long

---

[20]Many other studies of the relationship between Chronicles and the Deuteronomic History could have been used to support conclusions similar to Williamson's. For example, Auld, "The 'Levitical Cities,'" 194–206; Werner E. Lemke, "The Synoptic Problem in the Chronicler's History," *HTR* 58 (1965): 349–63; J. C. Trebolle, "Redaction, Recension, and Midrash in the Books of Kings," *BIOSCS* 15 (1982): 12–35; Eugene C. Ulrich, *The Qumran Texts of Samuel and Josephus* (HSM 19; Missoula, MT: Scholars Press, 1978). However, this general tendency does not always hold true. For example, although Steven L. McKenzie argues that the *Vorlage* of Chronicles is generally closer to the LXX of the Deuteronomic History (*The Chronicler's Use of the Deuteronomistic History* [HSM 33; Atlanta: Scholars Press, 1985]), McKenzie also demonstrates that this is not necessarily the case in Kings (*The Chronicler's Use of the Deuteronomistic History*, 119–58; "1 Kings 8: A Sample Study into the Texts of Kings Used by the Chronicler and Translated by the Old Greek" *BIOSCS* 19 (1986): 15–34).

[21]Person, *The Kings–Isaiah and Kings–Jeremiah Recensions*.

lapse of time; therefore, it is unlikely that the later redaction would fall within the remaining period of the exile (561–538 B.C.E.), suggesting that the later redaction must be postexilic.

(ii) If MT-Jeremiah is postexilic, as Tov has argued,[22] then the close textual relationship of MT-Jeremiah 52 with MT-2 Kgs 24:18–25:30 and LXX-2 Kgs 24:18–25:30 suggests that these two texts are also postexilic.

(iii) Studies comparing Chronicles with Joshua–Kings suggest that the *Vorlage* which the Chronicler used was generally closer to LXX-Samuel–Kings than MT-Samuel–Kings.[23] Therefore, either the later redaction had not yet occurred or the later redaction had not yet gained the same authority and popularity as had the earlier redaction. Either of these possibilities would further support a postexilic date for the later redaction.

(iv) The phrase "a land of olive oil and honey" applied to Assyria in 2 Kgs 18:32 may be postexilic in origin. This phrase appears to be an addition for the following reason: it is a common phrase used in descriptions of the promised prosperity of the land (for example, Deut 8:8; 2 Chr 31:5), yet it cannot refer to Assyria, since Assyria's climate was not conducive to olive trees. Therefore, the redactor responsible for this addition probably lived in Israel. If this is the case, a preexilic or postexilic setting is most probable, since it is unlikely that a bureaucracy supporting scribes continued in Jerusalem during the exilic period. Since 2 Kings 20 is often understood as a foreshadowing of the Babylonian exile, the postexilic setting is the most likely setting for this addition.

(v) The occurrence of "the Jews" [היהודים] (2 Kgs 25:25 // MT-Jer 52:28,30 // LXX-Jer lacking) suggests a postexilic origin for the later redaction.[24]

---

[22]"Aspects," 166–67, "Literary History," 236–37. My arguments for the postexilic date of MT-2 Kings closely follow those of Tov concerning MT-Jeremiah.

[23]See above p. 40 n. 20.

[24]For all of the biblical references, see Person, *Kings–Isaiah and Kings–Jeremiah Recensions*, 112.

(vi) MT-Kings changes the original singular reading of verbs with collective subjects to plurals.[25] The rendering of collectives as plural is a feature of late biblical Hebrew[26] and, therefore, suggests a postexilic setting for MT-Kings.

Taken together, these arguments strongly suggest that MT-Kings is a product of the Deuteronomic school in the postexilic period.

All of these text critical studies compare favorably with many other text critical studies which also conclude that the LXX for the Deuteronomic History (often with support from Qumran, Chronicles, Josephus, and/or the Old Latin) generally preserves an earlier stage of the redaction process of the Deuteronomic History than the MT.[27] Together all of these studies suggest that the Deuteronomic History underwent, at least, a dual redaction. Since two of the text critical studies suggest a postexilic setting for the final Deuteronomic redaction, it is possible that the evidence for a later redaction in the other text critical studies should also be located within a postexilic setting. Such a possibility is especially supported by the evidence that the Chronicler used a *Vorlage* closer to the LXX than the MT for his material from Joshua, Samuel, and Kings, for the Chronicler may not have had access to the later redaction(s).

---

[25]For further discussion, see Person, *Kings–Isaiah and Kings–Jeremiah Recensions*, 103.

[26]Robert Polzin, *Late Biblical Hebrew: Toward an Historical Typology of Biblical Hebrew Prose* (HSM 12; Missoula: Scholars Press, 1976), 40–42.

[27]For example, Auld, "Judges 1 and History"; Auld, "Textual and Literary Studies in the Book of Joshua"; Pierre-M. Bogaert, "Les trois rédactions conservées et la forme originale de l'envoi du Cantique de Moïse (Dt 32,43)," in *Das Deuteronomium* (ed. N. Lohfink; BETL 68; Leuven: Leuven University Press, 1985), 329–40; Simon J. DeVries, "The Three Comparisons in 1 Kings XXII 4b and Its Parallel and 2 Kings III 7b," *VT* 39 (1989): 283–306; Leonard J. Greenspoon, *Textual Studies in the Book of Joshua* (HSM 28; Chico, CA: Scholars Press, 1983); Jos Luyten, "Primeval and Eschatological Overtones in the Song of Moses," in *Das Deuteronomium* (ed. N. Lohfink; BETL 68; Leuven: Leuven University Press, 1985), 341–47; McKenzie, *Chronicler's Use of the Deuteronomistic History*; James Donald Shenkel, *Chronology and Recensional Development in the Greek Text of Kings* (HSM 1; Cambridge: Harvard University Press, 1968); Eugene Charles Ulrich, *The Qumran Text of Samuel and Josephus* (HSM 19; Missoula, MT: Scholars Press, 1978).

Even though the text critical evidence suggests at least a dual-redaction of the Deuteronomic History, does this *necessarily* mean that the Deuteronomic school was responsible for the later redaction(s)? Although the answer to this question is "it is not necessarily so," some evidence suggests that the Deuteronomic school was responsible for some of the later redactions. In the following list, I provide quotes from the MT, which contain material that the above text critical studies have suggested are additions [given in italics]. In these examples, we find Deuteronomic language, strongly suggesting that these additions came from the hands of Deuteronomic scribes.

(1) Josh 20:4–6: "*He shall flee to one of these cities and present himself at the entrance to the city gate and plead his case before the elders of that city; and they shall admit him into the city and give him a place in which to live among them. Should the blood avenger pursue him, they shall not hand the manslayer over to him since he killed the other person without intent and had not been his enemy in the past. He shall live in that city until he can stand trial before the assembly until the death of the high priest who is in office at that time. Thereafter, the manslayer may go back to his home in his own town, to the town from which he fled.*"[28] This is a direct quote taken from Deut 19:4–6, which also has close affinities with Deut 4:41–43.

(2) Josh 1:7: "to observe faithfully according to *all the teaching* which Moses my servant enjoined to you."[29] The phrase "to observe faithfully according to *all the teaching*" is found in Deuteronomic literature frequently.[30]

(3) Josh 1:11: "The land which the Lord your God gives to you *as a possession.*"[31] This phrase occurs frequently in Deuteronomic literature.[32]

(4) Josh 24:17: "For it was the Lord our God who brought us and our fathers up from the land of Egypt *the house of bondage, and who*

---

[28]Rofé, "Joshua 20," 137–39. The translation is Rofé's. See also Tov, "Growth of the Book of Joshua," 335.

[29]Tov, "Growth of the Book of Joshua," 336. The translation is Tov's.

[30]Weinfeld, *Deuteronomy and the Deuteronomic School*, 336.

[31]Tov, "Growth of the Book of Joshua," 336. The translation is Tov's.

[32]Weinfeld, *Deuteronomy and the Deuteronomic School*, 342.

wrought those wondrous signs before our very eyes."[33] Two phrases in this addition suggest Deuteronomic origin: "*the house of bondage*"[34] and "*wondrous signs.*"[35]

(5) Jdgs 2:7: "*The people worshipped the Lord all the days of Joshua, and all the days of the elders who outlived Joshua, who had seen all the great work that the Lord had done for Israel.*" The phrase "*who had seen great work that the Lord had done*" is a Deuteronomic phrase.[36]

(6) Jdgs 2:11–13: "*Then the Israelites did what was evil in the sight of the Lord and worshipped the Baals; and they abandoned the Lord, the God of their ancestors, who had brought them out of the land of Egypt; they followed other gods, from among the gods of the peoples who were all around them, and bowed down to them; and they provoked the Lord, and worshipped Baal and the Astartes.*" This addition contains numerous Deuteronomic phrases: "*did what was evil in the sight of the Lord,*"[37] "*worshipped the Baals,*"[38] "*they followed other gods,*"[39] "*the gods of the peoples who were all around them and bowed down to them,*"[40] "*provoked the Lord,*"[41] and "*worshipped Baal and the Astartes.*"[42]

(7) Jdgs 2:17–23: "*Yet they did not listen even to their judges; for they lusted after other gods and bowed down to them. They soon turned aside from the way in which their ancestors had walked, who had obeyed the commandments of the Lord; they did not follow their example. Whenever the Lord raised up judges for them, the Lord was with the judge, and he delivered them from the hand of their enemies all the days of the judge; for the Lord would be moved to pity by their groaning because of those who persecuted and oppressed them. But whenever the judge died they would relapse and behave worse than their ancestors, following other gods,*

---

[33]Tov, "Growth of the Book of Joshua," 336. The translation is Tov's.

[34]Weinfeld, *Deuteronomy and the Deuteronomic School*, 326–27.

[35]Weinfeld, *Deuteronomy and the Deuteronomic School*, 330.

[36]Weinfeld, *Deuteronomy and the Deuteronomic School*, 329.

[37]Weinfeld, *Deuteronomy and the Deuteronomic School*, 339.

[38]Weinfeld, *Deuteronomy and the Deuteronomic School*, 320.

[39]Weinfeld, *Deuteronomy and the Deuteronomic School*, 320.

[40]Weinfeld, *Deuteronomy and the Deuteronomic School*, 321, 322.

[41]Weinfeld, *Deuteronomy and the Deuteronomic School*, 340.

[42]Weinfeld, *Deuteronomy and the Deuteronomic School*, 320.

worshipping them and bowing down to them. They would not drop any of their practices or their stubborn ways. So the anger of the Lord was kindled against Israel; and he said, 'Because this people has transgressed my covenant that I commanded their ancestors, and have not obeyed my voice, I will no longer drive out before them any of the nations that Joshua left when he died.' In order to test Israel, whether or not they would take care to talk in the way of the Lord as their ancestors did, the Lord had left those nations, not driving them out at once, and had not handed them over to Joshua. " This addition contains numerous Deuteronomic phrases, including: *"turned aside from the way,"*[43] *"obeyed the commandments,"*[44] *"behave worse,"*[45] *"following other gods,"*[46] *"worshipping them and bowing down to them,"*[47] *"transgressed my covenant,"*[48] *"drive out before them any of the nations,"*[49] *"to walk in the way of the Lord,"*[50] *"left those nations,"*[51] and *"not driving them out at once."*[52]

(8) 1 Sam 18:12: "Saul was afraid of David, *for the Lord was with him and had turned away from Saul.*"[53] The phrase *"the Lord ... had turned away from Saul"* suggests a Deuteronomic origin. The metaphorical use of "turning away" to denote apostasy has been noted before as characteristically Deuteronomic.[54] Closely related to this use is another

---

[43] Weinfeld, *Deuteronomy and the Deuteronomic School*, 339.
[44] Weinfeld, *Deuteronomy and the Deuteronomic School*, 337.
[45] Weinfeld, *Deuteronomy and the Deuteronomic School*, 340.
[46] Weinfeld, *Deuteronomy and the Deuteronomic School*, 320.
[47] Weinfeld, *Deuteronomy and the Deuteronomic School*, 321.
[48] Weinfeld, *Deuteronomy and the Deuteronomic School*, 340.
[49] Weinfeld, *Deuteronomy and the Deuteronomic School*, 342.
[50] Weinfeld, *Deuteronomy and the Deuteronomic School*, 333.
[51] Weinfeld, *Deuteronomy and the Deuteronomic School*, 344.
[52] Weinfeld, *Deuteronomy and the Deuteronomic School*, 343, 347.
[53] Emanuel Tov ("The Composition of I Samuel 16–18," 105) concluded that this addition comes from an independent tradition, which was conflated with the earlier tradition preserved in LXX. However, he did not discuss the possibility of this later redactor being Deuteronomic. The translation is Tov's.
[54] Weinfeld (*Deuteronomy and the Deuteronomic School*, 339) included the following phrases in his list of Deuteronomic phraseology: "to turn away," "to turn aside from the way," "to turn away from Yahweh," and "to turn right or left." To this list I add two other phrases that use a form of "turn" to describe apostasy: (1) "he did not turn

metaphorical use of "turning away"—the "turning away" of the Lord as punishment for the "turning away" of the apostates. Although such language occurs once in the book of Hosea (Hos 9:12),[55] all other occurrences of the Lord's "turning away" as punishment are within Deuteronomic literature.[56] Therefore, the metaphor of the Lord's "turning away" as punishment for the "turning away" of apostates betrays a Deuteronomic origin for this later addition.

(9) 1 Kgs 11:31–39: "And he said to Jeroboam, 'Take for yourself ten pieces; for thus says the Lord, the God of Israel, "Behold, I will tear the kingdom from the hand of Solomon and will give you ten tribes. *One tribe will be his, for the sake of my servant David and for the sake of Jerusalem, the city that I have chosen out of all the tribes of Israel. This is because they have forsaken me, worshipped Astarte the goddess of the Sidonians, Chemosh the god of Moab, and Milcom the god of the Ammonites. They have not walked in my ways, doing what is right in my sight and keeping the statutes and ordinances, as his father David did. Nevertheless I will not take the whole kingdom from him, but will make him a ruler all the days of his life, for the sake of my servant David whom I chose and who did keep my commandments and my statutes. But I will take the kingdom away from his son and give it—the ten tribes—to you. But to his son I will give one tribe, so that my servant David may always have a lamp before me in Jerusalem, the city where I have chosen to put my name. And you I will take and you will reign over all that your soul desires; you will be king over Israel. And if you will listen to all that I command you, walk in my ways, and do what is right in my sight by keeping my statutes and my commandments, as David my servant did, I will be with you and will build you an enduring house, just as I built for David, and I will give to you Israel. And I will punish the descendents of David for this reason, but not forever."*"[57] This addition

---

from the sins of Jeroboam" and its variants (2 Kgs 3:3; 10:29,31; 13:2,6,11; 14:24; 15:9,18,24,28; 17:22) and (2) "the high places were not taken [turned] away" (1 Kgs 15:14; 22:44; 2 Kgs 12:4; 14:4; 15:4,35).

[55]Num 14:9: "Their [the people of the land] protection is removed from them, and the Lord is with us." This verse may suggest such language, but the relationship between the Lord and the removal of the protection is not made explicit.

[56]Judg 16:20; 1 Sam 16:14,23; 18:12; 28:15,16; 2 Sam 7:15; 2 Kgs 24:3.

[57]Schenker, "Jeroboam and the Division of the Kingdom," 224–27.

contains numerous Deuteronomic phrases, including the following: *"for the sake of my servant David;"*[58] *"Jerusalem, the city that I have chosen out of all the tribes of Israel;"*[59] *"because they have forsaken me, worshipped [foreign gods];"*[60] *"walk in my ways;"*[61] *"doing what is right in my sight;"*[62] *"keeping the statutes and ordinances"/"keeping my commandments and my statutes;"*[63] *"whom I chose;"*[64] *"David may always have a lamp before me in Jerusalem;"*[65] and *"Jerusalem, the city where I have chosen to put my name."*[66]

(10) 1 Kgs 14:21b–24: "he was forty-one years old when he began to reign, and he reigned seventeen years in Jerusalem, *the city that the Lord has chosen to put his name there out of all of the tribes of Israel.* His mother's name was Naamah the Ammonite. Judah did what was evil in the sight of the Lord; *they provoked him to jealousy with their sins that they committed, more than all that their ancestors had done. For they also built for themselves high places, pillars, and sacred poles on every high hill and under every green tree; there were also male temple prostitutes in the land. They committed all the abominations of the nations that the Lord drove out before the people of Israel."*[67] Both additions in this passage contain Deuteronomic phrases: *"the city that the Lord has chosen to put his name there out of all the tribes of Israel;"*[68] *"they provoked him* [the Lord];"[69] *"on every high hill and under every green tree;"*[70] and *"the abominations of the nations that the Lord drove out."*[71]

---

[58] Weinfeld, *Deuteronomy and the Deuteronomic School*, 354.
[59] Weinfeld, *Deuteronomy and the Deuteronomic School*, 324, 325.
[60] Weinfeld, *Deuteronomy and the Deuteronomic School*, 320.
[61] Weinfeld, *Deuteronomy and the Deuteronomic School*, 333.
[62] Weinfeld, *Deuteronomy and the Deuteronomic School*, 335.
[63] Weinfeld, *Deuteronomy and the Deuteronomic School*, 336, 337.
[64] Weinfeld, *Deuteronomy and the Deuteronomic School*, 354.
[65] Weinfeld, *Deuteronomy and the Deuteronomic School*, 354.
[66] Weinfeld, *Deuteronomy and the Deuteronomic School*, 324, 325.
[67] Schenker, "Jeroboam and the Division of the Kingdom," 254–55.
[68] Weinfeld, *Deuteronomy and the Deuteronomic School*, 324, 325.
[69] Weinfeld, *Deuteronomy and the Deuteronomic School*, 340.
[70] Weinfeld, *Deuteronomy and the Deuteronomic School*, 322.
[71] Weinfeld, *Deuteronomy and the Deuteronomic School*, 323, 342.

(11) 2 Kgs 20:6: "I will defend this city for my own sake *and for the sake of David, my servant.*"[72] The phrase *"for the sake of David, my servant"* is clearly Deuteronomic[73] and is commonly associated with the Harvard school's Dtr[1].[74]

(12) 2 Kgs 24:19–20: *"And he did evil in the sight of the Lord, according to all that Jehoiakim had done. For because of the anger of the Lord it came to pass in Jerusalem and Judah that he cast them out from his presence."*[75] Two phrases in this addition suggest Deuteronomic origin: *"he did what was evil in the sight of the Lord "* and *"he [the Lord] cast them out from his presence."* The phrase *"to do what is evil in the sight of the Lord "* occurs numerous times throughout the Deuteronomic History (more than 50x) and in the Deuteronomic prose of Jeremiah (3x)[76] and this is not even taking into account the variations of this phrase such as "to do good in the sight of the Lord."[77] The phrase *"to cast away from the presence of the Lord "* is also typically Deuteronomic.[78] Therefore, the occurrence of these two phrases betrays a Deuteronomic origin for this postexilic addition.

The text critical studies summarized above have suggested that each of these passages contain post-LXX additions to the MT, most of which appear to be postexilic. The above discussion of these passages demonstrates that they also contain Deuteronomic language. These two observations strongly suggest that the Deuteronomic school redacted the Deuteronomic History in the postexilic period. I see no reason to postulate another scribal group for the postexilic redaction of the Deuteronomic History. Therefore, the text critical evidence alone suggests a postexilic setting for some

---

[72]Person, *Kings–Isaiah and King–Jeremiah Recensions*, 77.

[73]Weinfeld, *Deuteronomy and the Deuteronomic School*, 354.

[74]See Cross, "Themes and Structure," 281; Knoppers, *Two Nations under God*, 2:7, 43, 118, 119, 237.

[75]Person, *Kings–Isaiah and Kings–Jeremiah Recensions*, 110.

[76]Weinfeld, *Deuteronomy and the Deuteronomic School*, 339.

[77]Weinfeld, *Deuteronomy and the Deuteronomic School*, 335.

[78]Weinfeld, *Deuteronomy and the Deuteronomic School*, 347.

redactional activity of the Deuteronomic school in the Deuteronomic History.[79]

Oddly enough, those scholars who have analyzed the Deuteronomic History based solely upon the MT[80] have inadvertently supported my contention that the later additions in the final redaction of the Deuteronomic History —that is, the material unique to the MT—are also Deuteronomic. They have done so by basing their arguments upon the unity of Deuteronomic themes and language from the Deuteronomic History upon the final Deuteronomic redaction (MT). In other words, these postexilic additions in the final Deuteronomic redaction (those unique to the MT) have been incorrectly treated by many as originating in the exilic period at the hand of Deuteronomic redactors. These additions have been so treated because the themes and language therein are so similar to the material in the earlier redactions (represented in textual traditions such as the LXX, which have been generally ignored in redaction criticism) that these scholars could not discern a thematic or phraseological difference between what the text critical evidence suggests came from different stages of the redaction of the

---

[79]Römer has accepted the validity of this argument in his recent work on the Deuteronomic History. See Römer, "Transformations in Deuteronomistic and Biblical Historiography," 10–11.

[80]The following examples represent the Harvard school and the Göttingen school as well as some who still maintain a unity for the Deuteronomic History: Hans Jochen Boecker, *Die Beurteilung der Anfänge des Königtums in den deuteronomischen Abschnitten des I. Samuelbuches: Ein Beitrag zum Problem des deuteronomistischen Geschichtswerkes* (WMANT 31; Neukirchen: Neukirchener Verlag, 1969); Robert G. Boling, "In Those Days There Was No King in Israel," in *A Light unto My Path* (eds., H. Bream, R. Heim, and C. Moore; Philadelphia: Temple University Press, 1974), 33–48; Clements, "The Isaiah Narrative of 2 Kings 20:12–19 and the Date of the Deuteronomic History," 3:209–20; Cross, "Themes and Structure"; Richard Elliot Friedman, "From Egypt to Egypt: Dtr[1]and Dtr[2]," in *Traditions in Transformation* (eds. B. Halpern and J. D. Levenson; Winona Lake: Eisenbrauns, 1981), 167–92; Halpern, *First Historians*; T. R. Hobbs, *2 Kings* (WBC 18; Waco: Word Books, 1985); Jon Levenson, "The Last Four Verses in Kings" *JBL* 103 (1983): 349–63; Long, *I Kings*; Mayes, *Story of Israel*; Steven L. McKenzie, "The Prophetic History and the Redaction of Kings" *HAR* 9 (1985): 203–20; Nelson, *Double Redaction*; Noth, *Deuteronomistic History*; Gottfried Vanoni, "Beobachtungen zur deuteronomistischen Terminologie in 2 Kön 23,25–25,30," in *Das Deuteronomium* (ed. N. Lohfink; BETL 68; Leuven: Leuven University Press, 1985), 357–62.

Deuteronomic History. In other words, for the study of the Deuteronomic History, the stylistic and thematic criteria for redaction criticism have proven insufficient in discerning different redactional layers evident from text criticism. This insufficiency of the stylistic and thematic criteria can be explained by noting that the language and themes of the different redactional layers are so similar that the application of these criteria could not separate out the different layers. Because of this similarity, such redaction critical studies have fallen short and have also, inadvertently, pointed to the possibility of my thesis of postexilic, redactional activity of the Deuteronomic school.

THE THEME OF RESTORATION AND ITS IMPLICATIONS ON DATING

A theme within the Deuteronomic History that may suggest a postexilic setting for the final redaction of the Deuteronomic History is that of restoration following repentance. This theme is generally assumed to belong to the exilic period, thereby providing hope of the return to the exiles.[81] Although the exiles had a need for such reassurance, it was also needed by those who lived in postexilic Judah, who were struggling to rebuild the Temple and the community in the face of internal and external conflicts (see Haggai, Zechariah, Isaiah 56–66, Chronicles).[82] Therefore, there is no reason to assume that restoration themes in the Deuteronomic History necessarily point to an exilic rather than a postexilic setting. The following examples of texts from the Deuteronomic History contain restoration language and have been used to support the general assumption of an exilic setting of the final redaction of the Deuteronomic History. As such, they provide a framework for some representative interpretations of

---

[81]For example, Walter Brueggemann, "The Kerygma of the Deuteronomistic Historian," *Interpretation* 22 (1968): 387–402; Hans Walter Wolff, "The Kerygma of the Deuteronomic Historical Work," in *The Vitality of Old Testament Traditions* (eds. W. Brueggeman and H. W. Wollf; Atlanta: John Know, 1975), 83–100.

[82]In the "deutero-prophetic" literature that he discussed, David L. Petersen included as one characteristic of this literature the "eschatological scenario" (*Late Israelite Prophecy* [SBLMS 23; Missoula, MT: Scholars Press, 1977], 17). Such eschatological tendencies reassure postexilic communities; therefore, it is equally possible that the restoration theme in the Deuteronomic History also functioned in this manner.

these passages, which are based primarily upon the assumed exilic setting of the Deuteronomic History. Following this review, I will make some preliminary remarks concerning how these same passages could have functioned equally well in a postexilic setting.

The first three examples are taken from the book of Deuteronomy:

> When you are in distress and all these things come upon you, in the latter days you will return to the Lord your God and you will obey his voice, for the Lord your God is a merciful God; he will not fail you and he will not destroy you and he will not forget the covenant with your fathers which was sworn to them. (Deut 4:30–31)

> And if you surely obey the voice of the Lord your God, being careful to do all his commandments which I command you this day, the Lord your God will set you high above all the nations of the earth. And all these blessings shall come upon you and overtake you, for you obeyed the voice of the Lord your God. (Deut 28:1–2)

> When ... you remember them among all the nations where the Lord God has driven you; and when you return to the Lord your God and obey his voice in all that I command you this day, you and your children, with all your heart and with all your soul; then the Lord your God will reverse your captivity and have compassion upon you, and he will repent and gather you from all the peoples where the Lord your God has scattered you. (Deut 30:1–3)

According to A. D. H. Mayes, these three passages come from the hand of the exilic redactor, because they generally parallel the restoration language in Second Isaiah.[83] Richard Friedman argued that these three passages belong to the exilic Dtr[2] because they reflect the theme of "apostasy leading to exile and national dispersal, followed by repentance leading to restoration."[84] Ernest Nicholson suggested that the "turn again" motif in Deut 4:29–30 and Deut 30:1–6 is exilic, expressing hope to those exiled in Babylon for a future return.[85] According to Alexander Rofé, Deut 4:25–31 is exilic because these verses "explain the punishment of exile as for the

---

[83] Mayes, *Story of Israel*, 39.

[84] Friedman, "From Egypt to Egypt," 180–81, 183. See also Friedman, *The Exile and Biblical Narrative: The Formation of the Deuteronomistic and Priestly Works* (HSM 22; Chico: Scholars Press, 1981), 19, 25.

[85] Nicholson, *Preaching*, 76

making of images and speak of repentance in exile, but not of a return to the land."[86] Together, these representative commentators essentially argue that these three passages are exilic because they attempt to explain theologically the rationale for the exile and offer the hope of restoration without the explicit report of the restoration having taken place. In other words, these commentators have assumed the argument of an exilic setting for the final redaction of the Deuteronomic History and this assumption has influenced their understanding of the restoration language in these passages.

The next example is taken from the end of the book of Judges:

> And the people of Israel departed from there at that time, each to his tribe and clan, and they went out from there, each to his inheritance. In those days there was no king in Israel. Each man did what was right in his own eyes. (Judg 21:24–25)

According to Robert Boling, the use of the phrase "each man doing what is right in his own eyes" in Deut 12:8 and here in Judg 21:25 suggests what is required for Israel not only to enter the land and conquer its people (Deut 12:8), but also for Israel to "make a new beginning" once Israel is in the land.[87] Boling assigned Judg 19:1–21:25 to the exilic redactor and suggested that the language in this passage provided hope to the exiles—that is, this passage, which narrates the conquest, was added during the exilic period to give expression to the hope of making a new beginning, a restoration.[88] Again, the implicit restoration theme is illuminated against the assumed exilic setting of the final redaction of the Deuteronomic History.

---

[86]Rofé, "Monotheistic Argumentation," 442.

[87]Boling, "In Those Days," 44. A very similar line of argument for Judges 21:25 is given in William J. Dumbrell, "'In Those Days There Was No King in Israel; Every Man Did What Was Right in his Own Eyes'. The Purpose of the Book of Judges Reconsidered," *JSOT* 25 (1983), 23–33.

[88]Boling, "In Those Days," 41–44. See also James D. Martin, *The Book of Judges* (CBC; Cambridge: Cambridge University Press, 1975), 225–26.

The next two examples occur in the books of Kings:

> If they sin against you ..., then you are angry with them, and you give them to an enemy, so that they are carried away captive to the land of the enemy, distant or near. But if they take it to heart in the land to where they have been carried and they repent and they make supplication to you in the land of their captors, saying, 'We have sinned and we have acted perversely and we are evil.' If they return to you with all their mind and with all their heart ... and if they pray to you toward their land, which you gave to their fathers, the city which you have chosen, and the house which I have built for your name; then you will hear in heaven your dwelling place their prayer and their supplication, and you will maintain their cause and you will forgive your people who have sinned against you and all their transgressions which they have committed against you; and you will give them compassion in the sight of their captors that they may have compassion on them. (1 Kgs 8:46–50)

> And in the thirty-seventh year of the exile of Jehoiachin king of Judah, in the twelfth month, on the twenty-seventh day of the month, Evil-merodach king of Babylon, in the first year of his reign, lifted up Jehoiachin king of Judah from the house of bondage; and he spoke with him kindly; and he gave him a seat above the seats of the kings who were with him in Babylon. And Jehoiachin put off his garments of bondage and he dined regularly in his presence, all the days of his life. And for his allowance, a regular allowance was given to him from the king, a portion every day, all the days of his life. (2 Kgs 25:27–30)

According to Jon Levenson, 1 Kgs 8:22–53 belongs to the exilic redactor ("Dtr2") because both the theme of the foreign convert who makes a pilgrimage to Jerusalem (8:41–43) and the passage's theology of the Temple reflect "the Exilic or the immediate post-Exilic era."[89] Similarly, Levenson argued that 2 Kgs 25:27–30 is from the hand of the exilic redactor ("Dtr2") for the purpose of bringing "the legacy of the promisory

---

[89] Jon D. Levenson, "From Temple to Synagogue: 1 Kings 8," in *Traditions in Transformation* (Winona Lake, Ind.: Eisenbrauns, 1981), 158. On an exilic setting for 1 Kgs 8:22–53, see also Simon J. DeVries, *1 Kings* (WBC 12; Waco: Word Books, 1985), 126; John Gray, *I and II Kings: A Commentary* (OTL; Philadelphia: Westminster Press, 1970), 226; Gwilyn H. Jones, *1 and 2 Kings* (2 vols.; NCB; Grand Rapids: Eerdemans, 1984), 1:204; Richard D. Nelson, *First and Second Kings* (IBC; Atlanta: John Knox, 1981), 52–55; Ernst Würthwein, *Die Bücher der Könige: 1 Könige 1–16* (ATD 11, 1; Göttingen: Vandenhoeck and Ruprecht, 1977), 95.

covenant with David into line with the new historical reality effected by the events of 587 B.C.E."[90] Although he gave parallels to postexilic literature (Isaiah 56–66),[91] Levenson gave no reason why these passages in Kings are exilic rather than postexilic. If these themes reflect "the Exilic or the immediate post-Exilic era,"[92] then why does he reject the postexilic period as a possible setting? Since he gave no reason, we must assume his reason proceeds from his assumption of the exilic setting for the final redaction of the Deuteronomic History.

We have briefly reviewed some of the interpretations concerning restoration language in the Deuteronomic History and how they fit within the commentators' understanding of the redaction of the Deuteronomic History. Once again, we see a general assumption at work concerning the interpretations of these passages. This assumption concerns Noth's imprecise argument for the exilic setting of the final redaction of the Deuteronomic History. In other words, the assumption of an exilic setting for the final redaction of the Deuteronomic History suggests that all restoration language in the Deuteronomic History is *vaticinia pro eventu* (prophecy before the event) rather than *vaticinia ex eventu* (prophecy after the event).

Although it would be equally imprecise to assume that all restoration language is *vaticinia ex eventu* and, therefore, postexilic; we must acknowledge the possibility that restoration language in the Deuteronomic History may have a postexilic setting. This acknowledgement is based upon the realization that restoration language clearly occurs in postexilic literature as the following example from the book of Zechariah illustrates:

---

[90]Levenson, "Last Four Verses," 361. On an exilic setting for 2 Kgs 25:27–30, see also Halpern, *First Historians*, 158; Siegfried Herrmann, *Prophetie und Wirklichkeit in der Epoche des babylonischen Exils* (Stuttgart: Calwer, 1967), 12–113; Hobbs, *2 Kings*, 367–69; Nelson, *First and Second Kings*, 265–69; Nicholson, *Preaching*, 78–79; Gerhard von Rad, *Old Testament Theology* (trans. D. M. G. Stalker; 2 vols.; New York: Harper & Row, 1962), I:334–47, esp. 343; E. Zenger, "Die deuteronomistische Interpretation der Rehabilitierung Jojachins," *BZ* 12 (1968): 30.

[91]Levenson, "1 Kings 8," 158–59.

[92]Levenson, "1 Kings 8," 158.

I will strengthen the house of Judah, and the house of Joseph I will save. I will bring them back for I have compassion on them, and they will be as if I had not rejected them; for I am the Lord their God and I will answer them. (Zech 10:6)

With the possibility of both an exilic and a postexilic setting in mind, the restoration themes in the Deuteronomic History need to be reevaluated in order to determine, if possible, the redactional setting of each passage. Unfortunately, as argued in Chapter 1, redaction critical tools often prove incapable of such precise delineation of Deuteronomic literature without the aid of text critical controls. Since text critical controls are not often available and when they are the results from them remain quite limited, a tremendous difficulty remains in determining when a passage with restoration language originated in the exilic or postexilic period.

Below in Chapters 5 and 6, I will present interpretations of various texts in the Deuteronomic History in a postexilic setting, but here I give some preliminary remarks concerning how the restoration themes in the Deuteronomic History could be understood in the context of a postexilic setting. Two themes concerning the land can be easily understood against a postexilic setting: (1) the theme in Deuteronomy concerning the covenantal requirements upon Israel before they enter the land and (2) the theme in Judges concerning the conquest of the land, which could be lost if the Lord's commandments are not kept. These themes can be understood as narrative forms of the admonition of what was required for the return of the exiles to Judah and for the continuing restoration of the people of God. In other words, the postexilic community of Judah could be addressed in narrative through the speeches of Moses and other prominent figures in the Deuteronomic History to obey the Lord concerning what is required of them, like their ancestors, to remain and flourish in the land. The passages given above from the books of Kings could easily be viewed against the backdrop of the Second Temple (1 Kgs 8:46–50) and the postexilic hope for the Davidides (2 Kgs 25:27–30). Nothing in the narrative of any of these passages requires an exilic, rather than a postexilic, setting. They are equally, and possibly better, understood when they are placed within a postexilic setting.

A disclaimer is required before proceeding further. My criticism of the above interpretations does *not* suggest that they require, rather than an

exilic setting, a postexilic setting. The assumption in favor of the final redaction of the Deuteronomic History in the exilic period should be seriously questioned and, therefore, the themes of restoration need to be reevaluated so that the possibilities of exilic *and* postexilic settings can be taken seriously. Therefore, it may be that further research will show that some of the above passages were produced in the exilic period, while others were produced in the postexilic period.

SOCIO-POLITICAL CONTEXT FOR THE DEUTERONOMIC SCHOOL

With the deportations of 597 and 587 B.C.E., the leadership of Judah was removed from the land and taken into exile in Babylonia. In 539 B.C.E., the Babylonian empire fell to the Persian king, Cyrus the Great. In the following year, Cyrus gave an edict which proclaimed royal support for the return of the exiles to Jerusalem under Sheshbazzar and the rebuilding of the temple, thus beginning the return of the exiles to Jerusalem and the establishment of the province of Judah. After Cyrus' death in 530 B.C.E., his son Cambyses I ascended to the Persian throne. With Cambyses' death in 522 B.C.E., revolts broke out and a struggle for the accession to the throne occurred. In late 522 B.C.E., Darius I gained control of the throne and consolidated his empire. Early in his reign, Darius appointed Zerubbabel as governor of Judah. Zerubbabel, as governor, and Joshua ben Jehozadak, as high priest, led more exiles to Jerusalem in order to renew the effort to rebuild the temple. Zerubbabel and Joshua found prophetic support in the messages of the prophets Haggai and Zechariah. In 516/515 B.C.E., the Jerusalem temple was rededicated.

During the reign of Darius I (522–486 B.C.E.), the Persian empire, including the province of Judah, experienced a high degree of stability. However, following Darius' death in 486 B.C.E., another period of instability in the empire began. In 486 B.C.E., Egypt rebelled against Persian control and, in 482 B.C.E., the Babylonians assassinated their satrap. Again in 460 B.C.E., Egypt revolted against the empire, this time with the support of the Athenian navy. Shortly after this revolt was put down, Megabyzus, the satrap of Beyond the River, rebelled against the Persian throne. Within this context of instability, the missions of two other

appointees, Ezra (458 B.C.E.) and Nehemiah (445 B.C.E.), occurred.[93] Through the missions of both Ezra and Nehemiah, Artaxerxes I (465–424 B.C.E.) strove to consolidate Persian control of the small, but strategically important, province of Judah.[94] As with previous appointees and their missions to Jerusalem, both Ezra and Nehemiah were accompanied by more returnees.

As is evident in the above brief review of history, Persian imperial administration included the return of displaced peoples to their ethnic homelands as well as the restoration of local sanctuaries and their native cults. This strategy is evident in various missions to Jerusalem, including the missions of Sheshbazzar, Zerubbabel, Ezra, and Nehemiah. An important element of this strategy included the return of scribal groups who were responsible for the codification and preservation of religious literature associated with the restored sanctuary. This Persian strategy is most clearly illustrated in the mission of Udjahorresnet to Sais, Egypt.[95]

Assuming that the Deuteronomic school returned to Judah with Persian support, there are several possible missions in which they may have participated—that is, the returns under Sheshbazzar, Zerubbabel, Ezra, and

---

[93]My position does not require firm agreement with these dates of Ezra and Nehemiah nor with an understanding that the entire material in the book of Ezra and Nehemiah are somehow historically reliable. Obviously, there are theological motives involved in the writing of this material, and not all of the details are historically reliable. (For criticism of such assumptions concerning Ezra, see Lester L. Grabbe, "What was Ezra's Mission?" in *Second Temple Studies: 2. Temple and Community in the Persian Period* [eds. T. C. Eskenazi and K. H. Richards; JSOTSup 175; Sheffield Academic Press, 1994], 286–99 and David Janzen, "The 'Mission' of Ezra and the Persian-Period Temple Community," *JBL* 119 [2000]: 619–43.) However, the narrative clearly presents the Persian emperor as behind the missions of Ezra and Nehemiah and I think that there is some historical kernel behind this perspective. This does not require the idea that the Persians were generous in their policies toward foreign religious cults. On the contrary, the reestablishment of temple cults and the maintenance of some administrative control over them provided the imperial administration with a source of taxes and a way to influence the masses through their own religious traditions.

[94]For the most thorough discussion of the context of Ezra and Nehemiah's missions within the Achaemenid empire, see Kenneth G. Hoglund, *Achaemenid Imperial Administration in Syria-Palestine and the Missions of Ezra and Nehemiah* (SBLDS 125; Atlanta: Scholar Press, 1992).

[95]On Udjahorrsenet, see further Chapter 3 below.

Nehemiah. The return under Zerubbabel is to be preferred for several reasons.[96] First, the other possibilities appear to be unlikely. The return under Sheshbazzar failed to accomplish its mission of rebuilding the Jerusalem temple and may have lacked the necessary support from Persian authorities and the exiles in Babylon. The missions of Ezra and Nehemiah occurred quite late after the temple cult had clearly been reestablished—for example, Ezra's lawbook competed with a body of religious literature that already existed in Jerusalem. Therefore, the return under Zerubbabel seems the most likely. Second, Darius I's concern for reestablishing religious literature associated with restored local temples is obvious in the contemporary mission of Udjahorresnet. That is, Darius' commission of Zerubbabel to rebuild the temple and its cult in Jerusalem most likely included the return of a scribal group of exiles. The Deuteronomic school is the most likely candidate for this group. Together these arguments strongly suggest that the Deuteronomic school returned to Jerusalem under Zerubbabel with the likely task of preservation and codification of earlier literature for the restored temple.

The Deuteronomic theological interpretation of Israel's history would have prepared the Deuteronomic school for collaboration with the Persian administration's effort to rebuild Jerusalem and the temple cult. On the one hand, they interpreted the destruction of Israel by the Assyrians and Babylonians as the Lord's judgment for disobeying the Lord's commandments (for example, 2 Kgs 17:1–18; 25:1–21). On the other hand, they understood that the Babylonians would also be divinely judged for their treatment of Israel, a judgment that would ultimately lead to the restoration of Israel (for example, 1 Kgs 8:46–50; Jer 25:11–14). Like the prophet of Second Isaiah (Isa 44:24–45:13), the Deuteronomic school may have viewed the conquest of Babylon by the Persians and the Persian policy of return and restoration as fulfillment of the Lord's plan.[97] Therefore, the

---

[96]In his work on Jeremiah, Yohanan Goldman independently concluded that the Deuteronomic school returned under Zerubbabel (*Prophétie et royauté au retour de l'exil* [OBO 118; Freiburg: Universitätsverlag Freiburg, 1992]).

[97]For a fuller discussion of the Deuteronomic school's theology in the postexilic period, see further Chapters 5 and 6 below.

Deuteronomic school would have seen themselves as collaborating with the Lord more so than with the Persians.

This theological understanding of history may have cut both ways though. Although it allowed the Deuteronomic school to collaborate with the Persian-supported administration in Jerusalem in the early Persian period, it probably led to increasing conflict with this same Persian-supported administration as time went by. That is, the Deuteronomic school's theological understanding of history included certain expectations about what would occur if the people returned to Jerusalem and restored the temple cult, including political autonomy for Judah and the restoration of the Davidic king. As time went on, it became increasingly clear that this was not going to happen under the Persian-supported administration, which would have led to increasing conflict between the Deuteronomic school and the other groups in the administration. It is in this context of Deuteronomic disillusionment with and distancing from the Jerusalem leadership that I place a growing eschatological perspective.[98]

This disillusionment and conflict with the Jerusalem administration probably affected the fate of the Deuteronomic school. The mission of Ezra, who is depicted as bringing with him "the law of the God of Heaven," suggests that the Deuteronomic school had lost favor with the temple administration in Jerusalem and Persian authorities. Although the exact character of Ezra's legal material cannot be ascertained, it most likely was not identical to that of the Deuteronomic school. The description of Ezra as the one who brings "the law" with him itself suggests that this "law" was to have a new status in Judah and thus conflicted with the "law" established under previous returns. Hence, Ezra's introduction of "the law of the God of Heaven" probably was an attempt by the Persian authorities to reassert some control over the Jerusalem political and religious establishment in face of antagonism caused by the increasingly disenfranchised Deuteronomic school.[99] This reassertion of Persian control appeared in the form of replacing one legal system (in the Deuteronomic canon) with another

---

[98]See Chapter 6 below.

[99]This is consistent with Hoglund's suggestion that "general defection" in Jerusalem may be the situation to which Ezra's mission was the Persian administration's response (*Achaemenid Imperial Administration*, 230).

(Ezra's law), a strategy not unknown elsewhere in the Persian empire. Ezra's mission, which included social as well as legal reforms, may have thus undermined the political and social support upon which the Deuteronomic school depended, thereby contributing to its demise.

There is a growing tendency among scholars to date at least the final redactions of many biblical books to the Persian period and even the Hellenistic period. Ehud Ben Zvi has recently argued, however, that the early Persian period (Persian I; 538–450 B.C.E.) did not have the required social resources that are conducive to literary production and that the late Persian period (Persian II; 450–332 B.C.E.) was more conducive to such literary activity.[100] Although he does not deal only with the Deuteronomic school, Ben Zvi's general comments concerning the "literati" in Persian Judah conflict to some degree with the above reconstruction of the social setting of the Deuteronomic school in the postexilic period. Therefore, a careful critique of his position is given below as well as my argument that the Persian I period was also conducive to literary production.

I share Ben Zvi's presuppositions concerning the necessary social resources available for the support of a scribal group, such as the Deuteronomic school:

> The presence of a group of literati ... presupposes (1) availability of the resources necessary for educating and continuously supporting their activities (including writing, reading, re-reading, copying, training of readers and copyists, etc.), and (2) a need for such activity in society.[101]

Where we disagree is whether or not these conditions can be met in Persian I period.

Ben Zvi draws heavily from the demographic work of Charles Carter.[102] Carter draws from both archaeological data for Persian Judah and

---

[100]Ehud Ben Zvi, "The Urban Center of Jerusalem and the Development of the Literature of the Hebrew Bible," in *Urbanism in Antiquity* (Sheffield: Sheffield Academic Press, 1997), 194–209.

[101]Ben Zvi, "Urban Center," 196.

[102]Charles E. Carter, "The Province of Yehud in the Post-Exilic Period: Soundings in Site Distribution and Demography [graphs, maps, tables]," in *Second Temple Studies* (2 vols.; Sheffield: JSOT Press, 1994), 2:106–145. Since Ben Zvi's work, Carter has published a fuller presentation of his thesis (*Emergence of Yehud in the Persian Period: A*

sociological models for estimating population based on the size of settlements. Carter estimates the population of Persian I Judah as about 13,350 and Persian II Judah as about 20,650.[103] Carter concludes, "according to my estimates, the province of Yehud was both relatively small and relatively poor for much of the Persian period."[104] Carter's work is clearly the most methodologically sophisticated study of the demography of Persian Judah and I do not question his conclusions. However, I do not agree with Ben Zvi's use of Carter's conclusions. In fact, although he did not have access to Ben Zvi's essay, Carter himself foresees interpretations of his demographic data that are similar to Ben Zvi's and explicitly rejects them.[105]

Ben Zvi argues that, since Persian Judah was so small and poor, there could not have been the necessary resources, especially in the Persian I period, to support the type of literary production often imagined. When Carter deals specifically with the question of a small and relatively poor Judah producing a significant amount of literature, he concludes that "the level of literary creativity traditionally attributed to the Persian period need not be questioned on the grounds either of a small province or a small Jerusalem."[106] Even in agrarian societies, such as Persian Judah, urban elites

---

Social and Demographic Study [JSOTSup 294; Sheffield: Sheffield Academic Press, 1999]).

[103] Ben Zvi ("Urban Center," 194) reported Carter's figures (11,000 and 17,000 respectively) from his earlier work ("The Province of Yehud in the Post-Exilic Period," 108). Based on new archaeological surveys, Carter revised his figures upward to 13,350 and 20,650 (*Emergence of Yehud*, 201).

[104] Carter, "The Province of Yehud in the Post-Exilic Period," 108. Even with the revised figures, this conclusion obtains (*Emergence of Yehud*, 246).

[105] See also the arguments by John Kessler against Ben Zvi ("Reconstructing Haggai's Jerusalem: Demographic and Sociological Considerations and the Quest for an Adequate Methodological Point of Departure," in *Every City Shall Be Forsaken: Urbanism and Prophecy in Ancient Israel and the Near East* [eds. L. Grabbe and R. Haak; JSOTSup 330; Sheffield: Sheffield Academic Press, 2001], 137–58).

[106] Carter, *Emergence of Yehud*, 288

See also David Vanderhooft, "New Evidence Pertaining to the Transition from Neo-Babylonian to Achaemenid Administration in Palestine," in *Yahwism after the Exile* (eds. Rainer Albertz and Bob Becking; Studies in Theology and Religion; Assen-Maastricht: Van Gorcum, forthcoming 2002). Vanderhooft analyzes epigraphic evidence and

may account for less than 10 percent of the population. These elites provide a variety of specialized skills, including often scribal skills. Therefore, it is possible that Ben Zvi's "literati" existed throughout the Persian period.[107] Carter also demonstrates that, even though Persian Judah itself was small and poor, as an administrative unit of the Persian empire it was not necessarily isolated or insignificant. In fact, the biblical text suggests that the Persians helped to finance the rebuilding of the Jerusalem temple and restoration of its cult as well as the rebuilding of the city and its defensive walls, because Jerusalem's location was strategically significant (for example, Ezra 1; 5; Nehemiah 2).[108] The biblical text also suggests that some of the Jewish returnees who lived in surrounding provinces supported the rebuilding of Jerusalem and the temple cult (for example, Nehemiah 3). Moreover, the archaeological data suggests that there was a vibrant trade between Persian Judah with surrounding provinces. In other words, even within a small and relatively poor Jerusalem, an urban elite that included scribes for literary production could have been supported by a combination of local support, support from Jews in surrounding provinces, and the support of the Persian imperial administration.[109]

Carter's contention is consistent with what Elayi, Crowley, and Sapin have called "one of the most characteristic phenomena" of the Beyond the River satrapy, the Persian administrative area to which Persian

---

determines that the Persian administration greatly expanded opportunities for Jewish scribes, both in Judah and other areas of the empire.

[107]Carter, *Emergence of Yehud*, 287.

[108]For an excellent discussion of how this fits into the larger Persian empire's political strategy, see Hoglund, *Achaemenid Imperial Administration*.

[109]The arguments presented by some for Palestine being the location of an exilic redaction (for example, Noth's "Deuteronomistic Historian," Dietrich's "DtrP," and Veijola's "DtrG," DtrP," and "DtrN") are also to be rejected. First, the sociological conditions required to support such literary activity in exilic Palestine were certainly lacking, as implied in Ben Zvi's and Carter's arguments summarized above. Second, any perspectives within the Deuteronomic History that might hint at a setting in Palestine can be explained by these elements being present in pre-exilic sources used or being added by postexilic Deuteronomic redactors in Jerusalem. See Noth, *Deuteronomistic History*, 142 n. 9; Dietrich, *Prophetie und Geschichte*, 143–44; Timo Veijola, *Die ewige Dynastie: David und die Entstehung seiner Dynastie nach der deuteronomistischen Darstellung* (AASF 193; Helsinki: Suomaleinen Tiedeakatemia, 1975).

Judah belonged—that is, "the overlapping of powers that sometimes strangely resembled a system of nesting boxes."[110] Elayi, Crowley, and Sapin give the example of the city of Ashkelon, which had its own monarchy but was nevertheless dependent politically on the city-state of Tyre. Tyre was under Persian control of a provincial authority, which was also under the control of a Persian satrap. Therefore, although Ben Zvi's characterization of the limited resources that Persian I Jerusalem had itself may be accurate, his argument against the possibility of a "literati" in Jerusalem during this time should be rejected, because resources from outside Jerusalem could have easily been utilized. In fact, Carter has provided archaeological data that can support the contention of this study—that is, the social circumstances of the early Persian period not only could provide adequate resources to support the Deuteronomic school, but the scribal skills of the Deuteronomic school also served a bureaucratic necessity within the Persian imperial administration, including the restoration of the Jerusalem temple cult and the preservation and production of religious literature associated with the temple cult.

---

[110]Josette Elayi, J. Edward Crowly, and Jean Sapin, *Beyond the River: New Perspectives on Transeuphratene* (JSOTSup 250; Sheffield: Sheffield Academic Press, 1998), 145.

CHAPTER 3

SCRIBAL SCHOOLS IN THE
ANCIENT NEAR EAST

As stated in the Introduction, I understand the Deuteronomic school to be a guild of scribes who collected, preserved, and composed literary texts, including the Deuteronomic History and Jeremiah. This understanding is influenced by comparative discussions of scribal schools in the ancient Near East. Below I begin by reviewing the evidence for scribal schools in the ancient Near East and the common arguments for the existence of scribal schools in ancient Israel specifically. This discussion will demonstrate clearly that at least some scribes in the ancient Near East were involved in functions other than copying and transcribing. That is, some scribes were themselves composers of literary texts. All redactors were trained as scribes, although not all scribes were redactors. Therefore, a review of the role of scribes and scribal schools in the ancient Near East may illumine the role of the Deuteronomic redactors.

SCRIBAL SCHOOLS IN THE ANCIENT NEAR EAST: A REVIEW OF
LITERATURE[1]

SCRIBES AND SCRIBAL SCHOOLS PRIOR TO THE PERSIAN
PERIOD

During the Old Babylonian period, the institution of the *edubba*s
("tablet-houses") provided for the education of artisans, especially reading
and writing. According to Å. W. Sjöberg,[2] Sumerian was no longer a living
language; therefore, instruction began in Babylonian with the goal of
bilingualism (Sumerian and Babylonian). Other than the study of Sumerian,
the curriculum in *edubba*s included mathematics, surveying, music,
agriculture, construction, and literature. The study of literature in the
*edubba*s was of primary importance and included dictation, composition,
and the ability to identify isolated quotes within its proper literary context.
Concerning the leaders within these *edubba*s, Samuel Noah Kramer wrote:[3]

> In the *edubba*s of Nippur and Ur, for example, there flourished the scholar and
> man of letters, the academic and humanist, who studied, enlarged, and
> expanded whatever linguistic, literary, and theological lore was current in his
> day.

In his survey of "The Sage in Mesopotamian Palaces and Royal
Courts,"[4] Ronald Sweet included a discussion of the palace scribe, who was

---

[1] This section is heavily dependent upon John G. Gammie and Leo G. Perdue, eds.,
The Sage in Israel and the Ancient Near East (Winona Lake: Eisenbrauns, 1990). In this
volume, the designation "sage" is sufficiently broad so as to include discussions of
scribes.

[2] This paragraph on *edubba*s is based primarily upon Å. W. Sjöberg, "The Old
Babylonian Eduba," in *Sumeriological Studies in Honor of Thorkild Jacobsen on his
Seventieth Birthday* (ed. S. Liebermann; AS 20; Chicago: University of Chicago Press,
1975), 159–79.

[3] Samuel N. Kramer, "Sage in Sumerian Literature: A Composite Portrait," in *The
Sage in Israel and the Ancient Near East* (eds. J. G. Gammie and L. G. Perdue; Winona
Lake: Eisenbrauns, 1990), 31–32.

[4] Ronald F. G. Sweet, "The Sage in Mesopotamian Palaces and Royal Courts," in
The Sage in Israel and the Ancient Near East (eds. J. G. Gammie and L. G. Perdue;
Winona Lake: Eisenbrauns, 1990), 99–107.

"indispensable for administration of the scale and complexity practiced in Mesopotamia."[5] Sweet noted that by the Ur III period the institution of the "palace scribe" (*dub-sar-é-gal*) was well established with eighteen different scribal titles used. Although many scribes dealt primarily, or maybe even exclusively, with administrative texts, some scribes were involved in the composition and transmission of various literary genres, including royal inscriptions, collections of legal material, year-lists, king lists, chronicles, hymns of praise, and disputation texts. Therefore, the Mesopotamian palace scribe was not necessarily a mere transcriber or copyist, rather some were composers in their own right.[6]

In his review of Egyptian literature, Ronald Williams has described the practice of scribal training in ancient Egypt, beginning in the Old Kingdom. According to his reconstruction, youths underwent four years of elementary instruction in basic skills (for example, arithmetic) with a strong emphasis on the art of writing, beginning with hieratic then hieroglyphic script.[7] After this elementary education, there were various types of advanced studies. Some of the youths were granted the title "scribe" and undertook more advanced classes; others may have continued their studies within an apprenticeship; still others may have attended trade schools.[8] Those who became scribes hoped to attain a position in the "House of Life," a scribal institution which not only copied texts but also produced them.[9] Usually located near a temple, the "House of Life" contained archives that included religious texts. Given the functions of the "House of Life," an

---

[5]Sweet, "Sage in Mesopotamian Palace," 103. His discussion of palace scribes is on 103–05.

[6]See Rivkah Harris, "The Female 'Sage' in Mesopotamian Literature (with an Appendix on Egypt)," in *The Sage in Israel and the Ancient Near East* (eds. J. G. Gammie and L. G. Perdue; Winona Lake: Eisenbrauns, 1990), 3–17. Harris reached a similar conclusion concerning female scribes in Mesopotamia. Her discussion included the female scribe as bureaucrat, poetess, and scholar.

[7]Ronald J. Williams, "Scribal Training in Ancient Egypt," *JAOS* 92 (1972): 216, 219.

[8]Williams, "Scribal Training in Ancient Egypt," 216.

[9]Ronald J. Williams, "The Sage in Egyptian Literature," in *The Sage in Israel and the Ancient Near East* (eds. J. G. Gammie and L. G. Perdue; Winona Lake: Eisenbrauns, 1990), 26–27; Williams, "Scribal Training in Ancient Egypt," 220–21.

accomplished Egyptian scribe would have been much more than a mere copyist, he (or possibly she) would have become a compiler, a librarian, and, possibly, an author.

With respect to the Ugaritic evidence, Loren Mack-Fisher criticized Albright's conclusion that there was no didactic material[10] and the continuing influence of his conclusion upon contemporary works. After re-assessing the existing Ugaritic corpus, Mack-Fisher concluded that Ugaritic scribes produced various types of didactic literature, which betray strong Babylonian influence.[11] He then reconstructed a list of Ugaritic scribes in relationship to the Ugaritic kings under whom they served.[12] In his discussion of some of these Ugaritic scribes, he noted various roles that the Ugaritic scribe might play, including counselor to the king, librarian, and composer of literary works. As in Egypt and Mesopotamia, a scribe in Ugarit was not necessarily a mere transcriber or copyist, nor even confined to literary matters such as composition.

The extent of the diffusion of educational institutions and literacy in preexilic Israel remains widely debated. For example, André Lemaire has concluded that schools existed in every major city of preexilic Judah and that the general populace had access to these schools; therefore, the rate of literacy was high.[13] On the other hand, Roger Whybray has concluded that there were no schools at all in preexilic Judah and, therefore, a relatively low rate of literacy.[14] Despite this variety, there appears to be a movement towards a more minimalist view of literacy and schools for instruction in

---

[10]Loren R. Mack-Fisher, "A Survey and Reading Guide to the Didactic Literature of Ugarit: Prolegomenon to a Study on the Sage," in *The Sage in Israel and the Ancient Near East* (eds. J. G. Gammie and L. G. Perdue; Winona Lake: Eisenbrauns, 1990), 67.

[11]Mack-Fisher, "Didactic Literature of Ugarit."

[12]Loren R. Mack-Fisher, "The Scribe (and Sage) in the Royal Court at Ugarit," in *The Sage in Israel and the Ancient Near East* (eds. J. G. Gammie and L. G. Perdue; Winona Lake: Eisenbrauns, 1990), 111–12.

[13]André Lemaire, "The Sage in School and Temple," in *The Sage in Israel and the Ancient Near East* (eds. J. G. Gammie and L. G. Perdue; Winona Lake: Eisenbrauns, 1990), 165–181.

[14]Roger N. Whybray, "The Sage in the Israelite Royal Court," in *The Sage in Israel and the Ancient Near East* (eds. J. G. Gammie and L. G. Perdue; Winona Lake: Eisenbrauns, 1990), 139.

ancient Israel, so much so that Graham Davies has concluded that "viewed as a whole, the tenor of scholarly discussion has moved from confident assertion [of the existence of schools] to doubt and even denial in recent years."[15] The two most comprehensive, recent studies of the problem are works by James Crenshaw and Susan Niditch, both of whom understand a relatively low level of literacy in ancient Israel primarily limited to professional scribes. Susan Niditch wrote that "the presence of many documents, while it assures the existence of scribal classes of various sorts, does not offer evidence of general literacy in the modern sense."[16] Similarly Crenshaw wrote:[17]

> A few scribal guilds existed from early times and were conscripted, probably at their own initiative, by some monarchs to assist in propaganda, record keeping, and administrative activity. With the collapse of the monarchy, first in the north and later in Judah, a single guild may have continued to train scribes in exile and subsequently in Judah.

Therefore, although the tendency among scholars is to minimize the diffusion of educational institutions and general literacy, even many of these same scholars accept that there must have been some institutions for the training of professional scribes in preexilic Judah.[18]

---

[15]Graham I. Davies, "Were There Schools in Ancient Israel?" in *Wisdom in Ancient Israel: Essays in Honor of J. A. Emerton* (ed. J. Day, R. P. Gordon, and H. G. M. Williamson; Cambridge: Cambridge University Press, 1995), 199.

[16]Susan Niditch, *Oral World and Written Word: Ancient Israelite Literature* (Louisville: Wesminster/John Knox Press, 1996), 50.

[17]James L. Crenshaw, *Education in Ancient Israel: Across the Deadening Silence* (ABRL; New York: Doubleday, 1998), 12.

[18]Although there is some variety among the following concerning the extent of scribal guilds, the following argue that some institution must have provided formal instruction for the training of professional scribes in the bureaucracy: Crenshaw, *Education in Ancient Israel*, 85–113; Menahem Haran, "On the Diffusion of Literacy and Schools in Ancient Israel," in *Congress Volume: Jerusalem 1986* (ed. J. A. Emerton; VTSup 40; Leiden: E. J. Brill, 1988), 81–95; David W. Jamieson-Drake, *Scribes and Schools in Monarchic Judah: A Socio-Archeological Approach* (JSOTSup 109; Sheffield: Almond Press, 1991); Lemaire, "The Sage in School and Temple," 165–181; Niditch, *Oral World*, 39–77; Puech, "Les écoles dans l'Israël preéxilique: données épigraphiques," in *Congress Volume: Jerusalem 1986* (ed. J. A. Emerton; VTSup 40; Leiden: E. J. Brill, 1988), 189–203.

Arguments for the existence of formal training of scribes in preexilic Judah are based on four kinds of evidence: (1) The Hebrew Bible itself contains three kinds of evidence: (a) narratives that describe the activity of professional scribes (for example, 2 Kgs 22:8–13),[19] (b) the mention of the existence of source materials, which presumably would have come from the royal court,[20] such as "the Book of the Chronicles of the Kings of Israel"[21] and "the Book of the Chronicles of the Kings of Judah";[22] and (c) vocabulary reflecting the technical language of scribalism.[23] (2) The administrative complexity of the institution of the monarchy required the service of professional scribes; therefore, in order to fulfill this need, scribal schools were established.[24] (3) Scribal schools existed throughout the ancient Near East; hence, by analogy, ancient Israel may have also had scribal schools.[25] (4) Archaeological evidence, especially epigraphic sources, increasingly suggests the existence of professional

---

[19]For example, Joseph Blenkinsopp, "The Sage, the Scribe, and Scribalism in the Chronicler's Work," in *The Sage in Israel and the Ancient Near East* (eds. J. G. Gammie and L. G. Perdue; Winona Lake: Eisenbrauns, 1990), 308–09; Michael Fishbane, *Biblical Interpretation in Ancient Israel* (Oxford: Oxford University Press, 1985), 25; Heaton, *The School Tradition of the Old Testament*, 32–36; Weinfeld, *Deuteronomy and the Deuteronomic School*, 158–78.

[20]For example, Philip R. Davies, *Scribes and Schools: The Canonization of the Hebrew Scriptures* (Louisville, Ky: Westminster/John Knox Press, 1998), 86; Halpern, *First Historians*, 207–18; Mayes, *Story of Israel*, 121–24; McCarter, *I Samuel*, 23–27; Noth, *Deuteronomistic History*, 36, 42–43, 63–68; Weippert, "Die 'deuteronomistischen' Beurteilungen der Könige von Israel und Juda und das Problem der Redaktion der Königsbücher"; John Van Seters, "Histories and Historians of the Ancient Near East: The Israelites," *Orientalia* 50 (1981), 137–85.

[21]1 Kgs 14:19; 15:31; 16:5, 14, 20, 27; 22:39; 2 Kgs 1:18; 10:34; 13:8, 12; 14:15, 28; 15:11, 15, 21, 26, 31

[22]1 Kgs 14:29; 15:7, 23; 22:45; 2 Kgs 8:23; 12:19; 14:18; 15:6, 36; 16:19; 20:20; 21:17, 25; 23:28; 24:5

[23]Fishbane, *Biblical Interpretation*, 29–32.

[24]For example, Walter Brueggeman, "The Social Significance of Solomon as a Patron of Wisdom," in *The Sage in Israel and the Ancient Near East* (eds. J. G. Gammie and L. G. Perdue; Winona Lake: Eisenbrauns, 1990), 117–32; Davies, *Scribes and Schools*, 15–19; Niditch, *Oral World*, 4.

[25]For example, Davies, *Scribes and Schools*, 15–30; Heaton, *The School Tradition of the Old Testament*, esp. 24–64; Lemaire, "Sage in School and Temple," 168–70.

scribes who were trained with some amount of standardization.[26] Although such reasoning has justifiably been used to make what Crenshaw has called "extravagant claims,"[27] it nevertheless suggests that schools for the training of professional scribes existed in preexilic Judah and that these scribes were not necessarily mere copyists. It is in this context that the emergence of the Deuteronomic school is often located.

SCRIBES AND SCRIBAL SCHOOLS IN PERSIAN ADMINISTRATION PERTAINING TO PERSIA AND EGYPT

In "Sages and Scribes at the Courts of Ancient Iran,"[28] James Russell discussed various court activities of Persian scribes, including religious duties, interactions with non-Persians, and scribal tasks. Among their scribal tasks, Persian scribes kept administrative records and compiled royal annals. He concluded that during the Persian period "a majority of the *dabir*s—the term refers primarily to transcribers, translators, and lower-level bureaucrats—were non-[Persian]."[29]

His conclusion that most of the *dabir*s were non-Persians brings us closer to the question of the role of scribes in the administration of the Persian empire outside of Persia, for it shows that, because of language barriers, the Persian imperial administration required the service of non-Persian scribes to serve as translators, especially in the outlying satraps. Moreover, since Persian strategy for controlling various ethnic groups

---

[26]For example, Heaton, *The School Tradition of the Old Testament*, 30–32; Davies, *Scribes and Schools*, 77–78; Jamieson-Drake, *Scribes and Schools in Monarchic Israel*; Davies, "Were There Schools in Ancient Israel"; Puech, "Les écoles dans l'Israël preéxilique;" Niditch, *Oral World*, 39–59; James L. Crenshaw, "Education in Ancient Israel," *JBL* 104 (1985): 601–15.

[27]"Education in Ancient Israel," 601. Crenshaw used "extravagant claims" in reference to Lemaire's reconstruction of schools for the general population at all of the major cities of the preexilic Judah.

[28]In *The Sage in Israel and the Ancient Near East* (eds. J. G. Gammie and L. G. Perdue; Winona Lake: Eisenbrauns, 1990), 141–46. Russell's article refers to scribes during three different periods: Achaemenid (550–333 BCE), Parthian (250 BCE–224 CE), and Sasanian (224–651 CE); however, he noted that the "inherent conservativism in pre-Islamic Iranian thought" allowed some collation of the material.

[29]"Sages and Scribes in the Ancient Court of Iran," 146.

involved the reestablishment and preservation of the native religious practices at their original cultic sites and also the codification of religious legal material, local scribes were involved in a wider range of literary activities. This strategy is illustrated well in the mission of Udjahorresnet.[30]

As is known from the inscription on his mortuary statue, Udjahorresnet was an Egyptian scribe whose duties included the supervision of lesser scribes at Sais.[31] When Cambyses I conquered Egypt, Udjahorresnet collaborated with the Persians and later influenced Cambyses to restore the dynastic sanctuary at Sais. After this restoration, he went to Susa as a royal counselor on Egyptian affairs. Early in the reign of Darius I, he was commissioned to return to Sais and to reestablish the "House of Life," a scribal institution which had been closely related to the Sais temple.

> The institution known as the House of Life had not one but many locations, usually—but not exclusively—in the proximity of temples. It was more than a mere scriptorium or library, although it was a center for the composition, preservation, study, and copying of texts. These were mainly of a religious nature, intended for cult use. However, the range of works extended to magical

---

[30]This discussion of Udjahorresnet's mission is based upon the following works: Joseph Blenkinsopp, "The Mission of Udjahorresnet and Those of Ezra and Nehemiah," *JBL* 106 (1987): 409–21; A. B. Lloyd, "The Inscription of Udjahorresnet: A Collaborator's Testament," *JEA* 68 (1982): 166–80.

Blenkinsopp noted that the mission of Udjahorresnet had other parallels within the Achaemenid empire ("Mission of Udjahorresnet," 413).

Blenkinsopp's position has been criticized by Lester L. Grabbe ("What was Ezra's Mission?" 294–95) and David Janzen ("The 'Mission' of Ezra and the Persian-Period Temple Community"). Their criticisms primarily concern how well the analogy between Udjahoresnet and Ezra holds and, although some of their criticisms may be valid, Ezra nevertheless must have had some sort of Persian support for his mission, even if the mission was primarily a matter internal to Jerusalem and Judah. Such a position is certainly suggested by the careful analysis of Persian administration in Hoglund, *Achaemenid Imperial Administration*. See also the critique of Janzen's argument by Richard C. Steiner ("The *MBQR* at Qumran, the *EPISKOPOS* in the Athenian Empire, and the Meaning of *LBQR'* in Ezra 7:14: On the Relation of Ezra's Mission to the Persian Legal Project," *JBL* 120 [2001]: 623–646). However, even if the analogy has its weaknesses between Udjahoresnet and Ezra, the analogy I am drawing between Udjahoresnet and the Deuteronomic School remains strong.

[31]Udjahorresnet's role fits with Williams' description of the role of ancient Egyptian scribes ("Sage in Egyptian Literature," 25).

and medical texts, dream-books, and hemerologies. Academy may be an inaccurate as well as an anachronistic term for it, but it was the resort of the intellectuals of the day.[32]

Although it is unclear to what extent Williams' above description of this institution can be related to Udjahorresnet's commission to reestablish the "House of Life" at Sais, Udjahorresnet's "House of Life" probably served the function of a scriptorium and a library for religious texts associated with the Sais temple. Because the institution of the "House of Life" was an Egyptian scribal school consisting of priests who redacted and preserved religious texts, Udjahorresnet's mission is in all likelihood associated with Darius I's order (preserved in the *Demotic Chronicle*) that a commission be established in order to codify Egyptian laws which were in force at the end of Amasis' reign (526 B.C.E.).

SCRIBES AND SCRIBAL SCHOOLS IN PERSIAN ADMINISTRATION PERTAINING TO JUDAH

The use of non-Persian scribes in the administration of the Persian empire involved administrative duties, such as record keeping, and also the collection and preservation of native religious texts. It is within this context that the mission of Ezra must be placed.[33]

In Ezra 7:12, Ezra is addressed as "Ezra the priest, the scribe of the law of the God of Heaven." Whether or not the phrase "the scribe of the law of the God of Heaven" is an imperial title or a Jewish title,[34] Ezra is depicted as a learned scribe who was commissioned by the Persian king, Artaxerxes I, to reassert Persian control over the Jerusalem temple cult. This reassertion was to be accomplished by Ezra's reintroducing the "true" law of Moses and by insuring that this law was strictly obeyed. Ezra's

---

[32]Williams, "Sage in Egyptian Literature," 27.

[33]For discussion of the context of Ezra's mission within the Persian empire, see Blenkinsopp, "Mission of Udjahorresnet"; Blenkinsopp, "Sage, the Scribe, and Scribalism in the Chronicler's Work"; and Hoglund, *Achaemenid Imperial Administration*.

[34]See Hoglund, *Achaemenid Imperial Administration*, 226–36 and the literature cited there.

entourage probably included other scribes.[35] Thus, Ezra's mission to Jerusalem paralleled Udjahorresnet's mission to Sais in that both were scribes who were sent by Persian kings to their native cultic center to reassert imperial control through the codification of cultic laws.[36]

SCRIBAL PRACTICES AND QUMRAN

The earliest and best evidence concerning the transmission of biblical texts comes from the Dead Sea Scrolls found in the caves near Khirbet Qumran. In fact, the Qumran literature includes many manuscripts of books that are not in the Hebrew Bible and in some cases were unknown until their discovery in the 1940s. This collection of manuscripts constitutes an important Jewish library from the early first century C.E. and from this collection we can learn much about Jewish scribal practices of the time.

The Qumran community was clearly organized along hierarchical lines. The following quote from the *Manual of Discipline* or the *Rule of the Community* describes the hierarchy of the community (*yahad*) during the annual covenant renewal ceremony:

> Thus shall they do, year by year, as long as the dominion of Satan endures. The Priests shall enter first, ranked one after another, according to the perfection of their spirit; then the Levites; and thirdly, all the people one after another in their Thousands, Hundreds, Fifties, and Tens, that every Israelite may know his place in the Community of God according to the everlasting design. No man shall move down from his place nor move up from his allotted position. For according to the holy design, they shall all of them be in a Community of truth and virtuous humility, of loving kindness and good intent one towards the others, and (they shall all of them be) sons of the everlasting Company. (2.19–25)[37]

---

[35]Ezra's entourage included "Levites," some of which were probably scribes. See 2 Chr 34:13 (Christine Schams, *Jewish Scribes in the Second Temple Period* [JSOTSup 291; Sheffield: Sheffield Academic Press, 1998], 64).

[36]Blenkinsopp, "Mission of Udjahorresnet"; Hoglund, *Achaemenid Imperial Administration*, 235–36.

[37]From the translation by Geza Vermes (*The Dead Sea Scrolls in English* [Sheffield: Sheffield Academic Press, 1987], 65) cited in James VanderKam, *The Dead Sea Scrolls Today* (Grand Rapids: Eerdemans, 1994), 111–12.

The head of the hierarchy was called the *maskil* ("instructor" or "master").[38] His duties included instruction concerning the will and mysteries of God, assessing the initiates and members according to the standards of God's will, presiding at the community's meetings, and certain liturgical duties. As the head of the community responsible for knowledge of God's will and, therefore, the protection of the community by insuring that it and its members followed God's will, the *maskil* must have been somehow involved in the preservation and transmission of the community's authoritative literature and its written interpretations of this literature. This is certainly suggested by the description of the *maskil* in the *Damascus Document* as "the one who has mastered all the secrets of men and the languages of all their clans" (14:9–10).[39] If the "secrets of men" are to be found in the authoritative literature or the "scripture" of the Qumran community, then it would make sense that the *maskil* was expected to know how to read and write "the languages of all their clans" (certainly Hebrew and Aramaic, possibly Greek). At the same time, the *maskil* certainly could not have single-handedly undertaken the task of the preservation and transmission of the community's literature and would have required the skills of other scribes in the community. Therefore, most likely the *maskil* was the head of the group of scribes at Qumran, who were probably further delineated according to a hierarchy of their scribal skills and their knowledge of the will and mysteries of God.

The study of the Qumran literature has also revealed that the Qumran community had a hierarchical understanding of the literature that it preserved. For example, James VanderKam has developed some criteria to determine if the Qumran community considered a particular work authoritative. If a book presents itself as a revelation from God and this same book is quoted in some of the manuscripts authored at Qumran, it was likely considered authoritative. Moreover, if a book itself became the subject of one of the community's commentaries (*pesharim*), it was likely

---

[38]See Carol A. Newsom, "The Sage in the Literature of Qumran: The Functions of the *Maskil*," in *The Sage in Israel and the Ancient Near East* (eds. John G. Gammie and Leo G. Perdue; Winona Lake: Eisenbrauns, 1990), 373–82.

[39]From the translation by Geza Vermes (*The Dead Sea Scrolls in English*, 116) cited in Newsom, "The Sage in the Literature of Qumran," 375.

considered authoritative. With these criteria, VanderKam has determined the following to have been strictly authoritative for the Qumran community: most (but not all) of the Hebrew Bible, 1 Enoch, Jubilees, and the Temple Scroll (11QTemple).[40] This implies that some of the preserved works were given more authority than others and, of course, it is likely that some literature simply was considered so profane as to not deserve any effort on the part of the community to preserve it. Therefore, we can agree with Shemaryahu Talmon's statement comparing the rabbinic sages and the Qumran scribes (the "Covenanters"):

> We may assume that, like the Sages, the [Qumran] Covenanters also invested certain writings with various grades of authority and holiness, and considered others to be altogether profane and not binding.[41]

As is well known, even among the books that VanderKam has designated as strictly authoritative, there are variant text forms preserved at Qumran. Some of the manuscripts of these authoritative texts were produced by other Jewish groups and brought to Qumran where they were used and stored. Others were clearly copied at Qumran. In fact, Emanuel Tov has demonstrated that the biblical manuscripts can be assigned to two general categories: (1) those that are proto-Masoretic and (2) those that reflect the "Qumran practice."[42] The proto-Masoretic manuscripts not only agree more with the MT, but also are more likely to reflect the rabbinic prescriptions for the copying of biblical texts and their *Vorlagen* were probably copied more exactly. Tov generally assigns this group of manuscripts to Pharisaic scribes—that is, outside of the Qumran

---

[40]VanderKam, *The Dead Sea Scrolls Today*, 149–57.

[41]Shemaryahu Talmon, "The Community of the Renewed Covenant: Between Judaism and Christianity," in *The Community of the Renewed Covenant: The Notre Dame Symposium of the Dead Sea Scrolls* (eds. E. Ulrich and J. VanderKam; Notre Dame: University of Notre Dame, 1994), 17.

[42]Emanuel Tov, "Scribal Practices Reflected in the Documents from the Judean Desert and in the Rabbinic Literature: A Comparative Study," in *Texts, Temples, and Traditions: A Tribute to Menahem Haran* (ed. M. V. Fox; Winona Lake: Eisenbrauns, 1996), 383–403; Emanuel Tov, "The Textual Base of the Corrections in the Biblical Texts Found at Qumran," in *The Dead Sea Scrolls: Forty Years of Research* (eds. D. Dimant and U. Rappaport; STDJ 10; Leiden: E. J. Brill, 1992), 299–314.

community. The "Qumran practice" manuscripts not only diverge more from the MT (often agreeing with the LXX and/or the Samaritan Pentateuch), but are less likely to follow the rabbinic prescriptions for the copying of biblical texts and contain more scribal interventions—that is, "corrections" and other changes to their *Vorlagen* (additions, omissions, substitutions). Tov generally assigns this group of manuscripts to the Qumran scribes themselves. Therefore, we can see that the Qumran community preserved literature from other groups that it considered authoritative, even when these manuscripts may have differed somewhat from their own manuscripts of the same works, and that the Qumran community allowed a certain amount of variety even among the copies of works that the community itself copied.

Sometimes the scribal interventions in materials found at Qumran were so extensive as to constitute new compositions. For example, the Reworked Pentateuch from Cave 4 (4QRP) is a (pre-Qumran) paraphrase of the entire Pentateuch with numerous additions, omissions, and reorderings of the biblical text according to the author's notion of what presents a more coherent understanding of the Torah.[43] Since the sources for 4QRP—that is, the books of the Pentateuch—were also found at Qumran, the community preserved not only 4QRP (in at least five different manuscripts) but also its sources. Furthermore, since 4QRP may have been a source for the Temple Scroll and Jubilees, the community preserved 4QRP as well as later documents that drew from it. In sum, the Qumran community preserved a variety of text types for some of the documents it preserved as well as various works derived from earlier sources that it also continued to preserve.

The variety among the Qumran materials concerning the amount of scribal interventions leads us to the conclusion that scribes at Qumran worked in two different ways. First, they often simply reproduced their

---

[43] See Sidnie White Crawford, "The Rewritten Bible at Qumran," in *The Hebrew Bible and Qumran* (ed. J. H. Charlesworth; N. Richland Hills: BIBAL Press, 2000), 173–95; Emanuel Tov, "Biblical Texts as Reworked in Some Qumran Manuscripts with Special Attention to 4QRP and 4QParaGen–Exod," in *The Community of the Renewed Covenant: The Notre Dame Symposium of the Dead Sea Scrolls* (eds. E. Ulrich and J. VanderKam; Notre Dame: University of Notre Dame, 1994), 111–34.

Vorlagen as carefully as possible with minimal scribal interventions. Indeed, the fact the manuscripts include evidence of scribes "correcting" their own work or the work of another scribe certainly suggests that faithful reproduction of the *Vorlagen* was often the goal of the scribes.[44] Second, they sometimes intentionally revised their *Vorlagen* by various forms of scribal interventions (additions, omissions, substitutions, reordering). In fact, occasionally these scribal interventions were so great that they may have created new texts.[45]

With this range of diversity for how the copying of manuscripts occurred at Qumran, the obvious question should be "Could any Qumran scribe make as many changes as he wanted?" The answer is "Most certainly not." Given the hierarchical structure of the community, there must have been some hierarchy among the scribes. Most of the Qumran scribes in the lower ranks were probably assessed on their scribal abilities by how accurately they reproduced their *Vorlagen*. This would certainly explain the practice of some scribal "corrections" in the manuscripts coming from the hand of a scribe other than the scribe who originally copied the manuscript. However, scribes who have reached a higher status within the community (perhaps limited only to the *maskil*) had more latitude for scribal interventions and could even produce new compositions. This would not only explain how the Qumran community could produce new compositions, but also later recensions of these same texts (for example, the two recensions of the previously unknown War Scroll [=1QM and 4QM1]). The Qumran community, therefore, provides us with the best evidence of a community in which a group of scribes composed and transmitted the community's literature within its own hierarchical bureaucracy.

---

[44]For example, Millar Burrows demonstrates that the scribe of the Isaiah Scroll (1QIsa[a]) corrected his own work. See *The Dead Sea Scroll of St. Mark's Monastery, 1: The Isaiah Manuscript and the Habakkuk Commentary* (ed. M. Burrows; New Haven: The American Schools of Oriental Research, 1950), xv; Millar Burrows, "Variant Readings in the Isaiah Manuscript," *BASOR* 111 (1948): 16–26; 113 (1949): 24–32. For a good discussion of scribal interventions (including "corrections"), see Tov, "Textual Base of the Corrections."

[45]See similarly, Tov, "Textual Base of the Corrections," 302–03; Eugene Ulrich, *The Dead Sea Scrolls and the Origins of the Bible* (Grand Rapids: Eerdemans, 1999), 11.

THE DEUTERONOMIC SCHOOL AS A SCRIBAL SCHOOL

At the end of Chapter 2, I noted that, according to Charles Carter, Jerusalem in the Persian I period could have supported a small elite group of literati and then I argued that the Deuteronomic school most likely was this group. That is, the Deuteronomic school returned to Jerusalem with Zerubbabel to serve the bureaucratic needs of the Persian-supported administration in Jerusalem with their scribal skills, especially related to the rebuilding of the Jerusalem temple and the reestablishment of the temple cult. As we have seen in this chapter, this reconstruction of a scribal school associated with a temple is consistent with evidence throughout the ancient Near East and is especially consistent with Persian administrative policy that returned exiled peoples to their homelands and reestablished their local religious cults (for example, the missions of Udjahoresnet and Ezra).

The evidence from Qumran suggests that the collection of documents preserved by a group may be somewhat diverse. The Qumran literature includes texts composed much earlier than the formation of the community, including copies of some of these texts from other contemporary Jewish groups; various recensions of texts composed by others and composed at Qumran; in some cases both texts and their source texts; and texts that were considered more authoritative than other texts which were also preserved. This diversity is consistent with arguments for the Deuteronomic school. The Deuteronomic school seems to have preserved some of the sources that it used (for example, "the Book of the Annuals of the Kings of Judah") and produced various recensions of its own compositions. Certainly, the Deuteronomic school may have preserved earlier documents that it did not compose as well (for example, the book of Amos), although it may have redacted some of these texts at some point in their transmission.

This understanding of a diverse collection of texts is consistent with evidence from the ancient Near East. In his study of 253 archives and libraries throughout the ancient Near East from 1500 to 300 B.C.E., Olof Petersén notes a little bit more than half (127 of the 253) of the archives and libraries were found in official buildings (palaces, temples, etc.) and the remaining were found in large private homes.[46] The libraries in private homes for the most part were private economic and legal documents, but the libraries in official buildings often included not only administrative texts but also literary, historical, and scientific texts. Thus, the production of such administrative texts (especially reports to Persian authorities) probably was also an important part of the Deuteronomic school's work for the Jerusalem administration. This work, however, clearly would not have been the work of most interest or of the most importance from the perspective of the Deuteronomic school itself. The Deuteronomic school would have been most theologically interested in the composition, redaction, and transmission of its religious texts.

We have also seen how scribal communities were sometimes organized hierarchically. This is certainly implicit in the missions of the scribes of Udjahoresnet and Ezra, who led groups of scribes to reintroduce religious texts, and is also evident in the hierarchical structure of the Qumran community. Likewise the Deuteronomic school's scribal duties strongly suggests a hierarchy of scribes. That is, the training of Deuteronomic scribes would have consisted of the careful study and reproduction of authoritative texts. The lower ranked scribes would have probably devoted much of their time to the administrative duties expected of the Deuteronomic school as well as the simple copying of authoritative texts. Those Deuteronomic scribes who were the most accomplished would have moved up in the guild hierarchy until they reached the status wherein they could leave their own imprint on the authoritative literature, thus becoming more than mere copyists but rather composers and redactors. Such a process would have promoted a conservative transmission of distinctive Deuteronomic characteristics (phraseology, themes) in that all Deuteronomic redactors would have firstly learned their scribal craft from copying authoritative texts that contain such characteristics and secondly achieved their status with a guild structure which existed primarily (at least from the Deuteronomic school's own perspective) for the preservation of these authoritative texts as possible instruction of others based on these

---

[46]Olof Petersén, *Archives and Libraries in the Ancient Near East 1500–300 B.C.* (Bethesda: CDL Press, 1998).

texts. This conservativism would not, however, have completely denied all creativity, for different Deuteronomic redactors dealt with various authoritative traditions and literary genres within different periods of the Deuteronomic school's history.[47]

---

[47]This view is somewhat similar to that of Moshe Weinfeld: "The fact that the Deuteronomist and the editor of the prose sermons in Jeremiah used idioms and expressions not found in the book of Deuteronomy proper points to a continuous ideaological and literary development within the deuteronomic circle and attests to the dynamism of the school. Indeed, an examination of the linguistic and ideaological fabric of the deuteronomic movement shows that its development progressed from Deuteronomy through deuteronomic historiography to the prose sermons in the book of Jeremiah" (*Deuteronomy and the Deuteronomic School*, 4).

CHAPTER 4

THE DEUTERONOMIC SCHOOL IN
ITS ORAL WORLD

Beginning with Noth, scholars have generally striven to identify the specific individuals responsible for the Deuteronomic History. Noth identified the Deuteronomistic Historian. Although Cross rejected a single Deuteronomist, he nevertheless identified two distinct individuals, a Josianic Deuteronomist (Dtr[1]) and an exilic Deuteronomist (Dtr[2]). Likewise Smend identified three distinct individuals: the Deuteronomistic Historian (DtrG), the prophetic redactor (DtrP), and the nomistic redactor (DtrN). The social location of these variously identified individuals is generally ignored beyond a general date and provenance and some assumption that they are connected by a common theology and the language in which they express their theology. Questions such as "How did Dtr learn to read and write?" and "For what institution or patronage did Dtr write?" are generally overlooked.[1] The differences between the various Dtr's are assumed to stem from either a different temporal setting (especially concerning Dtr[1] and Dtr[2]) or a somewhat different theological approach (especially concerning DtrG, DtrP, and DtrN). Their similarities are generally understood to come

---

[1]The most notable exception are the discussions of the Josianic Dtr[1], who as a part of Josiah's bureaucracy supported the reform.

from working with the same material and/or being in the same theological tradition. However, questions such as "How does the common theological tradition span the years between the various Dtr's?" and "How did this literature survive from one Dtr to another?" are also generally overlooked.

Below I argue that this individualistic way of thinking about ancient writers is anachronistic, drawing too close an analogy to the enterprises of modern scholarship. For example, I can talk about the Harvard school founded by Cross, in which there is a common approach to the redaction history of the Deuteronomic History and even some common language for describing the approach. When I describe the Harvard school, however, I can specify exactly who has contributed to its various arguments and who has created the variant understandings within the school (for example, when the pre-exilic redaction occurred), because I know the authors of the books and articles that comprise their literature. That is, for modern scholars it is professionally critical that their names be associated with their work. Thus, we tend to want to identify who the individual authors/redactors of biblical texts are and, since we rarely know their names, we often give them one (for example, "the Deuteronomist," "the Chronicler," "the Jahwist").[2] Such concern for individual attribution, however, was not as important in ancient Israel as should be obvious from the fact that the literature rarely gives any information that we might use, justifiably or not, to name its author. (An example of an exception to this observation concerns the book of Jeremiah. Since Baruch the scribe is mentioned in Jeremiah, some scholars have argued that he wrote some early form of the Jeremiah tradition).[3]

Our modern concern for knowing who the individual authors of texts were is most likely an outgrowth of the individualism that is a byproduct of our society being highly literate. As we will see below, societies in which literacy is absent or limited to a small proportion of the

---

[2]Admittedly, this work also participates somewhat in this tendency by my continued use of "Deuteronomic school." The only difference is that I refrain from identifying specific individuals within this school.

[3]After the texts had a certain degree of authority in ancient Israel, the early tradition often associated the literature with a major character in the biblical text. For example, the book of Psalms is attributed to David and the book of Proverbs to Solomon. In this way, our modern tendencies are also found in the pseudepigraphical nature of the ancient tradition to some extent.

population have a very different understanding of composition—that is, these societies are primarily oral, even though writing can be found within segments of the society. In order to understand this better, I will review arguments from the study of oral traditions in relationship to composition of literary texts and to their transmission before discussing the implications of this work on our understanding of the Deuteronomic school.

ORAL TRADITION AND THE COMPOSITION OF BIBLICAL TEXTS

In contrast to modern Western society, societies based primarily on oral transmission of culture rarely preserve information about who originated the narratives repeatedly performed. This insight was first emphasized strongly in Western scholarship by Milman Parry.[4] At that time in Homeric studies a debate was raging concerning who Homer was and even if he ever existed. The two sides of the debate were those who argued for a single author, Homer, and those who argued for a long redactional history of the Homeric epics in which numerous "Homers" systematically reworked the tradition. Parry saw that the discussion was at a complete impasse, since neither side seemed completely reasonable given the contradictory evidence. Parry's solution was to bypass the discussion of how many authors/redactors were responsible for the epics by emphasizing rather a continuing traditional process. In his master's thesis of 1923, Parry wrote:[5]

> Just as the story of the Fall of Troy, the tale of the House of Labdakos, and the other Greek epic legends were not themselves the original fictions of certain authors, but creations of a whole people, passed through one generation to another and gladly given to anyone who wished to tell them, so the style in which they were to be told was not a matter of individual creation, but a popular tradition, evolved by centuries of poets and audiences, which

---

[4]The below discussion of Parry and Lord is based on John Miles Foley, "Oral Theory in Context," in *Oral Traditional Literature: A Festscrift for Albert Bates Lord* (ed. J. M. Foley; Columbus: Slavica Publishers, 1981), 27–122, esp. 27–51.

[5]"A Comparative Study of Diction as One of the Elements of Style in Early Greek Epic Poetry," in *The Making of Homeric Verse: The Collected Papers of Milman Parry* (ed. A. Parry; Oxford: Oxford University Press, 1971), 421 (cited in Foley, "Oral Theory in Context," 30).

the composer of heroic verse might follow without thought of plagarism, indeed, without knowing that such a thing existed.

This initial idea suggested that poets in oral traditional societies do not understand themselves as authors who are creating something new, but rather as performers of a long standing tradition. However, they are more than mere performers in that they are also composers. Whereas many modern performers will generally repeat what they have memorized, the oral poets compose extemporaneously the traditional epics by drawing from the system of formulae, themes, and story patterns available within the tradition. As Albert Lord noted, "the picture that emerges is not really one of conflict between preserver of tradition and creative artist; it is rather one of the preservation of tradition by the constant re-creation of it."[6] On the one hand, one cannot speak of the original composer of a traditional oral epic because the tradition produced the epic. On the other hand, one can identify many composers of the epic in every performer, including future performers within the tradition.

Parry tested his own early notions of oral tradition concerning Homer by conducting fieldwork in the former Yugoslavia among the *guslar*s, the oral poets of the Serbo-Croatian epic traditions. Parry was joined by his student, Albert Lord, who continued Parry's work after his untimely death. The work begun by Parry and Lord has been expanded further by many others to include fieldwork in various contemporary cultures and the application of these observations to many other bodies of literature. Clearly the leader in this field today is John Miles Foley, who founded and edits the journal *Oral Tradition* and whose own research is primarily in Homeric epic, Old English literature, and Serbo-Croatian epic.[7]

---

[6]Albert B. Lord, *Singer of Tales* (Cambridge: Harvard University Press, 1960), 29.

[7]John Miles Foley, *The Theory of Oral Composition: History and Methodology* (Bloomington: Indiana University Press, 1988); John Miles Foley, *Traditional Oral Epic: The Odyssey, Beowulf, and the Serbo-Croatian Return Song* (Berkeley: University of Californa Press, 1990); John Miles Foley, *Immanent Art: From Structure to Meaning* (Bloomington: Indiana University Press, 1991); John Miles Foley, *The Singer of Tales in Performance* (Bloomington: Indiana University Press, 1995); and John Miles Foley, *Homer's Traditional Art* (University Park: Pennsylvania State University Press, 1999).

Although biblical scholars have talked about oral traditions behind the biblical text for many years (especially since Gunkel), it was not until the 1970s and the 1980s that the Parry-Lord approach to the study of oral traditions was applied to biblical texts. The early work of applying the Parry-Lord theory to biblical texts was done by Robert Culley, Robert Coote, Burke Long, Werner Kelber, and Albert Lord among others.[8] The most comprehensive and authoritative application of the Parry-Lord approach to the Hebrew Bible is the 1998 monograph by Susan Niditch, *Oral World and Written Word*.

Niditch concluded that "Israelite writing is set in an oral context."[9] From our modern, literate perspective, this conclusion may sound contradictory—that is, how can writing be understood in an oral context? In fact, until recently scholars of orality and literacy emphasized what Werner Kelber has called "the great divide thesis"[10]—that is, a tremendous gulf was envisioned between oral cultures and literate cultures. It was as if, when an oral epic was written down, it was completely removed from its traditional culture, never again to be influenced by that culture, and even the earliest readers of this new text were ignorant of its traditional culture. Recent studies, however, discuss an oral–literate continuum, thereby narrowing the supposed gap between oral and literate cultures, especially as it relates to the interaction of orality and literacy in transitional cultures like ancient Greece and medieval Europe.[11] Even though Niditch's conclusion *seems* contradictory from our modern perspective on literacy, it is consistent with contemporary scholarly understandings of the interaction of literacy and orality in ancient and transitional cultures. Therefore, as Niditch states,

---

[8]For an excellent review of these studies and others, see Robert C. Culley, "Oral Tradition and Biblical Studies." *Oral Tradition* 1 (1986): 30–65.

[9]Niditch, *Oral World*, 88.

[10]"Scripture and Logos: The Hermeneutics of Communication," (paper presented at the annual meeting of the SBL, Kansas City, November 1991).

[11]For example, M. T. Clanchy, *From Memory to Written Record: England, 1066-1307* (Cambridge: Harvard University Press, 1979); Brian Stock, *The Implications of Literacy: Written Language and Models of Interpretation in the Eleventh and Twelfth Centuries* (Princeton: Princeton University Press, 1983); Brian Stock, *Listening for the Text: On the Uses of the Past* (Baltimore: Johns Hopkins University Press, 1990); Rosalind Thomas, *Oral Tradition and Written Records in Classical Athens* (Cambridge: Cambridge University Press, 1989).

"Israelite literacy in form and function is not to be confused with modern literacy and ... ancient Israelite literacy has to be understood in the context of an oral-traditional culture."[12]

Niditch's conclusions have implications for how the composition and transmission of the Hebrew Bible are understood. Niditch offers four models for the "genesis of the Hebrew Bible":

> (1) the oral performance, which is dictated to a writer who preserves the text in an archive, creating a fixed text out of an event; (2) the slow crystallization of a pan-Hebraic literary tradition through many performances over centuries of increasingly pan-Israelite tales to audiences with certain expectations and assumptions about shared group identity; late in the process authors write down the shared stories; (3) a written imitation of oral-style literature to create portions of the tradition; (4) the production of a written text that is excerpted from another written text by a writer who deftly edits or recasts the text in accordance with his own view of Israelite identity.[13]

Although each of these models moves from one end of the oral-literate continuum to the other, Niditch capably demonstrates that even the most literate of these models—that is, a written composition based upon written sources—is nevertheless influenced by an oral mindset. For example, Chronicles is based upon Samuel–Kings but does not displace or replace it as would be expected in a culture with a literate mindset.[14] Therefore, even if the biblical text being studied was created by a literate redactor working with various written sources, the redactor and the redactor's work was still heavily influenced by the contemporary oral culture.

ORAL TRADITION AND THE TRANSMISSION OF BIBLICAL TEXTS

Niditch's emphasis is clearly upon the composition of the Hebrew Bible. After referring to some recent text critical works, however, she suggests that the "transmission of this tradition may well have involved complex interplays between written and oral processes."[15]

---

[12]Niditch, *Oral World*, 99.
[13]Niditch, *Oral World*, 130.
[14]Niditch, *Oral World*, 130.
[15]Niditch, *Oral World*, 77.

As we saw in the previous chapter, the division made between composition and transmission is often difficult to make, because many scribes were not mere copyists. As Michael Fishbane has written, "the boundary-line between scribes and authors is often quite difficult to draw in biblical literature, and, in some cases, involves precarious judgments."[16] We will see below why this is the case, as I develop Niditch's suggestion concerning transmission more fully. By drawing from both the text critical study of the Hebrew Bible and the study of oral traditions, I will argue the following: The ancient Israelite scribes were literate members of a primarily oral society. As members of a primarily oral society, they undertook even their literate activity—that is, the copying of texts—with an oral mindset. When they copied their texts, the ancient Israelite scribes did not slavishly write the texts word by word, but preserved the texts' meaning for the on-going life of their communities in much the same way that performers of oral epic re-present the stable, yet dynamic, tradition to their communities. In this sense, the ancient Israelite scribes were not mere copyists, but were also performers of the tradition.[17]

ORAL TRADITION AND THE UNDERSTANDING OF "WORD"

As Niditch argues so well, ancient Israelite literature must be understood from the perspective of the aesthetics of an oral tradition. One

---

[16]Fishbane, *Biblical Interpretation*, 85; see also 27, 37, 41, 78–79, 83–88.

[17]This position is similar to the arguments by Alger N. Doane and Katherine O. O'Keefe concerning Anglo-Saxon scribes. See Alger N. Doane, "The Ethnography of Scribal Writing and Anglo-Saxon Poetry: Scribe as Performer," *Oral Tradition* 9 (1994): 420–39 and Katherine O. O'Keefe, *Visible Song: Transitional Literacy in Old English Verse* (Cambridge: Cambridge University Press, 1990).

See also the recent treatment of scribes and early Christian literature by Kim Haines-Eitzen (*Guardians of Letters: Literary, Power, and the Transmitters of Early Christian Literature* [Oxford: Oxford University Press, 2000]) and the articles in the recent edition of the journal *Oral Tradition* on rabbinic literature (Martin S. Jaffee, "Oral Tradition in the Writings of Rabbinic Oral Torah: On Theorizing Rabbinic Orality," *Oral Tradition* 14 [1999]: 3–32; Steven D. Fraade, "Literary Composition and Oral Performance in Early Midrashim," *Oral Tradition* 14 [1999]: 33–51; Yaakov Elman, "Orality and the Redaction of the Babylonian Talmud," *Oral Tradition* 14 [1999]: 52–99; Elizabeth Shanks Alexander, "The Fixing of the Oral Misnah and the Displacement of Meaning," *Oral Tradition* 14 [1999]: 100–39).

aspect of oral traditions concerns the understanding of the basic unit of
meaning. Studies in oral traditions demonstrate that the understanding of
"word" differs from our own highly literate understanding—that is, a unit
of meaning in a primarily oral culture may be equivalent to what we would
call a line, a stanza, or even the entire epic.[18] This general observation is
illustrated well in the interview between Milman Parry's Yugloslavian
assistant Nikola Vujnovic and the Serbo-Croatian oral poet (*guslar*) Mujo
Kukuruzovic:

> Nikola: Let's consider this: "Vino pije licki Mustajbeze" ("Mustajbeg of Lika was
> drinking wine"). Is this a single word?
> Mujo: Yes.
> N: But how? It can't be *one*: "Vino pije licki Mustajbeze"
> M: In writing it can't be one.
> N: There are four words here.
> M: It can't be one in writing. But here, let's say we're at my house and I pick up the
> *gusle* [a traditional single-stringed instrument]—"Pije vino licki
> Mustajbeze"—that's a single word on the *gusle* for me.
> N: And the second word?
> M: And the second word—"Na Ribniku u pjanoj mehani" ("At Ribnik in a drinking
> tavern")—there.[19]

In this interview, we can see a clash of cultures as the literate Yugoslav
insists that "Vino pije licki Mustajbeze" is not one word but four, while the
oral poet insists that it is only one word. In fact, the oral poet's conception
of the entire phrase being one word even allows for some variation. Notice
that Nikola is discussing the phrase "Vino pije licki Mustajbeze," but, when
Mujo imagines playing his *gusle* (a one-string instrument) and singing this
phrase, he says what from a highly literate viewpoint might be considered a
different phrase because of the inversion of the first two "words," that is,
"Pije vino licki Mustajbeze." For Mujo, the oral poet, both "Vino pije licki
Mustajbeze" and "Pije vino licki Mustajbeze" are not only one "word," but
the *same* "word."

---

[18]John Miles Foley, "Editing Oral Epic Texts: Theory and Practice," *Text* 1 (1981)
77–78; Foley, *Traditional Oral Epic*, chaps. 4–6.
[19]Cited in Foley, "Editing Oral Epic Texts," 92 n. 11.

We can see a similar phenomenon in the semantic range of the Hebrew word דבר. דבר is the closest Hebrew equivalent to the English term "word," but it can also mean "utterance," "speech," or "message." For example, in Deut 4:13 and 10:4, we can translate עשרת הדברים literally as "the ten words" and imagine an analogous argument concerning how many "words" there are in each of "the ten commandments" (as it is usually translated). Is "observe the sabbath day and keep it holy" (Deut 5:12) only one "word" among "the ten words"? It certainly looks like more than one "word" to us modern, literate readers! We must keep in mind, however, that the ancient Israelite unit of meaning or "word" may not correspond to our own highly literate understanding of "word" as we struggle to understand more about the primarily oral culture in which the ancient Israelite scribes lived and worked.

TEXT CRITICAL VARIANTS OF "WORDS"

The text critical evidence of the Hebrew Bible that suggests most strongly that the ancient Israelite scribes also had an oral mentality are the numerous synonymous readings found in the Hebrew Bible.[20] Shemaryahu Talmon defined synonymous readings as follows:

> The class of synonymous readings will include only those variants which do not affect the subject matter of the text, are derived correctly according to Hebrew grammatical and stylistic rules, cannot be accounted for as being deliberate or due to slips of the pen or lapses of memory, and (as far as our knowledge goes) do not spring from different linguistic strata distinguishable from one another in point of time, place, or class in society.[21]

Below are two examples of synonymous readings taken from 2 Kings 18–20 // Isaiah 36–39 and one from 2 Kings 25 // Jeremiah 52.[22]

---

[20]See Shemaryhu Talmon, "Synonymous Readings in the Textual Traditions of the Old Testament," (*ScrHier* 8 [1961]: 335–83) for a detailed discussion of numerous examples.

[21]Shemaryahu Talmon, "Observations on Variant Readings in the Isaiah Scroll (1QIsa[a])," *The World of Qumran from Within: Collected Studies* (Jerusalem: Magnes Press, 1989), 122.

[22]These examples and many others from these passages are discussed in Person, *The Kings–Isaiah and Kings–Jeremiah Recensions*.

(1)   2 Kgs 18:25:   עַל הַמָּקוֹם הַזֶּה against this place
         Isa 36:10:   עַל הָאָרֶץ הַזֹּאת against this land

Since מָקוֹם and אָרֶץ sometimes occur in synonymous parallelism (for
example, Isa 5:8; 7:23–24), these two phrases are synonymous readings that
probably occurred at an early stage of development.

(2)   MT-2 Kgs 19:9:   וַיָּשָׁב וַיִּשְׁלַח מַלְאָכִים
                                         And he returned and he sent messengers
         MT-Isa 37:9:   וַיִּשְׁמַע וַיִּשְׁלַח מַלְאָכִים
                                         And he heard and he sent messengers
         1QIsaª 37:9 (= LXX)   וַיִּשְׁמַע וַיָּשָׁב וַיִּשְׁלַח מַלְאָכִים
                                         And he heard and he returned
                                         and he sent messengers

MT-Kings and MT-Isaiah contain synonymous readings that are conflated
in the Isaiah Scroll of Qumran (and LXX-Isaiah).

(3)   MT-2 Kgs 25:30 (=LXX):   כָּל יְמֵי חַיָּו
                                         All the days of his life
         LXX-Jer 52:34:   עַד יוֹם מוֹתוֹ
                                         Until the day of his death
         MT-Jer 52:34:   עַד יוֹם מוֹתוֹ כָּל יְמֵי חַיָּו
                                         Until the day of his death,
                                         all the days of his life

The formulae in MT-Kings and LXX-Jeremiah are synonymous. MT-
Jeremiah conflates the readings.

As we can see in these examples, what Talmon called synonymous
readings might be called synonymous "words"—that is, although the
synonymous readings might contain more than one of our "words," each
phrase is itself a unit of meaning and, therefore, could be understood as a
דָּבָר, a "word," analogous to each of the "ten commandments" being
understood as a "word." This is certainly the case with synonymous
formulae as in example (3). According to Talmon, the parallel structure of
Hebrew poetry fixed some of the synonymous readings together as pairs.
Talmon wrote, "pairs of words ... which were regularly used as synonyms
... became so closely wedded to each other that the mention of one pair

automatically evoked the mention of the other."[23] If this is the case, and I agree that it is, we can easily understand how one reading is substituted by its synonymous reading, especially within a primarily oral culture.

Another class of text critical variants that suggests that the ancient Israelite scribes may have approached the task of copying texts with an oral mindset are additions providing specificity. As Tov, McKane, and others have noted, the majority of variants between LXX-Jeremiah and MT-Jeremiah consist of additions of titles, proper names, adjectives, adverbs, divine names and epithets, and standard prophetic formula in the expansive MT.[24] A few examples follow with the MT additions in italics:

> addition of titles:
> > 28:5: And Jeremiah *the prophet* said to Hananiah *the prophet*
> addition of proper names:
> > 21:2: *Nebuchadrezzar*
> > 52:16: *Nebuzaradan*
> addition of patronymics:
> > 28:4: Jeconiah, *son of Jehoiakim, king of Judah*
> > 36:8: Baruch, *son of Neriah*
> addition of divine names and epitets:
> > 29:21: Thus says the Lord *of Hosts, the God of Israel*

Again, if we keep in mind that the ancient scribes' understanding of "word" is larger than our own, these variants are only variants from our literate point of view. Those familiar with the tradition know that Jeconiah was the son of Jehoiakim and was king of Judah, so any combination of these labels for Jeconiah (including his other names "Coniah" and "Jehoiachin") all refer to the same individual—that is, they could all be understood as the same דבר, the same "word." This kind of variation in characters' names and titles is common in oral traditions. For example, John Miles Foley demonstrates that the two Homeric formulae "honored Hermes" and "mighty slayer of Argos" refer not only to each other, but to the entire

---

[23]Talmon, "Synonymous Readings," 337.

[24]See Tov, "Aspects"; Tov, "Literary History"; Emanuel Tov, *Textual Criticism of the Hebrew Bible* (Minneapolis: Fortress Press, 1992), 319–27; McKane, *Jeremiah*, l–lxxxiii; Louis Stulman, *The Prose Sermons of the Book of Jeremiah* (SBLDS 83; Atlanta: Scholars Press, 1986), 141.

mythic story of the Greek character Hermes, thereby explaining their interchangeability in the tradition.[25] In this sense, Talmon's comments concerning synonymous readings may also apply to this type of variant—that is, for example, the name "Jeconiah" is automatically associated with his patronym, titles, and events surrounding his reign, so that the copyist may not even be conscious that he is writing down what from our perspective includes additional words.

The most important information for scribal transmission comes from our understanding of the scribal process as practiced at Qumran, because of the presence of scribal interventions or "corrections" in the manuscripts.[26] For example, the Isaiah Scroll (1QIsa[a]) includes scribal interventions in a variety of forms, such as omissions by crossing out a word with a horizontal line or the use of cancellation dots as well as supralinear and marginal additions of letters, words, and phrases.[27] Sometimes these interventions are made by the original scribe himself; other times by a later scribe.[28]

Some of the interventions suggest that the original scribe of 1QIsa[a] may have approached the task of copying his *Vorlage* with an oral mentality. For example, the scribe first wrote חזקיה מלך יהודה ("Hezekiah, king of Judah") in 36:4. The words מלך יהודה ("king of Judah") are to be omitted as suggested by the cancellation dots placed above each letter. Since the MT and the LXX of both Isaiah 36:4 and its parallel in 2 Kings 18:19 do not contain this title, it is most likely the result of the scribe unconsciously adding the phrase as he copied the *Vorlage*.[29] This is consistent with the argument made above for the influence of an oral

---

[25]Foley, *Singer of Tales in Performance*, 156–60.

[26]See Frank Moore Cross and Shemaryahu Talmon, eds., *Qumran and the History of the Biblical Text* (Cambridge: Harvard University Press, 1975) and Tov, "Textual Base of the Corrections." Tov uses the more neutral "scribal intervention" to denote that the "correction" may actually be moving further away from the original text. His language is used here.

[27]See Tov, "Textual Base of the Corrections" for a full discussion of the types of scribal interventions in the Qumran materials.

[28] Burrows, *Isaiah Manuscript*, xv; Burrows, "Variant Readings."

[29]For further discussion of this and other variants in 1QIsa[a] 36–39, see Person, *King–Isaiah and Kings–Jeremiah Recensions*, 8–79.

mentality in the copying of texts. The scribe associated unconsciously the name "Hezekiah" and the title "king of Judah" together and wrote both down. However, the original scribe clearly proofread his own text by comparing it to the *Vorlage* and made corrections, sometimes just the addition of one letter (for example, Isa 1:1: ישעיהו {"Is[a]iah"}, the ע is a supralinear addition correcting the misspelled name) and sometimes the addition of entire verses (for example, 37:6–7).[30] Such proofreading and correcting of the text betrays a literate mentality. In fact, 1QIsa[a] provides evidence of a later scribe also proofreading and correcting the text, possibly by comparing it with a Hebrew manuscript that was not the original scribe's *Vorlage*.[31] Therefore, the presence of מלך יהודה ("king of Judah") with supralinear cancellation dots provides evidence of an oral mentality *and* a literate mentality in the copying of the text. In other words, although some variant readings can be explained as the result of an oral approach in the copying of the texts, the proofreading and correction of texts is clearly a literate activity. This is consistent with Niditch's conclusion that "Israelite *writing* is set in an oral context."[32]

CONCLUSION: THE ANCIENT ISRAELITE SCRIBE AS PERFORMER

Although ancient Israelite scribes were among the most literate in their society, they were nevertheless influenced significantly by the primarily oral culture in which they lived. Therefore, the ancient Israelite scribes' oral mentality allowed for variation as they copied texts—that is, since their understanding of "word" probably included what we would call phrases and lines, what they possibly understood as a faithful copy of their *Vorlagen* we would understand as containing variants. This seems to provide an explanation for many of the variants that arose in the pre-Masoretic period, especially including but not limited to synonymous readings.

---

[30]Burrows, *Isaiah Manuscript*, xv; Burrows, "Variant Readings [Part 2]," 32.

[31]Burrows, *Isaiah Manuscript*, xv.

[32]Niditch, *Oral World*, 88 [emphasis mine].

This position builds upon the reevaluation of text criticism and its goals in light of the evidence from Qumran, but it goes further than text critics have been willing to go thus far. Shemaryahu Talmon is representative of how many text critics view their work. He has argued that the idea of a Hebrew *textus receptus* is anachronistic when applied to early Judaism.[33] If there was no *textus receptus*, then some of the "variant" readings should be understood simply as alternative readings. Concerning synonymous readings, Talmon wrote, "These alternative readings are not really 'variants,' since they originated at a time when there was not yet a standard text from which they could be said to have deviated."[34] Note that Talmon makes this observation concerning synonymous readings, which "cannot be accounted for as being deliberate or due to slips of the pen or lapses of memory."[35]

If Niditch is correct that all "Israelite writing is set in an oral context"[36] (as I think she is), then the ancient Israelite scribes' activity of copying their *Vorlagen* was influenced by an oral mentality. If this is the case, then Talmon's conclusions move in the proper direction but stop short. As Talmon suggests, the idea of a Hebrew *textus receptus* is anachronistic and some of what earlier text critics called "variants" must be understood now as alternative readings. Talmon's conclusions, however, appear to be based on a literate understanding of a unit of meaning ("word"), which allows for fewer alternative readings than suggested above. That is, Talmon's understanding of what is a "deliberate" change in a text is too narrowly defined. For example, the addition of a title to a proper name need not be understood as a "deliberate" addition providing specificity, as is often assumed. Rather, the oral mentality of the scribe might have been *unconsciously* influenced by his knowledge of that particular biblical character and possibly a general tendency in the tradition to provide such specificity. In addition, such a general tendency itself did not necessarily begin with a conscious decision of some scribe(s); the social environment

---

[33]Shemaryahu Talmon, "Aspects of the Textual Transmission of the Bible in the Light of Qumran Manuscripts," in *Qumran and the History of the Biblical Text* (eds. F. M. Cross and S. Talmon; Cambridge: Harvard University Press, 1975), 228.

[34]Talmon, "Observations on Variant Readings," 126–27.

[35]Talmon, "Observations on Variants Readings," 122.

[36]Niditch, *Oral World*, 88.

may have simply influenced the transmission process. Therefore, when the transmission process is understood within the context of an oral culture, Talmon's understanding of alternative readings needs to be broadened beyond synonymous readings to include various other types of "variants."

As noted above, at least some scribes proofread their work at Qumran. This would seem to support Talmon's literate understanding of "deliberate." Even though the initial copying may have been influenced by an oral mentality (as argued above), the process of proofreading and "correcting" the copy suggests the scribes' attempt to reproduce their *Vorlagen* verbatim (a more literate approach). That is, these scribes appear to be "deliberate" in "adhering *faithfully* to the MS which [they] had chosen, or had been assigned, as the *Vorlage* for [their] own copy."[37] Although this may be the case for most of the Qumran scribes, it is not necessarily the case for them all. Even if it is, this would not necessarily be the case for other scribes of early Judaism. In fact, the variety among the biblical texts from Qumran suggests that those scribes who were responsible for producing the pre-Qumran versions of these texts were probably not as "careful" and "deliberate" (in a literate sense) in their copying as the Qumran scribes were. Of course, earlier scribes who approached the copying of texts with a more oral mentality would certainly not understand themselves as producing inferior texts; rather, their own understanding of "deliberate" copying would have allowed more variation than Talmon suggests.

When we take seriously the possibility that even the literate activity of copying texts was influenced by an oral mentality, we may begin to understand more clearly how "careful" scribes in ancient Israel produced texts with what appears to us to be "variants." Rather than copying the texts verbatim in a good literate manner (what we expect of ourselves as modern scholars), the ancient Israelite scribes performed the texts faithfully for their communities in their act of copying, often without changing what they would understand as a "word." However, their understanding of "word" and ours differ; therefore, they produced texts with what we perceive as "variants."

---

[37]Talmon, "Aspects of the Textual Transmission," 256 [emphasis mine].

THE DEUTERONOMIC SCHOOL IN ITS ORAL WORLD

As noted at the beginning of this chapter, scholars generally have an anachronistic, individualistic understanding of biblical authors and often ascribe names to the imagined authors (for example, "the Deuteronomist," "the Chronicler," "the Jahwist"). We can see this tendency in the following quote from Christopher Begg concerning similarities he saw between Deuteronomy 9 and Deuteronomy 31:[38]

> These further parallels lend added credence to the supposition that xxxi 9–13, 24–29 and ix 7–10, 11 derive from the same author, i.e., the Deuteronomist who would have employed a like verbal schema in his account of the writing and storing up of the two fundamental legal documents, the "table of covenant" and the "book of the law."

As we see here, it is not uncommon for biblical scholars to assign the literary similarities between two passages, especially when these similarities involve similar phraseology, to the same individual author/redactor. In fact, this is generally presupposed in the standard application of source and redaction criticism.

This general tendency to theorize about individual biblical authors contributes to the lack of discussion concerning a variety of issues: "How did Dtr learn to read and write?"; "For what institution or patronage did Dtr write?"; "How does the common theological tradition span the years between the various Dtr's?"; and "How did this literature survive from one Dtr to another?" The discussion in chapter 3 and chapter 4 has prepared us to address these issues more clearly.

In chapter 3 on the basis of analogies with other scribal groups in the ancient Near East we saw how the Deuteronomic school as a scribal guild probably was involved in the training of its own scribes and scribal duties related to the Persian-supported Jerusalem administration. These scribal duties probably included the writing of administrative texts (for example, concerning taxation and defense) as well as the composition, redaction, and transmission of the religious texts associated with the temple cult. Since Deuteronomic scribes would have learned their scribal skills by

---

[38]Christopher T. Begg, "The Table (Deut x) and the Lawbook (Deut xxxi)," *VT* 33 (1983): 96–97.

studying and copying authoritative texts containing Deuteronomic language and themes, the training of the scribes itself led to a certain conservativism by steeping the scribes in Deuteronomic language and theology. Within this type of institution, the identity of individual Deuteronomic scribes would have been minimized within the structure of the guild, except for some of the most respected scribes who would have earned the right to compose and/or redact the literature rather than simply copy it.[39] However, even these most accomplished Deuteronomic scribes would still be steeped in the characteristic Deuteronomic language and theology; therefore, their compositions and redactions would still be produced within a more conservative setting.

The results of this chapter further suggest that the "new" compositions and redactions that such high ranking Deuteronomic scribes may have produced would not necessarily be understood within the Deuteronomic school as "new." On the one hand, the institutional hierarchy of the Deuteronomic school most likely ranked the scribes according to their scribal skills, requiring the lowest ranked scribes to be more precise in their copying of their *Vorlagen* (even though their definition of "precise" would still differ from our own). That is, the more literate mentality of exactly copying word for word one's *Vorlage* probably applied most clearly to the lowest ranked scribes, who were the most accountable to the Persian-supported bureaucracy in that they probably produced most of the administrative documents. But even this expectation for more "precise" reproduction in the work of the lower ranked scribes would have allowed for what from our modern, literate perspective would be understood as "variants," including the substitution of synonymous readings and the additions of titles, proper names, patronymics, epithets, etc. Therefore, even *if* this was the only kind of changes that occurred in Deuteronomic literature, we can see how over a long span of time and through a gradual build-up of such changes, significant redactional changes could have

---

[39]Others have minimized the identification of individual redactors and argued for scribal groups behind biblical literature, including the Deuteronomic History. For example, see Patricia Dutcher–Walls, "The Social Location of the Deuteronomists: A Sociological Study of Factional Politics in Late Pre-Exilic Judah," *JSOT* 52 (1991): 77–94.

occurred.[40] On the other hand, the primarily oral society in which these scribes lived and worked would not necessarily understand the significant revisions of the most accomplished Deuteronomic scribes as "new" recensions of an "earlier" work because, if the Deuteronomic redactor worked within the limits of the tradition using appropriate Deuteronomic language and theology, such "new" works may be understood simply as accurate performances of the tradition. In other words, the very hierarchical structure of the Deuteronomic school may have been based upon the intricate interplay of the oral and literate within the primarily oral society of ancient Israel by defining the limits of what is an acceptable production of the tradition, while at the same time allowing for significant (at least from our modern perspective) variations within these defined limits.

If this reconstruction is valid, we can easily see why redaction critical studies of the Deuteronomic History have produced such a diversity of results, thereby failing to explicate accurately the details of the redaction process that most certainly must have been gradual and complicated. That is, Deuteronomic scribes/redactors all worked within the same tradition, using Deuteronomic language and theology, so that it is virtually impossible to distinguish one Deuteronomic redactor from another strictly on the basis of phraseology and themes. The observation that this same tradition spanned a long period of time can explain why there are so many tensions within Deuteronomic literature (for example election versus explanation of exile, pro-monarchical versus anti-monarchical, historiographical versus prophetic versus nomistic), because certainly new historical circumstances influenced

---

[40]This notion of a gradual process leading to significant differences between versions of the same text is also found in William McKane's notion of a "rolling corpus" as an explanation for the differences between MT-Jeremiah and LXX-Jeremiah (*Jeremiah*, 1:l-lxxxiii). However, McKane's notion needs to be corrected by the approach of oral traditions in that his understanding assumes a highly literate mentality for the redactors. For my refinement of McKane's notion of a "rolling corpus" in Jeremiah, see Raymond F. Person, Jr., "A Rolling Corpus and Oral Tradition: A Not-So-Literate Solution to a Highly Literate Problem," in *Troubling Jeremiah* (eds. A. R. P. Diamond, K. M. O'Connor, and L. Stulman; JSOTSup 260; Sheffield: Sheffield Academic Press, 1999), 263-71.

the theology of the Deuteronomic school through time even as it maintained its basic theological perspectives and its distinctive language.[41]

In sum, the general tendency of striving to identify individual Deuteronomic redactors fails methodologically because of the character of the literature produced by the Deuteronomic school over the long span of its history. Rather we should strive to understand better the collective unity of the Deuteronomic school in its history and the literature that it produced, being fully aware that some individual Deuteronomic redactors may have had significant influences within this history. Unfortunately, we will have to settle with the best descriptions we can make for the Deuteronomic school as a whole and, in most cases, this will require a careful use of what text critical evidence there may be that can shed light on the redactional process of Deuteronomic literature.

---

[41]This of course does not rule out other possible explanations for some tensions as well. For example, the use of different sources in different books certainly could have led to tensions between different books in Deuteronomic literature such as the tensions between Joshua and Judges.

CHAPTER 5

DEUTERONOMIC LITERATURE DURING THE TIME OF ZERUBBABEL

As argued above, the Deuteronomic school continued to redact the Deuteronomic History into the Persian period, probably returning to Jerusalem with Zerubbabel. If this is the case, then a reinterpretation of Deuteronomic literature and its meaning within the setting of postexilic Judah is necessary. In this chapter and the next, such a reinterpretation of selected passages from the Deuteronomic History and Jeremiah is given. These passages were not selected because we have clear evidence that they are postexilic in origin. In fact, I know of no compelling arguments that would definitively assign any of these passages in their earliest forms clearly to the postexilic period rather than the exilic period (or possibly earlier). At the same time, I know of no compelling arguments that would definitively assign any of them to the exilic period. Whether they are exilic or postexilic in origin, they were read and preserved by the Deuteronomic school in the postexilic period. In this chapter, the interpretations concern what meaning these texts may have had for the Deuteronomic school in the early postexilic period, specifically during the governorship of Zerubbabel (520–510).[1]

Although the following reinterpretations assume the time of Zerubbabel as the theological setting for these passages, this must be seen as primarily a hermeneutical decision rather than an assertion that these passages were either written before Zerubbabel's administration and were reinterpreted then or written during Zerubbabel's governorship. In other words, I allow the possibility that one or more of these passages or sections of these passages may have been written after the time of Zerubbabel. The limitations of redaction criticism, however, do not allow the kind of precision that would enable a commentator to place any one of these passages so precisely in a historical context in order to provide the kind of contextualized reading I am proposing. Furthermore, this interpretive move can be justified in that these passages are often understood as important to the theological vision in the Deuteronomic History and, therefore, even if they are products of a later time, the meaning that I am drawing from them would not be completely inconsistent with their interpretation by the Deuteronomic school in their original historical context. It is with these disclaimers that I attempt such reinterpretations.

PRELIMINARY OBSERVATIONS CONCERNING DEUTERONOMIC THEOLOGY

Before looking specifically at these selected texts, it is helpful to recall the Deuteronomic school's general theological understanding of history. It is widely accepted that the Deuteronomic school understood the destruction of Jerusalem and the Babylonian exile as the Lord's just punishment of disobedient Israel and that this punishment could lead to Israel's repentance and purification so that the Lord would return Israel to the land. This theological understanding of political history certainly included the Lord's use of foreign powers in order to enact divine will. If the Deuteronomic school continued into the postexilic period, then this theological understanding of political history certainly would have

---

[1]The dates for Zerubbabel are taken from Carol L. Meyers and Eric M. Meyers, eds., *Haggai-Zechariah 1–8* (AB 25B; Garden City: Doubleday, 1987), 14.

influenced their understanding of the Persian conquest of the Babylonians and the Persian policy of returning exiled populations to their homelands with the reestablishment of the native religious cults. That is, the Deuteronomic school (much like Second Isaiah) would have believed that the Lord used Cyrus the Great to punish Babylon and to begin the return of his repentant chosen people to Jerusalem. With such a theology, the Deuteronomic school would not only support the mission of Zerubbabel, but would also be eager to participate in it. From their theological perspective, this was not simply a Persian policy to gain the loyalty of the empire's subjects and maintain control over the empire; it was the beginning of the Lord's plan to restore Israel.

The Persian policy clearly included the rebuilding of the Jerusalem temple and the political appointments of Davidides as governor, first Sheshbazzar and then Zerubabbel. These appointments would certainly have reinforced any exilic hopes in the return of a Davidic king and this hope would have culminated during the governorship of Zerubbabel under whose leadership the temple was rebuilt. Such hope, however, did not necessarily suggest that the Deuteronomic school placed its hope in the governorship of Zerubbabel; its hope was in the Lord's promise to restore Israel and was not necessarily tied to one particular human endeavor. This cautious hope is evident in the overall tenor of the Deuteronomic History for even the best of the Lord's chosen leaders—Moses, Joshua, David, Solomon, Hezekiah, Josiah—ultimately failed to establish Israel according to the Lord's command.[2] In sum, although the Deuteronomic school could see great possibilities in the Lord's work in the mission of Zerubbabel and would have supported his mission with their scribal skills, their understanding of history would also caution them to identify any particular human initiative as *necessarily* leading to the restoration of Israel as promised by the Lord. A mission like Zerubbabel's may have the potential to restore obedience to the law of God and as such deserved the Deuteronomic school's support, but

---

[2]Although I came to many of these insights on the theology of the Deuteronomic school in the postexilic period independently (see *Second Zechariah and the Deuteronomic School*, 176–201), the discussion here is significantly influenced by Ehud Ben Zvi, "Looking at the Primary (Hi)Story and the Prophetic Books as Literary/Theological Units within the Frame of the Early Second Temple: Some Considerations," *SJOT* 12 (1998): 26–43.

many similar past possibilities did not reach their potential. This is why the Deuteronomic school placed its hope on the Lord's promise and the divine initiative to restore Israel, a hope that led to the development of a Deuteronomic eschatology.

DEUTERONOMY 30:1–14[3]

The book of Deuteronomy is clearly not concerned simply with reporting about the past historical events of Moses' instruction to the Israelites in the wilderness. In fact, it is primarily legal material set within an historiographical context for the purpose of instructing its readers about the Lord's will for their present lives and the Lord's plan for the future. This is especially evident in Deuteronomy 30:1–14, which begins:

> And after all these things have come upon you, the blessings and the curses,
> … then the Lord your God will restore your fortunes and show mercy on you
> and he will return and gather you from all the peoples where the Lord your
> God had scattered you there. (30:1–3)

The phrase "the blessings and the curses" clearly refers to the stories of prosperity and calamity from the time after Moses to the Babylonian exile—that is, all of the events narrated in the rest of the Deuteronomic History. These times of "blessings and curses" are explicitly related to obedience to the Lord's commandments (see Deuteronomy 28).

---

[3]The following works were consulted on Deut 30:1–14: Peter C. Craige, *The Book of Deuteronomy* (NICOT; Grand Rapids: Eerdmans, 1976), 361–73; S. R. Driver, *A Critical and Exegetical Commentary on Deuteronomy* (ICC; Edinburg: T. & T. Clark, 1965), 328–32; A. D. H. Mayes, *Deuteronomy* (NCB; Grand Rapids: Eerdmans, 1979), 367-70; J. Gordon McConville, "1 Kings VIII 46–53 and the Deuteronomic Hope," *VT* 42 (1992): 67–79; Norbert Mendecki, "Dtn 30,3–4—nachexilisch?" *BZ* 29 (1985), 267–71; Anthony Phillips, *Deuteronomy* (CBC; Cambridge: Cambridge University Press, 1973), 194–202; Gerhard von Rad, *Deuteronomy: A Commentary* (OTL; Philadelphia: Westminster Press, 1966), 182–84.

The restoration promised by the Lord through Moses has begun for the readers of this text during the time of Zerubbabel. The Lord has returned them to Jerusalem, rebuilt the temple, and appointed a Davidide as governor, all of course through the Lord's control of the Persians. The text, however, also makes it clear that the Lord's work is not yet done.

> And the Lord your God will circumcise your heart and your children's heart so that you will love the Lord your God with all your heart and all your soul, so that you might live. (30:6)

Hope cannot be placed only in the present political possibilities of Zerubbabel's administration and the people's return to the Lord. The external covenant has been fulfilled by the required punishment of the exile, but other well-intentioned leaders in the past could not affect the fully restored Israel. This can come only at the Lord's initiative. Replacing the external covenant, the Lord will "circumcise" divine will into every Israelite's heart, thereby overcoming the possibility of later human transgression of an outward covenant.

> For this [new] commandment which I have commanded you today, it is not too difficult for you and it is not too distant. ... For the word is exceedingly near to you, in your mouth and in your heart, so that you can do it. (30:11, 14)

Because of this inner circumcision that will make obedience to the Lord much easier, the people of God will prosper greatly—"and [the Lord your God] will make you prosper and become numerous more than your fathers" (30:5).

For the Deuteronomic school during the time of Zerubbabel, Deut 30:1–14 clearly refers to the "curse" of the exile, the return to Jerusalem, and a future divine initiative, which will bring about a fully restored Israel.

JOSHUA 1:1–11[4]

Repeating some information given in Deuteronomy 34, Josh 1:1–9 introduces Joshua as Moses' successor and provides the reader with the Lord's command to Joshua to conquer the land promised to Moses. The Lord promises to protect Joshua: "No man will be able to stand before you all the days of your life; just as I was with Moses, I will be with you; I will not fail you and I will not abandon you" (1:5). This promise, however, contains the typical Deuteronomic condition of obedience to the law: "This book of the law shall not depart from your mouth, but you shall meditate on it day and night, so that you might obey carefully everything that is written in it, for then you will make your way prosperous and then you will succeed" (1:8; see also 1:7). Joshua 1:10–11 then provides the reader with Joshua's command for the people to prepare for crossing the Jordan to enter the land.

For the Deuteronomic school in postexilic Jerusalem, the entrance into the land not only occurred under Joshua, but also under Zerubbabel. The Deuteronomic school would likely apply the Lord's promise to be with Joshua (1:5) to Zerubbabel as well (see Hag 2:20–23). Now that the temple has been rebuilt and reconsecrated under Zerubbabel, the people will be more likely to obey the law as the Lord has commanded the people through Moses and Joshua.

---

[4]The following works were consulted on Josh 1:1–11: A. Graeme Auld, *Joshua, Judges, and Ruth* (Philadelphia: Westminster Press, 1984), 5–15; Robert G. Boling, *Joshua* (AB; Garden City: Doubleday & Company, 1982), 113–38; John Gray, *Joshua, Judges and Ruth* (NCB; London: Nelson, 1967), 48–51; J. Maxwell Miller and Gene M. Tucker, *The Book of Joshua* (Cambridge: Cambridge University Press, 1974), 19–25; J. Alberto Soggin, *Joshua: A Commentary* (OTL; Philadelphia: Westminster Press, 1972), 25; Marten H. Woudstra, *The Book of Joshua* (Grand Rapids: William B. Eerdmans, 1981), 55–64.

JUDGES 17:6; 21:25[5]

Two majors themes are found in the book of Judges. First, there is a critique of the period of the judges, because there was no stable, central government to prevent the anarchy that often arose. Second, because of this lack of a stable central government, Israel's existence during this period was characterized by a cycle of apostasy, divine punishment in the form of oppression by other peoples, and deliverance from oppression by a judge sent by the Lord. The phrase "In those days there was no king in Israel; each man did what was right in his own eyes" (17:6; 21:25; see also 18:1; 19:1) expresses succinctly both of these themes and the connection between them. In fact, Jdgs 21:25 is the last word of the book, thereby summarizing these themes so that the reader ends with this point.

If the Deuteronomic school supported Zerubbabel and placed its hope in his becoming king, this phrase would have obvious meaning in this context. That is, until Zerubbabel becomes a proper Davidic king who can govern over all the people, insuring that they strictly obey the law, there will remain a certain amount of apostasy with the likely consequences of divine punishment. The cycle of apostasy and divine punishment must be broken and Zerubbabel becoming king according to the Lord's plan would at least begin to break this cycle. Therefore, the critique of the period of the judges also applies to some degree to the period of the reconstruction of the temple; however, in this period the Deuteronomic school might interpret that there are clear signs of movement in the right direction.

At the same time, the phrase "every man did what was right in his own eyes" may also place the responsibility for obeying the law upon "every man." That is, since Zerubbabel is not yet king, then "every man" has a greater responsibility to being obedient to the Lord's commandments. The cycle of apostasy in Judges is clearly based not upon the wrong doings of a king, for "there was no king." Rather, the apostasy that led to divine

---

[5]The following works were consulted on Jdgs 17:6; 21:25: Auld, *Joshua, Judges, and Ruth*, 222–26; Boling, "In Those Days," 333–48; Robert G. Boling, *Judges* (AB; Garden City: Doubleday & Company, 1975), 254–59, 289–94; Dumbrell, "In Those Days There Was No King in Israel"; Gray, *Joshua, Judges and Ruth*, 362–65; Martin, *Judges*, 225–26.

punishment occurred because of the people's failure to obey the law. Therefore, this phrase both expresses hope for a future king to provide the proper environment for obedience to the law, while at the same time emphasizing each individual's responsibility to obey the law.

2 SAMUEL 7:1–17[6]

In 2 Samuel 5–6, David becomes king of all of Israel and makes Jerusalem his capital and the home of the ark of the covenant. 2 Samuel 7 begins:

> And when the king had dwelt in his house and the Lord had given rest to him from all the surrounding enemies, the king said to Nathan the prophet, "See now, I dwell in a house of cedar, but the ark of God dwells in a tent." And Nathan said to the king, "All that is in your heart, go, do; for the Lord is with you." (2 Sam 7:1–3)

Although Nathan the prophet here tells David to begin construction of the Jerusalem temple according to his wishes, the following verses (2 Sam 7:4–17) presents the Lord speaking to Nathan, correcting him. David will not build the house of the Lord, but David's offspring will build the house of the Lord. Rather than David building the Lord a house, the Lord promises to build David a house, a dynasty.

> When your days are full and you lie with your fathers, I will raise up your offspring after you, who shall come forth from your own body, and I will establish his kingdom. He will build my house for my name, and I will establish the throne of his kingdom forever. (2 Sam 7:12–13)

In the narrative of Samuel–Kings, this prophecy is fulfilled by Solomon, David's son, building the first Jerusalem temple (1 Kings 6–8); however, the wording here does not specify Solomon, but is simply David's "offspring." Although the singular pronoun "he" is used, the word

---

[6]The following works were consulted on 2 Samuel 7:1–17: Walter Brueggemann, *First and Second Samuel* (Interpretation; Louisville: John Knox Press, 1990), 253–61; Lyle Eslinger, *House of God or House of David: The Rhetoric of 2 Samuel 7* (JSOTSup 164; Sheffield: Sheffield Academic Press, 1994); P. Kyle McCarter, Jr., *II Samuel* (AB 9; Garden City: Doubleday, 1984), 190–231; Robert Polzin, *David and the Deuteronomist*, 71–84.

"offspring" often refers simply to descendents without specifying which generation. Therefore, there is nothing in 1 Samuel 7:1–17 that requires an interpretation of Solomon or even one of David's sons, thereby leaving open the possible interpretation that this word of the Lord simply refers to David's descendents.

Once again the text includes the divine promise of peace and prosperity.

> And I will appoint a place for my people, Israel, and I will plant them so that they will dwell in their own place, and will not be disturbed again, and violent men will not continue to afflict them as formerly. (2 Sam 7:10)

Clearly the Lord is promising David to establish an eternal dynasty for him, that (at least) one of his descendents will build a temple in Jerusalem, and that, after the temple is built, there will be peace and prosperity for Israel.

This passage easily lends itself to interpretation by the Deuteronomic school in postexilic Jerusalem. The contrast between David and the people of Israel living in fine homes and the Lord having no home is also found in Haggai (1:4, 9). The prophecy that one of David's descendents would build the Lord's house in Jerusalem certainly applies to Zerubbabel. Moreover, some in the postexilic community also thought that once the temple was rebuilt the Lord would grant peace and prosperity to his people (see Hag 2:15–19; Zech 8:9–13).

2 SAMUEL 23:1–7[7]

And these are the last words of David: (23:1a)

---

[7]The following works were consulted on 2 Samuel 23:1-7: Brueggemann, *First and Second Samuel*, 345–47; Bernard Gosse, "Isa 59,21 et 2 Sam 23,1–7, l'opposition entre les lignées sacerdotales et royales à l'époche post-exilique," *BN* 68 (1993): 10–12; McCarter, *II Samuel*, 476–86; Tryggve N. D. Mettinger, "'The Last Words of David': A Study of Structure and Meaning in II Samuel 23:1–7," *SEÅ* 41-42 (1977): 147-56; G. del Olmo Lete, "David's Farewell Oracle (2 Samuel XXIII 1-7): A Literary Analysis," *VT* 34 (1984): 414–38; Shlomo Naéh, "A New Suggestion regarding 2 Samuel XXIII 7," *VT* 46 (1996): 260–65; H. Neil Richardson, "The Last Words of David: Some Notes on II Samuel 23:1–7," *JBL* 90 (1971): 257–66.

2 Samuel 23:1–7 is a poetic oracle attributed to David and, within its immediate narrative context, it sums up much of the royal ideology found in Samuel–Kings. David is identified by his relationship with the Lord (23:1b), including the title "the anointed one of the God of Jacob." David now speaks, claiming that the Lord has spoken to him (23:2–3a), reporting what the Lord said (23:3b–4), and then reporting God's eternal covenant with him for a dynasty (23:5–7).

> For, does not my house stand firm with God?
> For he has made with me an everlasting covenant,
> Ordered completely and secure.
> For, will he not cause all of my help and my desire to prosper?
> But the wicked, like thorns, are all thrown away—
> For they cannot be taken in the hand,
> And the man who touches them will be filled with iron and the staff of a
>   spear—
> And by fire they will be utterly burned in the summer fires (23:5–7)[8]

Clearly, the Deuteronomic school during the time of Zerubbabel would understand the "everlasting covenant" to refer to Zerubbabel, thereby supporting hope in the institution of the Davidic monarchy (see also Haggai 2:23; Zech 6:9–15).[9] At the same time, an outright revolt against the Persian empire would obviously be suicidal, given the overwhelming military power of the empire. The reference to the "wicked, like thorns" here may express caution against such open rebellion. Thorns cannot be held or touched without injury, unless one has the proper tools. The proper military tools to use against the Persian empire would not be available to postexilic Judah; therefore, hope may be expressed here in the use of the divine passive. Note that all of the successful or certain actions in these verses are the work of God, in contrast to human initiative. That is, the implication is that the Lord will throw away and utterly burn up all the thorns in the near future.

---

[8]The translation of 2 Sam 23:7 is based on Shlomo Naéh, "A New Suggestion regarding 2 Samuel XXIII 7," 265.

[9]Bernard Gosse ("Isa 59,21 et 2 Sam 23,1-7") dates 2 Sam 23:1–7 to the postexilic period, drawing theological analogies between it and Isa 55:3; Ps 89:29; Isa 59:21.

1 KINGS 8[10]

1 Kings 8 begins with the gathering of "all the people of Israel" (8:2). At the historical level, this is clearly an exaggeration. It is unlikely that "all the people" of both north and south ever did anything together. However, at the ideological level of using history to motivate contemporary readers, this passage implicitly calls for "all the people" to be supportive of the rebuilding of the temple and its rededication under Zerubbabel. Such a call is reminiscent of Haggai 1, in which the prophet admonishes the people under Zerubbabel for not rebuilding the temple (Hag 1:9) and succeeds in that "Zerubbabel ... Joshua ... and all the remnant of the people obeyed the voice of the Lord their God" (Hag 1:12) to rebuild the temple.

Solomon's temple is closely associated with the promise to David (1 Kgs 8:16–21, 24–26, 66). Solomon reports that his father, David, wanted to build the house of God, but that the Lord proclaimed that David's son who will sit on the throne after him will build the temple (8:16–21). Solomon's prayer of praise connects the Lord's promise for a temple to the Lord's promise to David concerning his descendent sitting on the throne.

> Therefore, O Lord, God of Israel, keep for your servant my father David that which you promised him, saying, "There shall never fail you a successor before me to sit on the throne of Israel, if only your children look to their way, to walk before me as you have walked before me." (8:25)

As a descendent of David who has successfully led the people of Israel in rebuilding the temple, Zerubbabel would certainly be a serious candidate for the Lord keeping his promise by placing him on the throne. In other

---

[10]The following works were consulted on 1 Kings 8: Marc Brettler, "Interpretation and Prayer: Notes on the Composition of 1 Kings 8.15–53," in *Minhah le-Nahum* (eds. M. Brettler and M. Fishbane; JSOTSup 154; Sheffield: Sheffield Academic Press, 1993), 17–35; Jones, *1 and 2 Kings*, 1:204; Gary N. Knoppers, "Prayer and Propaganda: Solomon's Dedication of the Temple and the Deuteronomist's Program," *CBQ* 57 (1995): 229–54; Jon D. Levenson, "1 Kings 8," in *Traditions in Transformation: Turning Points in Biblical Faith* (ed. B. Halpern; Winona Lake: Eisenbrauns, 1981), 143–63; Linville, *Israel in the Book of Kings*, 272–301; McConville, "1 Kings VIII 46–53 and the Deuteronomic Hope," 67–79; J. Gordon McConville, "Narrative and Meaning in the Books of Kings," *Bib* 70 (1989): 31–49; Nelson, *First and Second Kings*, 52–55; De Vries, *1 Kings*, 126; Würthwein, *1 Könige 1–16*, 95.

words, the Lord has begun this process by the Persians defeating the
Babylonians and Darius I appointing Zerubbabel as governor. Once the
people of Israel demonstrate their obedience to the Lord there is hope that
the Lord will fulfill his promise to David by making Zerubbabel king.

Solomon's prayer also includes an explicit reference to the exile
and the return. He prays, "When your people Israel, having sinned against
you, are defeated before an enemy but turn again to you, confess your
name, pray and plead with you in this house, then hear in heaven, forgive
the sin of your people Israel, and bring them again to the land that you gave
to their ancestors" (8:33–34; see also 8:46–51). Of course, during the time
of Zerubbabel much of this prayer has been fulfilled. The people sinned and
were punished by exile. However, they repented, the Lord returned them to
the land, and they once again pray in the temple.

Solomon's prayer continues asking for relief from drought and
famine (8:35–40). This also recalls the prophecies of Haggai during the
time of Zerubbabel, when the Lord says to the people before they began
construction on the temple, "Therefore the heavens above you have
withheld the dew, and the earth has withheld its produce" (Hag 1:10). In
other words, the prayers of the people who returned to the land before the
temple was rededicated under Zerubbabel included prayers for relief from
drought and famine. Once the temple was rebuilt their prayers were
answered, just as Solomon had requested, for the Lord spoke through
Haggai, saying,

> Since the day that the foundation of the Lord's temple was laid, consider: Is
> there any seed left in the barn? Do the vine, the fig tree, the pomegranate, and
> the olive tree still yield nothing? From this day on I will bless you. (Hag
> 2:18b–19).

So the prayers of the returnees were answered under Zerubbabel, but only
partially. Their prayers may have also included the hope in a Davidic king
and political independence, both potentially politically dangerous thoughts
but already expressed in Solomon's prayer.

Solomon's prayer also includes Israel's defeat of its enemies.

> If your people go out to battle against their enemy, by whatever way you
> shall send them, and they pray to the Lord toward the city that you have

chosen and the house that I have built for your name, then hear in heaven their prayer and their plea, and maintain their cause. (1 Kgs 8:44–45)

Such a prayer would certainly have been understood by the Persians as treason, if it came from the lips of Zerubbabel or his contemporaries. It is placed, however, in the mouth of Solomon and could refer to various earlier enemies, for example, the Assyrians and Babylonians. Of course, the ideological nature of historiography may be exploited here to express something potentially dangerous in the Persian empire.

The interpretation of 1 Kings 8 during the time of Zerubbabel I have thus far proposed has little of the cautionary hope that I described as typical of the Deuteronomic school. It appears that there is much hope being placed in the rebuilt temple and Zerubbabel and there is, but there is also a cautionary note in Solomon's prayer. Once again, recalling the exile and return, Solomon prays,

If they sin against you—for there is no one who does not sin—and you are angry with them and give them to an enemy, so that they are carried away captive to the land of the enemy, far off or near; ... if they repent with all their heart and soul ... then hear in heaven your dwelling place their prayer and their plea, maintain their cause and forgive your people who have sinned against you. (8:46, 48, 49–50)

Although this has already been fulfilled in the time of Zerubbabel—that is, the exile and the return are now history—this prayer allows for the Lord's forgiveness. In other words, all humans sin and the Lord does not necessarily have to become angry with all sinners, especially with those who now worship in the temple. The admission that all sin would certainly include Zerubbabel. That is, just as Moses and David before him sinned, Zerubbabel also sins and cannot restore Israel to its divinely willed glory himself. Such a restoration can only come from the Lord, who can forgive sins. Therefore, even though there is much Deuteronomic hope during the time of Zerubbabel, this hope is not placed on Zerubbabel himself, but on the certainty that the Lord will fulfill his promises that he made to Moses (8:53) and David (8:25).

Solomon's prayer continues, asking the Lord to help the people overcome their sinfulness.

> The Lord our God be with us, as he was with our ancestors; but incline our hearts to him, to walk in his ways, and to keep his commandments, his statues, and his ordinances, which he commanded our ancestors. (8:57–58)

This prayer—May the Lord incline our hearts to him—is similar to the idea of the Lord circumcising hearts in Deut 30:6. After the confession that "there is no one who does not sin" (8:46), this plea for the Lord to "incline our hearts" is clearly a request for the Lord's compassionate initiative to overcome the difficulties in keeping the commandments. Solomon and the Deuteronomic school during the time of Zerubbabel are saying that their ancestors were unable to keep these commandments and that they are unable to fully keep these commandments; therefore, they pray to the Lord for the necessary change of heart and mind, so that they can do what they are unable to do—that is, fully obey the Lord.

For the Deuteronomic school, the dedication of the temple under Solomon has obvious connections to the dedication of the temple under Zerubbabel. Solomon's prayer includes petitions for things that the returnees have already experienced, including the return itself and an end to drought and famine. Solomon's prayer also includes those things that the returnees are still praying for, even if somewhat covertly, such as political independence and the restoration of the Davidic monarchy. But the reality of the hegemony of the Persian empire casts a caution to those who place their hope in human endeavors, for all human endeavors are influenced to some degree by sin. Hence, the full hope for a restored Israel rests with the Lord alone, who has the power to change human nature so that the Lord's people will be fully obedient to his commandments and ways.

2 KINGS 17[11]

2 Kings 17 begins with an account of the destruction of the northern kingdom of Israel by the Assyrian army as divine punishment for idolatry (17:1–23). 2 Kings 17:24–33 concerns what happened in the northern kingdom after the destruction and exile of the people of Israel. The Assyrians populated Samaria with other exiled peoples—"people from Babylon, Cuthah, Avva, Hamath, and Sepharvaim"—who brought their own religious beliefs and practices with them (17:24–26). These exiled peoples living in Samaria were being attacked by lions and the Assyrian king was told that the attacks were because the people "do not know the law of the god of the land" (twice in 17:26). The king therefore returns one of the exiled Israelite priests to teach these people "the law of the god of the land" (17:27) and the priest teaches them to "fear the Lord" (17:28). The people of Samaria then feared the Lord, but they also continued their own idolatrous practices and beliefs (17:29–41). According to the narrative, the absence of the Israelites from Samaria and the syncretistic religious practices of the people of Samaria continue "to this day" (17:23, 34, 41).

This passage is obviously a justification for the anti-Samaritan stance of the community—that is, the Samaritans are not descendents of Abraham, but of "the nations," and their religious practices and beliefs have been corrupted by pagan religion, even if they appear to worship the Lord. This passage lends itself easily to understanding how the Deuteronomic school might have interpreted it in the context of the postexilic period, in which such anti-Samaritan rhetoric was present (see Ezra 6:1–6; 2 Chronicles 30). That is, the Deuteronomic school could use this passage to

---

[11] The following works were consulted on 2 Kgs 17:24–34: Mordechai Cogan, "'For We, Like You, Worship Your God': Three Biblical Portrayals of Samaritan Origins," *VT* 36 (1988): 286–92; Gray, *I & II Kings*, 650–56; Jones, *1 and 2 Kings*, 2:542–56; Linville, *Israel in the Book of Kings*, 212–20; Burke O. Long, *2 Kings* (FOTL 10; Grand Rapids: Eerdmans, 1991), 180–90; Shemaryahu Talmon, "Polemic and Apology in Biblical Historiography—2 Kings 17:24–41," in *The Creation of Sacred Literature: Composition and Redaction of the Biblical Text* (ed. R. E. Friedman; Berkeley: University of California Press, 1981), 57–68; Pauline A. Viviano, "2 Kings 17: Rhetorical and Form-Critical Analysis," *CBQ* 49 (1987): 548–59.

require a distancing from the religious practices of Samaria and to require a strict adherence to doing as the Lord had commanded.

> The Lord made with them a covenant and commanded them, "You shall not fear other gods and you shall not bow down to them and you shall not serve them and you shall not sacrifice to them; for the Lord who brought you out of the land of Egypt with great power and with an outstretched arm you shall worship him and to him you shall bow down and to him you shall sacrifice. …" (17:35–36)

This same rhetoric may have also been used to justify the stance of the Deuteronomic school and other returnees from Babylon over the people who remained in the land, especially if they were understood to have intermarried with other peoples.[12] Certainly, postexilic literature includes such denigrating of the people who remained in Judah during the exile (Ezra 3:1–3; 4:1–5) and within that context this passage could prove useful to those with this stance. One of those in power among the returnees was the high priest Joshua ben Jehozadak (for example, see Haggai 1:1, 12, 14; 2:2, 4; Zech 3:1–10). Joshua's role in the reestablished temple cult would have been understood as much the same for the priest that Assyrian king returned to Samaria—that is, Darius the king of Persia sent Joshua the high priest to reestablish the true worship of the "god of the land," so that the people of the land would once again "fear the Lord." Therefore, we can easily see how this passage may have been understood by the Deuteronomic school in the time of Zerubbabel and Joshua, the high priest.

---

[12]Shemaryahu Talmon also interprets 2 Kings 17 similarly; however, he assumes that such a postexilic addition cannot be Deuteronomic ("Polemic and Apology in Biblical Historiography—2 Kings 17:24–41," 67). For a similar understanding of how anti-Samaritan rhetoric could also serve to discourage intermarriage between returnees and those who remained in the land, see Othniel Margalith, "The Political Background of Zerubbabel's Mission and the Samaritan Schism," *VT* 41 (1991): 312–23. See further Chapter 6, 126–27.

2 KINGS 25:27–30 (= JER 52:31–34)[13]

The Deuteronomic History (and the book of Jeremiah) ends with a report of Jehoiachin's release from prison.

> In the thirty-seventh year of the exile of King Jehoiachin of Judah, in the twelfth month, on the twenty-seventh day of the month, King Evil-merodach of Babylon, in the year that he began to reign, released King Jehoiachin of Judah from prison; he spoke kindly to him, and gave him a seat about the other seats of the kings who were with him in Babylon. So Jehoiachin put aside his prison clothes. Every day of his life he dined regularly in the king's presence. For his allowance, a regular allowance was given him by the king, a portion every day, as long as he lived. (2 Kgs 25:27–30)

Since the end of a literary work often has a certain importance in relationship to the work's purpose, the question arises as to why the Deuteronomic school ended the book of Kings and the Deuteronomic History as a whole with this report. Various answers have been given to this question, from providing hope in the restoration of the Davidic monarchy[14]

---

[13]The following works were consulted on 2 Kgs 25:27–30 (= Jer 52:31–34): Albertz, "Wer waren die Deuteronomisten?," 319–38; Bob Becking, "Jehojacin's Amnesty, Salvation for Israel? Notes on 2 Kings 25,27–30," in *Pentateuchal and Deuteronomistic Studies* (eds. C. Brekelmans and J. Lust; BETL 94; Leuven: Leuven University Press, 1990), 283–93; Christopher T. Begg, "The Significance of Jehoiachin's Release," *JSOT* 36 (1986): 49–56; Georg Fischer, "Les Deux Faces de Jérémie 52," *ETR* 74 (1999): 481–89; Georg Fischer, "Jeremia 52—ein Schlüssel zum Jeremiabuch," *Bib* 79 (1998): 333–59; Meik Gerhards, "Die Begnadigung Jojachins—Überlegungen zu 2 Kön 25,27–30 (mit einem Anhang zu den Nennungen Jojachins auf Zuteilungslisten aus Babylon)," *BN* 94 (1998): 52–67; Halpern, *First Historians*, 158; Siegfried Herrmann, *Prophetie und Wirklichkeit in der Epoche des babylonischen Exils* (Stuttgart: Calwer, 1967), 12–113; Hobbs, *2 Kings*, 367–69; Jan Jaynes Granowski, "Jehoichin at the King's Table: A Reading of the Ending of the Second Book of Kings," in *Reading Between Texts: Intertextuality and the Hebrew Bible* (ed. D. N. Fewell; Louisville: Westminster/John Knox Press, 1992), 173–88; Nelson, *First and Second Kings*, 265–69; Levensen, "Last Four Verses," 353–61; Donald F. Murray, "Of All the Year of Hopes—or Fears? Jehoichin in Babylon (2 Kings 25:27–30)," *JBL* 120 (2001): 245–65; Person, *The Kings–Isaiah and Kings–Jeremiah Recensions*, 80–113; Zenger, "Die deuteronomistische Interpretation der Rehabilitierung Jojachins," 30; Römer, "Transformations in Deuteronomistic and Biblical Historiography," 10–11.

[14]Albertz, "Wer waren die Deuteronomisten?"; Levensen, "Last Four Verses."

to minimizing the Davidic monarchy from a pro-Babylonian position;[15] however, previous answers to this question have assumed an exilic setting.

When these verses are interpreted within the context of the governorship of Zerubbabel, they clearly provide hope in the restoration of the Davidic monarchy. That is, the process of restoration that the Lord began under the Babylonians with the release of King Jehoiachin from prison continued with the Persian defeat of the Babylonians, the return to Jerusalem, the appointment of Zerubbabel (Jehoiachin's grandson) as governor, and the rebuilding of the temple. Much like the prophet Haggai, the Deuteronomic school most likely understood that this divinely-initiated process would continue until Zerubbabel was proclaimed king and Judah had regained its political independence. It is in this way that the last four verses of the book of Kings (and the book of Jeremiah) provided hope in the restoration of the Davidic monarchy reinstituted by Jehoiachin's grandson, Zerubbabel. For this reason I agree with Thomas Römer's conclusion, "The last episode in Kings which tells of a sort of rehabilitation of the king Jehoiachin fits indeed better into the postexilic than into the exilic period."[16]

JEREMIAH 11:1–17[17]

This passage is commonly associated with the Deuteronomic school, either as based on an oracle by the historical Jeremiah supporting the Josianic reform or as a late Deuteronomic composition. But no matter when it originated, there is agreement that Jeremiah is portrayed here as prophetically proclaiming the covenant. The Lord summons Jeremiah (11:1–3), instructing him thrice what to say to the people concerning the covenant (11:3–5, 6–8, 9–13). The first instruction (11:3–5) reminds the people of Judah of the curses that will fall upon those who do not obey "the

---

[15]Becking, "Jehoiachin's Amnesty, Salvation for Israel?"; Begg, "Significance"; Gerhards, "Begnadigung Jojachins."

[16]Römer, "Transformations in Deuteronomistic and Biblical Historiography," 10–11.

[17]The following works were consulted on Jer 11:1–17: Brueggeman, *Jeremiah*, 109–12; Carroll, *Jeremiah*, 266–74; Clements, *Jeremiah*, 73–79; Holloday, *Jeremiah*, 1:345–56; McKane, *Jeremiah*, 1:236–53; Jack R. Lundbom, *Jeremiah 1–20* (AB 21A; New York: Doubleday, 1999), 614–33.

words of the covenant" which the Lord had made with their ancestors when he "brought them out of the land of Egypt" (11:3,4). The second instruction (11:6–8) implies that the Lord warned the people, the people continued to disobey, and, therefore, the Lord has punished disobedient Judah: "Therefore, I brought upon them all the words of this covenant which I commanded them to do, but they did not do" (11:8). The third instruction to Jeremiah (11:9–13) concerns the Lord's pronouncement of judgment against the rebellious, idolatrous people of Judah. Jeremiah is then commanded not to pray for the rebellious people of Judah (11:14) with reasons why such intercession would not be accepted given in the form of rhetorical questions and expressions of the wrath of God (11:15–17).

Although the passage is clearly referring to the destruction of Jerusalem and the Babylonian exile at the level of the narrative, it is nevertheless written in such a way that the theological message is predominant and the historical level is simply a vehicle to express the theological understanding of the covenant. Because of this, this passage could easily have been interpreted during the time of Zerubbabel as follows: the fulfillment of the Lord's punishment is at its end and, because of the rebuilt temple, there is an opportunity to renew the covenant, if the people obey the commandments. This renewal will restore the land to a "land flowing with milk and honey" (11:5).

DEUTERONOMIC THEOLOGY DURING THE TIME OF ZERUBBABEL

The Deuteronomic school's understanding of covenant underlies its postexilic theology. Strict adherence to the Lord's commandments is essential to receiving the Lord's blessings, including the promised land, the temple as the Lord's house, and the Davidic monarchy. Although the people of Judah (including Zerubbabel, Joshua, the Deuteronomic school) can cooperate with the Persian imperial government, this is not because one should cooperate with foreign (and therefore pagan) peoples. One should cooperate with the Persian imperial bureaucracy during the time of Zerubbabel only because it is the means by which the Lord is restoring Israel and ultimately by which the Lord will exalt Israel above the nations. That is, one is not really cooperating with the Persians as much as one is cooperating with the Lord, who will overcome the Persian empire for the security and prosperity of Israel. In fact, the Lord has made it clear that association and cooperation with the nations can lead one to disobedience against the commandments and, consequently, divine punishment.

Because of its understanding of the failure of even Judah's most righteous leaders—Moses, David, Solomon, Hezekiah, Josiah—to establish fully the security and prosperity of Israel as promised by the Lord, the Deuteronomic school understands that strict adherence to the law is required, but impossible. That is, the Deuteronomic school admonished the people to fully obey the law, while at the same realizing that absolute obedience to the law can only come from the Lord. Such absolute obedience will require the Lord's intervention in the form of changing human character by circumcising hearts—that is, internalizing the law so that obedience becomes an essential part of human nature (Deut 30:6; see also 1 Kgs 8:57–58).

The Deuteronomic school requires strict adherence to the law from the people and yet places its absolute hope in the divine initiative to fully restore Israel. The Deuteronomic school demands human initiative to move towards fully obeying the Lord's will, knowing that this is impossible. The striving for this goal, however, is the proper, faithful response to the Lord who will soon enable the people to reach this goal through divine intervention, so that the Lord's promises—including the restoration of the Davidic monarchy, the temple as the house of the Lord, and Israel presiding over the nations—will be fully realized.

CHAPTER 6

DEUTERONOMIC LITERATURE AFTER THE TIME OF ZERUBBABEL

In the previous chapter, reinterpretations of passages in the Deuteronomic History were given, assuming the setting of some time during the administration of Zerubbabel, when the Deuteronomic school probably returned to Jerusalem and participated in the effort to rebuild the temple and its cult. In this chapter, reinterpretations of passages in the Deuteronomic History are given assuming a setting after the governorship of Zerubbabel but before the mission of Ezra.[1] As argued above, the Deuteronomic school probably became somewhat disenfranchised by the failure of Zerubbabel to re-establish the Davidic monarchy and, therefore, probably better understood how the Persian-support of the temple cult meant a certain amount of Persian-control of the temple administration.

---

[1]Since I argued above that the mission of Ezra probably led to the demise of the Deuteronomic school, I would allow that the Deuteronomic school's redactional activity may have continued briefly after Ezra's arrival in Jerusalem. However, with its institutional support withdrawn, the Deuteronomic school probably would not have continued long after his arrival.

This disenfranchisement can be seen in the following interpretations of various passages from the Deuteronomic History.

As in the previous chapter, these passages were not selected because we have clear evidence that they are postexilic in origin. However, since the setting in which I place these passages for their interpretation is at the end of the Deuteronomic school's redactional activity, if they did not originate after the time of Zerubbabel, they were at least read and interpreted within this setting.

I begin this chapter with a discussion of Deut 30:1–14, simply because I began the previous chapter with this same passage. That is, since in this chapter I am interpreting selected passages from the end of the Deuteronomic school's redaction of the Deuteronomic History, each of the passages discussed in the previous chapter could possibly be discussed again here with a somewhat different interpretation because of the end of Zerubbabel's leadership, in whom much hope was cautiously placed. The remainder of the chapter contains new interpretations of other passages in Deuteronomic literature.

DEUTERONOMY 30:1–14[2]

Although the cautious hope placed on Zerubbabel would have been negated by history, the confident hope in the Lord's restoration promised by the Lord would continue.

> And after all these things have come upon you, the blessings and the curses,
> … then the Lord your God will restore your fortunes and show mercy on you
> and he will return and gather you from all the peoples where the Lord your
> God had scattered you there. (30:1–3)

In fact, the Deuteronomic school might now be understanding the Persian-support of the Jerusalem temple cult less as a "blessing" and more as a "curse," especially *if* Zerubbabel's mysterious disappearance from the biblical narrative can be explained by his being removed from power by the

---

[2] The following works were consulted on Deut 30:1–14: Craige, *Deuteronomy*, 361–73; Driver, *Deuteronomy*, 328–32; Mayes, *Deuteronomy*, 367–70; McConville, "1 Kings VIII 46–53 and the Deuteronomic Hope," 67–79; Mendecki, "Dtn 30,3–4—nachexilisch?," 267–71; Phillips, *Deuteronomy*, 194-202; von Rad, *Deuteronomy*, 182–84.

Persians because of increasing hope in the political independence of Judah with Zerubbabel as the Davidic king. But whatever the fate of Zerubbabel may have been, the Lord's work was understood to be not yet complete, because in the future the Lord will circumcise the people's hearts so that they might obey the Lord's commandments and live abundantly in the land (30:5–14). This remains something in which the Deuteronomic school can continue to place their hope.

DEUTERONOMY 4:29–31[3]

The book of Deuteronomy begins with Moses reciting Israel's history. In Deut 4:25–28, Moses the prophet predicts the exile as the Lord's scattering of disobedient Israel among the peoples.

> When you have begotten children and children's children and have grown old in the land, if you act corruptly and you make a graven image in the form of anything and do evil in the sight of the Lord, your God, so as to provoke him, … you will soon utterly perish from the land which you are going over the Jordan to possess. (Deut 4:25–26)

Since this prophecy has been fulfilled, the postexilic Deuteronomic school would continue to hope for fulfillment of the Lord's promise in Deut 4:30: "When you are in tribulation and all of these things come upon you at the end of days, you will return to the Lord and you will obey his voice."

This passage follows the standard progression in eschatological thought—that is, the tribulation of the people of God is followed by divine deliverance.[4] Of course, the punishment-restoration sequence itself does not constitute an eschatological perspective. The phrase "at the end of days" (Deut 4:30), however, is often found in eschatological contexts (see Jer 23:20; 30:24; 48:47; 49:39; Dan 10:4) and its presence here suggests that the Deuteronomic school may have become increasingly eschatological as

---

[3]The following works were consulted on Deut 4:29–31: Craige, *Deuteronomy*, 338–41; Driver, *Deuteronomy*, 73–75; Mayes, *Deuteronomy*, 156–57; McConville, "1 Kings VIII 46–53 and the Deuteronomic Hope," 67–79; Phillips, *Deuteronomy*, 35–37; von Rad, *Deuteronomy*, 446–52; Wolff, "Kerygma," 96–97.

[4]Wolff, "Kerygma," 98–99.

its hopes in human institutions, such as Zerubbabel's administration and perhaps the temple, subsided.[5]

JUDGES 3:1–6[6]

The book of Judges begins by listing the failure of the tribes of Israel to drive out all of the inhabitants of the land (Judges 1) and by summarizing the consequences of this failure—that is, the cycle of apostasy, divine punishment at the hand of the remaining inhabitants, and divine deliverance by the judges (Judges 2).[7] Since the theological perspective of the book (and the Deuteronomic History as a whole) assumes that the Lord controls history, an explanation of why the inhabitants of the land were allowed to remain (Jdgs 3:1–6) follows.

> These are the nations that the Lord left in order to test Israel by them, that is, all [of Israel] who had not experienced any war in Canaan. ... They existed to test Israel by them, to know whether they [Israel] would obey the commandments of the Lord, which he commanded their fathers by Moses. And the people of Israel dwelt among the Canaanites, the Hittites, the Amorites, the Perizzites, the Hivites, and the Jebusites; and they took their [the inhabitants'] daughters to themselves as wives and they gave their [the Israelites'] daughters to their [the inhabitants'] sons; and they served their [the inhabitants'] gods. (Jdgs 3:1, 4–6)

As noted by Marvin Sweeney, Jdgs 3:1–6 introduces "the theme of intermarriage with the pagan nations as the basis for a critique of the northern tribes that focuses especially on Ephraim and Bethel," the dominant theme in Judges 3–21.[8] Such intermarriage of the Israelites with

---

[5]On eschatological thought in Deuteronomy, see von Rad, *Deuteronomy*; Gerhard von Rad, "The Promised Land and Yahweh's Land in the Hexateuch," in *The Problem of the Hexateuch and Other Essays* (trans. E. W. Trueman Dicken; New York: McGraw-Hill, 1966), 92; Gerhard von Rad, *Studies in Deuteronomy* (SBT 9; London: SCM Press, 1953).

[6]The following works were consulted on Jdgs 3:1–6: Auld, *Joshua, Judges, and Ruth*, 140–45; Boling, *Judges*, 77–79; Gray, *Joshua, Judges and Ruth*, 259–60; Martin, *Judges*, 38–41; Marvin A. Sweeney, "Davidic Polemics in the Book of Judges," *VT* 46 (1997): 517–29.

[7]Sweeney, "Davidic Polemics in the Book of Judges," 527.

[8]Sweeney, "Davidic Polemics in the Book of Judges," 518.

the pagan inhabitants is explicitly forbidden in Deuteronomic law (Deut 7:1–4), because it will lead to serving other gods.

Intermarriage was common among the people of Judah in the postexilic period, at least common enough that the Ezra tradition refers to intermarriage as a problem requiring reform (Ezra 4:3; 6:21; 9:1–15; see also Mal 2:10–12). Hence, it is not difficult at all to understand the meaning this text would have for the Deuteronomic school in postexilic Judah—that is, intermarriage with the inhabitants of the land (possibly including the descendents of Israelites who remained in the land during the Babylonian exile) is strictly forbidden and, when it occurs, will lead to divine punishment.

1 SAMUEL 16–18[9]

The story of David and Goliath is one of the most widely known stories of the Deuteronomic History and even the Hebrew Bible as a whole. There are a variety of theological themes found in this story and its larger narrative context (1 Samuel 16–18), two of which fit especially well into a postexilic context: (1) the Lord's preference of David over Saul and (2) David's triumph over Goliath with divine aid.

(1) In 1 Sam 16:1, Samuel is grieving over Saul, because the Lord has rejected Saul. The Lord tells Samuel to go to Jesse the Bethlehemite among whose sons Samuel will find the next king. Samuel anoints David as a young boy (16:13) and later David is brought to serve Saul by comforting him with music (16:14–23). When the Philistines gather for battle led by their champion Goliath, all of the Israelite soldiers, including Saul, are petrified with fear (17:1–11, 23–25), but David the shepherd boy, with the

---

[9]The following works were consulted on 1 Samuel 16–18: Dominique Barthélemy, David W. Gooding, Johan Lust, and Emanuel Tov, eds., *The Story of David and Goliath* (OBO 73; Fribourg: Éditions Universitaires Fribourg; Göttingen: Vandenhoeck und Ruprecht, 1986); Brueggemann, *First and Second Samuel*, 119–34; Antony F. Campbell, "From Philistine to Throne (1 Samuel 16:14–18:16)," *ABR* 34 (1986): 35–41; McCarter, *I Samuel*, 284–314; Robert Polzin, *Samuel and the Deuteronomist: A Literary Study of the Deuteronomic History* (San Francisco: Harper & Row, 1989), 152–86; Rofé, "The Battle of David and Goliath," 117–51; Stoebe, "Die Goliathperikope 1 Sam. 17,1-18,5 und die Text-Form der Septuaginta," 397–413; Tov, "The Composition of I Samuel 16-18," 97–130; De Vries, "David's Victory over the Philistine as Saga and Legend," 23–36.

confidence that comes from being in the presence of the Lord, boldly
approaches Goliath and slays the champion warrior (17:26–51). David's
speech before he slays Goliath, demonstrates his confidence in the Lord.

> And David said to the Philistine, "You come to me with a sword and with a
> spear and with a javelin, but I come to you in the name of the Lord of Hosts,
> the God of the armies of Israel, whom you have taunted. This day the Lord
> will deliver you into my hand and I will strike you down and I will cut off
> your head. (17:45–46a)

That is, David the shepherd boy did single-handedly what Saul and his
warriors could not do together, thereby demonstrating that the Lord had
forsaken Saul and had chosen David.

With Zerubbabel as governor, hope in the Davidic monarchy was
strengthened. When Zerubbabel was no longer governor, hope in the
Davidic monarchy continued and this hope probably generated some
animosity towards governors who were not Davidides. If this is the case, the
conflict in the story between Saul and David and the Lord's clear choice of
David over Saul would have possible political implications for the
Deuteronomic school after Zerubbabel's governorship, both in their
theological understanding of the illegitimacy of the administration and in
their placement of hope less so in human institutions and more so in divine
intervention.

(2) In the narrative, the theme of David triumphing over Saul
obviously is closely related to the theme of David triumphing over Goliath
the champion warrior of the Philistines. Despite the Philistines' military
might, a shepherd boy can overcome them because of the Lord's presence.
This theme is described well in the words of Kyle McCarter:[10]

> Here is David, small, apparently defenseless, with none of the bearing or
> equipment of a trained soldier—the perfect personification of the tiny nation
> of Judah. And against him stands the gigantic enemy, heavily armed and
> evidently irresistible, as the enemies of Judah so often seemed. David has no
> real hope in force of arms, and despite his courage and wit he finally must rely
> on the one good hope that Judah, too, had in times of danger. "You come
> against me with sword and spear and scimitar," he cries to the Philistine, "but

---

[10]McCarter, *I Samuel*, 297.

I come against you with the name of Yahweh Sabaoth, god of the ranks of Israel!" (v. 45).

In David's speech to Goliath in 17:45, he uses the singular second person pronoun, indicating that his speech here is directed specifically at Goliath. David's speech in 1 Sam 17:46–47, however, changes to the plural second person pronoun, indicating all of the Philistines.

> This day the Lord will deliver you (sing.) into my hand and I will strike you (sing.) down and I will cut off your (sing.) head; and I will give the body (sing.) of the army of the Philistines this day to the birds of the air and to the beasts of the earth and all the earth may know that there is a god in Israel and that all of this assembly may know not by sword or spear does the Lord save, for to the Lord belongs the battle and he will give you (pl.) into our hands. (17:46–47)

The interpretation of David representing Judah and Goliath representing the Philistines is explicit in these verses. In the story, David kills only Goliath, but in his speech he equates the body of Goliath with the army of the Philistines and he ends his speech with "he [the Lord] will give you [the Philistines] into our [the Israelites'] hands." In fact, once David kills Goliath, the Philistines flee in fear and the Israelite soldiers are emboldened to pursue and kill them.

As noted above,[11] Alexander Rofé dates the story of David and Goliath in MT-1 Sam 16–18 to the postexilic period, specifically sometime during the late fifth or early fourth centuries B.C.E. Commenting on the change from the singular to the plural in 17:47, Rofé writes:[12]

> All of a sudden, the subject of the story is a future war against all the Philistines. This is a war that will establish a new monarchy that will never be destroyed or surrendered to another people.

That is, if the Philistines represent the enemies of Israel, this verse can certainly be understood in connection with eschatological hopes in a Davidic king. Rofé continues:[13]

---

[11]Chapter 2, 38–39.
[12]Rofé, "The Battle of David and Goliath," 139.
[13]Rofé, "The Battle of David and Goliath," 140.

> We do not know what became of Zerubbabel, but clearly the Persian monarchy did not fall, and no Davidic kingdom arose in its place. Indeed, the reality was the complete reverse of what Jews had desired. No one from the Davidic line took Zerubbabel's place as the focus of expectations that the monarchy would be restored. Persia, on the other hand, was stabilized under Darius's leadership and went on to become a world empire of dimensions hitherto unknown in the East. As a result, the nature of the Jewish concept of redemption underwent a fundamental change. Until now, hopes of salvation had been rooted in the actual, historical sphere and had centered on real personalities and events, i.e., Cyrus and the fall of Babylonia, Zerubbabel and the rebuilding of the Temple. Now they became metahistorical.

As suggested in the previous chapter, the Deuteronomic school's cautious hope in Zerubbabel never advocated a military rebellion against the Persian empire, but rather placed its hope in the Lord's initiative. This same understanding is especially present here—"that all of this assembly may know not by sword or spear does the Lord save, for to the Lord belongs the battle," 17:47). David's remark here is not simply that the Philistines (representing the nations) may know, but that "all of this assembly," including the Israelite army, may know that the battle belongs to the Lord. That is, despite the Deuteronomic school's growing animosity towards the Jerusalem administration controlled by the Persians and headed by a non-Davidide, the Deuteronomic school did not advocate armed rebellion against the militarily superior Persians. The Deuteronomic school believed that the Lord would keep his promise to David and to his people Israel and would fight the battle himself.

1 KINGS 21:1–20[14]

This passage is a part of the longer narrative concerning Ahab, who was more wicked than all of the kings before him.

> And Ahab, son of Omri, did evil in the sight of the Lord, more than all that were before him. And as if it had been a light matter for him to walk in the sins of Jeroboam the son of Nebat, he took a wife, Jezebel, the daughter of

---

[14]The following works were consulted on 1 Kgs 21:1-20: Gray, *I & II Kings*, 433-43; Jones, *1 and 2 Kings*, 349-60; Long, *1 Kings*, 223-30; Rofé, "The Vineyard of Naboth," 89-104; William M. Schniedewind, "History and Interpretation: The Religion of Ahab and Manasseh in the Book of Kings," *CBQ* 55 (1993): 649-61.

Ethba'al, king of the Sidonians. And he went and served Ba'al and worshiped him. (1 Kgs 16:30–31)

1 Kings 21:1–20 is one of the stories that illustrates how Ahab's marriage to Jezebel, a foreign woman, was so wicked.

Next to Ahab's palace was a vineyard owned by Naboth the Jezreelite. Ahab wanted to acquire the vineyard to enlarge his vegetable garden, but Naboth refused Ahab's offer due to his understanding of traditional custom to keep property within one's family (21:1–3). Ahab became disappointed that his wishes were not met and Jezebel criticizes Ahab's inaction and takes matters into her own hands to acquire the vineyard for him (21:4–7). She orchestrates a plan to have Naboth falsely accused of blasphemy, so that he will be stoned to death and then Ahab can acquire the vineyard (21:8–16). The plan succeeds. The Lord then speaks through Elijah, condemning Ahab for the crime (21:17–20).

As noted above,[15] the Deuteronomic schoool criticized inter-marriage, asserting that it leads to corrupted religious and social practices. Again, this passage obviously fits within the postexilic setting. Alexander Rofé presents linguistic and thematic evidence, strongly suggesting a postexilic setting for this passage. He concludes:[16]

> If we recapitulate our findings, saying that in the 5th or 4th century an author retold the old story of Naboth, shifting the guilt from King Ahab (2 Kings ix 25–6; 1 Kings xxi 17–20) to Queen Jezebel and to the *horim* (1 Kings xxi 1–16), the aim of the present narrative becomes all too obvious. Jezebel, the sinner and seducer, is the foreign wife of Ahab. Through her, foreign women in general are stigmatized.

Rofé continues noting that "the historical setting is the fight of Ezra and Nehemiah against intermarriage."[17]

---

[15]See 126–27.
[16]Rofé, "The Vineyard of Naboth," 101.
[17]Rofé, "The Vineyard of Naboth," 102.

JEREMIAH 7:1–15[18]

In this narrative, the Lord commands Jeremiah to proclaim a message to the devout people of Judah who worship at the temple (7:2). The message is one of repentance and a direct challenge to an ideology of the Jerusalem temple as a divine refuge for God's people. The devout trust in their own "lying words" (7:4, 8)—that is, the words "the temple of the Lord, the temple of the Lord, the temple of the Lord is this" (7:4) and "we are delivered" (7:10). Through Jeremiah the Lord condemns the people's ideology that the Jerusalem temple is a refuge for the chosen people of God, where they will always find safety from their enemies. The efficacy of the temple depends not upon the Lord, but on the very worshippers who enter it. Since the temple had become "a den of robbers" (7:11), the Lord proclaims its destruction, drawing a parallel between the destruction of the sanctuary at Shiloh and the northern kingdom of Israel, on the one hand, and the coming destruction of the Jerusalem temple and the southern kingdom of Judah, on the other (7:14–15). Therefore, this "temple sermon" criticizes the ideology based on divine favor for a particular place and emphasizes the obedience of all the people of Judah to the Lord's commandments as the condition to living securely in the land (7:5–7, 9).

Certainly, the Deuteronomic school after the governorship of Zerubbabel understood this passage to have import for their own understanding of the temple. The truth claims made at the narrative level had been fulfilled in that the Jerusalem temple had been destroyed and the Babylonian exile was a thing of the past. This passage now became a warning against exaggerated claims some may have made about the rebuilding of the Jerusalem temple. That is, the rebuilding of the temple itself will not bring about the Lord's intervention on behalf of Judah, thereby restoring the Davidic monarchy and establishing Judah above the nations. The people of Judah must amend their ways (7:5), becoming obedient to the Lord's commands, in order for such hopes to be realized. This message, therefore, can explain why the hope placed in the temple and

---

[18]The following works were consulted on Jer 7:1-15: Brueggeman, *Jeremiah*, 77–85; Carroll, *Jeremiah*, 206–12; Clements, *Jeremiah*, 43–46; Holloday, Jeremiah, 1:234–49; McKane, *Jeremiah*, 1:158–69; Lundbom, *Jeremiah 1–20*, 453–73.

the governorship of Zerubbabel has not yet been realized as well as instruct the people in what they must do. In fact, unless they amend their ways the possibility of another destruction of the temple remains.

JEREMIAH 30:1–3; 31:27–34, 38–40[19]

Jeremiah 30–31 contains the fullest expression of the restoration theme in the book of Jeremiah. Within these chapters are four prose sections (30:1–3; 31:27–30, 31–34, 38–40), all of which contain prophetic messages that begin with the eschatological phrase "behold, the days are coming" (30:3; 31:1, 27, 38). Jeremiah 30:3 announces the restoration in terms of the Lord returning the people of Israel and Judah to the land and their taking possession of it. Jeremiah 31:27–30 announces the restoration of the "house of Israel and the house of Judah" in the last days by which the divine standard of judgment will no longer be as a collective people whereby the entire nation will be punished, but rather "everyone will die for his own sin" (31:30). This more individualistic understanding will allow more permanence in relationship to the Lord's promise concerning Jerusalem and the people of Israel. Jeremiah 31:31–34 then announces the "new covenant" (31:31):

> I will put my law within them, and on their hearts I will write it. And I will be their God and they will be my people. And no longer will each teach his neighbor and each his brother saying, "Know the Lord," for all of them will know me, from the least to the greatest. (Jer 31:33–34)

That is, since each will be judged individually (31:30), the Lord will graciously inscribe each one's heart with the law, so that this internalization of the law will lead to obedience of the law and, therefore, full restoration and an everlasting peace and security for God's people (see similarly Deut 30:6). Jeremiah 31:38–40 announces the geographical dimensions of the eschatologically rebuilt Jerusalem, which because of the new standard of divine retribution according to individual's sin and the internalization of the

---

[19]The following works were consulted on Jer 31:27–34, 38–40: Brueggeman, *Jeremiah*, 264–300; Carroll, *Jeremiah*, 568–618; Clements, *Jeremiah*, 175–93; Bernard Gosse, "La menace qui vient du nord, les retournements d'oracles contre Babylone et Jérémie 30–31," *EstBib* 56 (1998): 289–314.

law "shall not be uprooted and shall not be overthrown again for ever" (31:40). Together these prose passages present the following scenario of history leading to the eschaton: after the judgment of Israel and Judah, the Lord's new covenant will be written on the hearts of the people so that each person will be accountable for sin and will be more capable of the required obedience. Since obedience will be internalized and no collective judgment will befall the people, the rebuilt Jerusalem will stand forever. In other words, in the last days the Lord will take the initiative to overcome human sin in order to permanently keep the promises made to Moses and David.

This scenario has obvious meaning for the Deuteronomic school after the time of Zerubbabel. Although the Babylonian exile has ended with the return of the people and the rebuilding of the temple, all the people of Israel and Judah have not yet been returned and the Persians remain in control of the land. Therefore, even the announcement of restoration in Jer 30:3 has not yet been fulfilled. The Deuteronomic school maintains hope not in the human institutions of the temple and the monarchy, although it appears to support these institutions at least in their best forms. However, since these institutions are corrupted by human sin, the Deuteronomic school places its hope in the promises of the Lord who will come in the last days to fully restore Israel and Judah and to change human nature itself, so that the people of God will innately obey the Lord's commandments, thereby faithfully fulfilling the covenant's conditions so that they continue to receive the Lord's blessings in Jerusalem forever.

DEUTERONOMIC THEOLOGY AFTER THE TIME OF ZERUBBABEL

The end of Zerubbabel's governorship and, therefore, the end of Davidic leadership in Judah brought about a reevaluation of the Deuteronomic school's theology. Although the Deuteronomic school's hope in Zerubbabel and the rebuilt temple was cautious, this hope undergirded much of the Deuteronomic school's theological rationale for its participation in the Persian-supported bureaucracy in Jerusalem. That is, the rebuilding of the temple and the governorship of Zerubbabel would initiate a heightened obedience to the law, thereby hastening fulfillment of the Lord's promise for a fully restored Israel.

The end of Zerubbabel's governorship led to a certain level of disillusionment concerning how the Deuteronomic school understood itself in relationship to the Persian-supported temple cult. As the Deuteronomic school became disillusioned with its involvement in the Jerusalem administration, this disillusionment affected its understanding of the efficacy of human institutions in general, including the temple cult. In other words, the Deuteronomic school's cautious hope in the declining authority of the Davidides and the increasingly status quo of the temple became even more cautious, relying less on human initiative and more on divine initiative. This shift led to a heightened eschatological perspective within the Deuteronomic school.

Although the Deuteronomic school became disillusioned with the Jerusalem authorities, the Deuteronomic school nevertheless remained realistic in relationship to armed rebellion against the military might of the Persian empire, which it understood as obviously futile. At the same time, its increasingly eschatological vision would have been understood by the Persian imperial administration and by the Jerusalem authorities who were accountable to the Persian empire as increasingly defiant of the Persian empire and, therefore, potentially dangerous. If this sketch of the history of the Deuteronomic school's theology is correct, it would explain both the demise of the Deuteronomic school and the mission of Ezra. Ezra was commissioned to reform the Jerusalem administration and temple by the imposition of a new law and brought with him a different group of scribes to displace the Deuteronomic school and its increasingly eschatological critique of the Jerusalem administration. Therefore, one reason for Ezra's mission would be to lessen the authority of the Deuteronomic school to state what the law is.

CHAPTER 7

THE DEUTERONOMIC SCHOOL
AND OTHER POSTEXILIC
LITERATURE

In the two preceding chapters, I have provided an interpretation of the Deuteronomic History in the context of the Second Temple period, both during and after the governorship of Zerubbabel. This interpretation necessarily depended heavily on what we know about the Persian period from the books of Haggai, Zechariah, Ezra, and Nehemiah. In fact, many of the themes used in these interpretations—hope in the Davidic monarchy (especially related to Zerubbabel's administration), the expectation that the rebuilt temple will bring prosperity, anti-Samaritan rhetoric, and condemnation of intermarriage—were justified by reference to the books of Haggai, Zechariah, Ezra, and Nehemiah. Due to the importance of these postexilic works to the argument of this entire volume, an explicit, but brief, discussion of how the Deuteronomic school may have related to these other postexilic texts is given below, first concerning the prophetic books of Haggai and Zechariah and then the historiographic books of Chronicles, Ezra, and Nehemiah.

THE DEUTERONOMIC SCHOOL AND THE BOOKS OF HAGGAI AND ZECHARIAH

The above reconstruction suggests that the Deuteronomic school returned to Jerusalem to support the rebuilding of the temple under Zerubbabel—that is, the rebuilding of the temple required scribal skills that the Deuteronomic school provided to Zerubbabel and his administration. Since Zerubbabel also had the support of the prophets Haggai and Zechariah, it is likely that the Deuteronomic school understood the prophets Haggai and Zechariah as true prophets sent by the Lord. Just as the Deuteronomic school probably understood itself as fulfilling its divine mission of supporting the rebuilding of the temple under Zerubbabel, the Deuteronomic school probably understood Haggai and Zechariah as fulfilling their divine mission of supporting the rebuilding of the temple. As those responsible for the scribal activity associated with the rebuilding of the temple, it would seem likely that the Deuteronomic school would be the group responsible for the writing down of the prophecies of the prophets Haggai and Zechariah and perhaps the later redaction of their prophecies, which are now found in Haggai and Zechariah 1–8.

Although a full discussion of the evidence relating to the likelihood that the Deuteronomic school was somehow involved in the preservation of the prophecies of Haggai and Zechariah is certainly beyond the scope of this work, some observations made by earlier researchers in Haggai and Zechariah 1–8 are quite suggestive that this may be the case. I know of no commentator who has argued for the Deuteronomic redaction of Haggai or Zechariah 1–8; however, some have argued for strong "Deuteronomistic" influence on the redactors of these works. I suspect that the notion of the Deuteronomic redaction of these works was not entertained, because of the prevailing view that the Deuteronomic school ceased to exist in the exilic period and, therefore, by definition could not have redacted these postexilic works. But despite the strong influence of this assumption, some scholars have assigned redactional material in Haggai and Zechariah 1–8 to redactors who were influenced by "Deuteronomistic" thought and language. With the above argument that the Deuteronomic school continued in the postexilic period, this Deuteronomic influence may now suggest actual Deuteronomic redaction. Below I briefly review some studies that suggest possible Deuteronomic redaction of Haggai and Zechariah 1–8.

In "The Purpose of the 'Editorial Framework' of the Book of Haggai," Rex Mason critiqued Beuken's argument that the redactor that created the editorial framework lived in a "Chronistic milieu" and found that the evidence suggests that the redactor of the book of Haggai should be more closely associated with the "Deuteronomists" than with the Chronicler.[1] Mason understands the "editorial framework" to be the following: Hag 1:1, 3, 12, 13a, 14, 15; 2:1, 2 (probably), 10, 20. When he reviews Beuken's arguments for why this material is in a "Chronistic milieu," he finds that Beuken's observations apply much better to a "Deuteronomistic" influence. First, Mason argues that the formula "the word of the Lord came by the hand of Haggai the prophet" (Hag 1:1, 3; 2:1) betrays Deuteronomistic influence (1 Kgs 12:15; 15:29; 16:12, 17, 34; 17:16; 2 Kgs 9:36; 14:25; 17:13, 23; 21:10).[2] Second, the redactional material places a greater emphasis on the leaders of Zerubbabel and Joshua adapting Haggai's oracles into an "installation to office," a form that is also found in the Deuteronomic History (e.g., Deuteronomy 31; Joshua 1; 10:25; 2 Samuel 11).[3] Third, Hag 1:12 contains two phrases Mason associates with Deuteronomic language: "listening to the voice of the Lord their God" and "the people feared before the Lord."[4] For Mason, these arguments combined to strongly suggest "Deuteronomistic" influence on the redactor of the book of Haggai.

Influenced by Mason's argument for Deuteronomistic influence on the redactor of Haggai, David Petersen suggests that the genre of the book of Haggai itself may have been influenced by "the deuteronomistic

---

[1]Rex A. Mason, "The Purpose of the 'Editorial Framework' of the Book of Haggai," *VT* 27 (1977): 413–21. W. A. Beuken, *Haggai-Sacharja 1–8* (Assen, Netherlands: Van Gorcum, 1967).

[2]Mason, "Purpose of 'Editorial Framework' of Haggai," 414–15. See similarly Hans Walter Wolff, *Haggai: A Commentary* (Minneapolis: Augsburg, 1988), 37.

[3]Mason, "Purpose of 'Editorial Framework' of Haggai," 416–17.

[4]Mason, "Purpose of 'Editorial Framework' of Haggai," 418. See similarly Meyers and Meyers, *Haggai–Zechariah 1–8*, 34; Wolff, *Haggai: A Commentary*, 50–51.

tradent."[5] He identifies the genre of the book of Haggai as a "brief apologetic historical narrative," a genre also found in Deuteronomic literature (2 Kgs 22–23; Jer 26; 36; 37–41).[6] Petersen concludes:

> The book is, in sum, a short apologia, comprising Haggai's words placed within a historical narrative. The book of Haggai is not a typical prophetic collection, but is rather an apologetic history that uses prophetic oracles as its essential source.[7]

That is, Petersen explicitly associates the form of the book of Haggai with sections of Deuteronomic prose narratives in the book of Jeremiah, thereby emphasizing the Deuteronomic influence.

The introduction to Zechariah 1–8 (Zech 1:1–6) has been recognized by a variety of commentators as being influenced by Deuteronomic thought and language. For example, Joseph Blenkinsopp wrote:[8]

> This is the message and the language of the Deuteronomists, and there are indications that both Malachi and the author of Zech 1.1–6 have modeled themselves on this source. Zech 1.1–6 reminds the hearers that "the former prophets" (1.4; cf. 7.7, 12) and "my servants the prophets" (1.6; a Deuteronomic expression) preached repentance to the Israel of an earlier day, that their message fell on deaf ears, and that the result was disaster. Their predictions were verified, and it was left to the forefathers to acknowledge the justice of God and lament their mistakes during the exile. It will be obvious that this is nothing else but a summary of Deuteronomic teaching.

Similarly, Eric and Carol Meyers noted that Zech 1:1–6 contains language borrowed from Deuteronomic literature ("earlier prophets" in 1:4; "words and statues" in 1:6; "overtake" in 1:6) and was familiar with Jeremiah; thus, they concluded that Zech 1:1–6 has a "Deuteronomic flavor."[9] Stephen Swanson looked more closely at the "Deuteronomistic stream of tradition" in which he understood Zechariah 1–8, focusing primarily upon Zech

---

[5]David L. Petersen, *Haggai and Zechariah 1-8: A Commentary* (OTL; Philadelphia: Westminster Press, 1984), 36.
[6]Petersen, *Haggai and Zechariah 1–8*, 35–36.
[7]Petersen, *Haggai and Zechariah 1–8*, 36.
[8]Blenkinsopp, *A History of Prophecy in Israel*, 235.
[9]Meyers and Meyers, *Haggai–Zechariah 1–8*, 94–96.

1:2–6. Comparing these verses with Deut 30:1–10; Jdgs 2:10–23; 1 Sam 12:1–25; 1 Kgs 8:46–53; 2 Kgs 17:7–23; Jer 7:22–29; 25:3–11; 32:30–44; 35:12–17, Swanson noted the following commons elements: (1) "Yahweh's anger at the sins of the people"; (2) the use of the term "return" (שוב); (3) "reference to the 'evil ways' of the people"; (4) "the 'decrees' of Yahweh, which were given to the people"; and (5) the phrase "my servants the prophets."[10] Swanson also noted that the theological presentation of history is similar:[11]

> The logical progression of the pattern discernible in the dtr passages and Zech 1:2–6 and 7:1–14 is consistent throughout: 1) the sins of the people, 2) the anger of Yahweh, 3) the warning given by the prophets, 4) the rejection of these warnings, and 5) the execution of judgment.

Therefore, it is quite clear that the redaction of Zechariah 1–8 was significantly influenced by Deuteronomic thought and language, at least in Zech 1:1–6.

The above arguments certainly suggest Deuteronomic influence on the redaction of Haggai and Zechariah 1–8 and I am inclined to conclude that they further suggest Deuteronomic redaction of Haggai and Zechariah 1–8, even though the presence of characteristic Deuteronomic language is relatively minimal. Since the redaction of Haggai and Zechariah 1–8 is generally agreed to have occurred shortly after the prophecies were given during the time of Zerubbabel, the Deuteronomic school is the most likely candidate for the scribal group responsible for this—that is, assuming the above reconstruction of the history of the Deuteronomic school is accurate. The minimal character of the Deuteronomic redaction may be explained in two ways. First, the prophecies of Haggai and Zechariah were so closely related to Deuteronomic thought of the time that there was little need ideologically to redact the material closer to Deuteronomic thought. Second, the lapse of time between the prophecies and their being written down may have been extremely small. That is, for example, since Jeremiah's prophecies differed from Deuteronomic thought and occurred

---

[10]Stephen Swanson, "Zechariah 1–8 and the Deuteronomistic Stream of Tradition" (paper presented at the Annual Meeting of SBL, Chicago, November 1988), 8–9.

[11]Swanson, "Zech 1–8 and the Deuteronomistic Stream of Tradition," 9.

before the destruction of Jerusalem, the Deuteronomic school in the exilic and postexilic periods was more likely to transform Jeremiah's prophecies through the redactional and transmission process, thereby creating long redactional additions; in contrast, the prophecies of Haggai and Zechariah did not need to be corrected to conform with Deuteronomic thought nor updated to a new time and place, thereby requiring minimal redaction.

My inclination to conclude that Haggai and Zechariah 1–8 was redacted by the Deuteronomic school is also influenced by my argument that the prose sections of Zechariah 9–14 are Deuteronomic prose, analogous to the Deuteronomic prose in the book of Jeremiah. That is, Zechariah 9–14 is Deuteronomic prose from later in the Deuteronomic school's history—after the time of Zerubbabel—which was created for the purpose of updating Zechariah 1–8 according to the increasing disillusionment of the Deuteronomic school and its increasingly eschatological theology. This argument—given in my *Second Zechariah and the Deuteronomic School*—is based on the prevalence of Deuteronomic language and theological themes throughout the prose material in Zechariah 9–14. In contrast to the book of Jeremiah where redactional material occurs throughout the book and the redactional process spanned a long period of time, the Deuteronomic prose in Zechariah 9–14 was appended to an earlier redaction of Zechariah 1–8 near the end of the redactional activity of the Deuteronomic school.

Taken together, these arguments suggest that the Deuteronomic school possibly redacted Haggai and Zechariah 1–8 during the time of Zerubbabel and later updated Zechariah 1–8 with the addition of the redactional material in Zechariah 9–14.

THE DEUTERONOMIC SCHOOL AND THE BOOKS OF CHRONICLES, EZRA, AND NEHEMIAH

The possibility just suggested for the books of Haggai and Zechariah expands the category of Deuteronomic literature. As stated in the introduction, however, this expansion does not constitute any sort of "pan-Deuteronomism." To clarify this point further I will discuss how the Deuteronomic school may have related to the postexilic books of Chronicles, Ezra, and Nehemiah.

The book of Chronicles is another presentation of the history of Israel beginning with Adam and ending with Cyrus, king of Persia. As such, Chronicles draws upon the biblical stories found in Genesis through Kings with the short addition concerning Cyrus as its ending (2 Chr 36:22–23). Whether Chronicles is based upon a redaction of the Deuteronomic History that is earlier than the version found in the MT[12] or both Chronicles and the Deuteronomic History are from a common source,[13] clearly Chronicles differs significantly from the Deuteronomic History in ways that suggest two different scribal groups with their differing theological traditions.

The books of Ezra and Nehemiah have long been associated with the book of Chronicles and with each other. These books continue the history of Israel from where Chronicles left off (Cyrus, king of Persia) to the mission of Ezra to restore the purity of the temple cult and the mission of Nehemiah to rebuild Jerusalem's defensive city walls. The missions of both Ezra and Nehemiah can be understood as the Persian imperial administration's attempt to strengthen its control over the administration of the Jerusalem temple and Judah, missions that could have led to conflict with the existing Jerusalem bureaucracies. As argued above, it is in this period of conflict that the demise of the Deuteronomic school can be located. Ezra was commissioned by Artaxerxes, king of Persia, to return to Jerusalem and take control of the Jerusalem temple cult by the "introduction" of the law of Moses. Nehemiah was commissioned for the more overt purpose of restoring the military fortifications of the city wall. Whatever the exact contents of Ezra's lawbook was, it most likely differed somewhat from the lawbook used in Jerusalem from the time of Zerubbabel to Ezra.[14] If the Deuteronomic school is associated with the lawbook used

---

[12]McKenzie, *The Chronicler's Use of the Deuteronomistic History.*

[13]A. Graeme Auld, *Kings without Privilege: David and Moses in the Story of the Bible's Kings* (Edinburgh: T. & T. Clark, 1994).

[14]I do not find any of the current arguments for identifying exactly what Ezra's lawbook contained (P, the complete Pentateuch, etc.) convincing, because of the lack of evidence for any of the proposals. However, I do find convincing the argument that the Persian administration did at times become involved in local legal issues (see especially Joseph Blenkinsopp, "Was the Pentateuch the Civic and Religious Constitution of the Jewish Ethnos in the Persian Period?" in *Persia and Torah: The Theory of Imperial*

under Zerubbabel and understood itself as the preserver of this tradition, Ezra's mission would have conflicted with the Deuteronomic school's self-understanding. Moreover, Ezra's entourage from Babylon probably included another scribal group that had its own self-understanding of preserving the "true" lawbook that Ezra was "introducing." It is the clash between these two scribal groups that eventually led to the demise of the Deuteronomic school and the rise of another scribal group in Judah. This scribal group that displaced the Deuteronomic school is probably responsible for the redaction of the books of Chronicles, Ezra, and Nehemiah.[15]

THE DEUTERONOMIC SCHOOL AND OTHER POSTEXILIC LITERATURE

The argument for the redaction of the Deuteronomic History continuing into the postexilic period in previous chapters certainly allows for the possibility that some of the other postexilic literature was redacted by the Deuteronomic school. This possibility has been examined here for the books that have had the greatest impact on the arguments in previous chapters, the books of Haggai, Zechariah, Chronicles, Ezra, and Nehemiah. The possibility of the Deuteronomic redaction of the books of Haggai and Zechariah has been affirmed, even though the amount of Deuteronomic language in Haggai and Zechariah 1–8 is minimal. The possibility of the Deuteronomic redaction of Chronicles, Ezra, and Nehemiah has been rejected. In fact, I have argued that the demise of the Deuteronomic school

---

Authorization of the Pentateuch [ed. James W. Watts, Symposium 17; Atlanta: Society of Biblical Literature, 2001], 41–62). Therefore, my argument does not depend on any particular understanding of exactly what Ezra's lawbook contained; it simply requires that Ezra's lawbook differed from the Deuteronomic school's.

[15]This view is not necessarily incompatible with the growing view that Chronicles, Ezra, and Nehemiah were composed by different authors (see James VanderKam, "Ezra-Nehemiah or Ezra and Nehemiah?" in *Priests, Prophets and Scribes: Essays on the Formation and Heritage of Second Temple Judaism in Honour of Joseph Blenkinsopp* [eds. Eugene Ulrich, et al., JSOTSup 149; Sheffield: Sheffield Academic Press, 1992], 55–75). That is, different scribes within this tradition may have authored the different books and, since the history of the redaction of these books probably did not span as long a period of time as the redaction of the Deuteronomic History, higher critical methods may still be able to discern the hands of different authors within this tradition.

is related to the rise of the scribal group that is responsible for the redaction of Chronicles, Ezra, and Nehemiah, the scribal group that most likely returned to Jerusalem with Ezra and was associated with Ezra's law of Moses.

CONCLUSION

The diversity of conclusions concerning the redaction history of the Deuteronomic History has occurred because of the nature of the literature itself. The Deuteronomic History underwent numerous, gradual redactional changes throughout the long span of its redaction within the Deuteronomic school, beginning in the exilic period and continuing into the postexilic period. Many of the changes (such as additions of titles, proper names, patronymics, epithets, characteristic Deuteronomic formulae) simply occurred as the Deuteronomic scribes copied their *Vorlagen* in a manner that from their perspective as members of a primarily oral society was a precise, deliberate reproduction. Moreover, even when more systematic redactions involving intentional revisions occurred (such as additions of entire passages and moving passages to new locations), the redactional changes were made by Deuteronomic redactors, all of whom used characteristic Deuteronomic language. Thus, redaction critics have failed to adequately detect differing redactional layers, because the language used by one Deuteronomic redactor is so similar to the language used by another Deuteronomic redactor that the redaction critical method has no basis for distinguishing the work of one from the other.

This study has tried to find a way forward in understanding the redaction history of the Deuteronomic History and the social history of the Deuteronomic school by focusing upon four new perspectives that are often overlooked in studies of Deuteronomic literature. First, redactional arguments of Deuteronomic literature can be refined when text critical results are used as objective controls for redactional arguments (Chapter 1). Second, the text critical evidence suggests that the Deuteronomic school continued its redactional activity into the postexilic period, most likely returning to Jerusalem under Zerubbabel (Chapter 2). Third, as the scribal school that served the Persian-supported administration in Jerusalem, the Deuteronomic school can be compared to analogous scribal guilds in the ancient Near East in order to learn something about its possible structure and organization (Chapter 3). Fourth, even though the Deuteronomic scribes were among the most literate members of their society, they nevertheless lived and worked in a primarily oral society and, therefore, they undertook even their literate tasks of copying and revising texts with an oral mentality (Chapter 4). These new perspectives lead to new understandings of the Deuteronomic school and its literature within the similar context of the postexilic prophets of Haggai and Zechariah and the books of Chronicles, Ezra, and Nehemiah (Chapters 5–7).

Most scholars have simply accepted Noth's exilic dating of the Deuteronomic History, even though his argument is based only on the assumption that its composition must have been shortly after its last recorded historical event, the release of Jehoiachin from prison in exile. This argument is clearly rejected when text critical evidence is utilized. Various text critical studies have demonstrated that the MT of the Deuteronomic History is generally a later, expanded revision of an earlier text often preserved in the LXX. Furthermore, many of these studies present linguistic evidence that the MT of the Deuteronomic History is also a postexilic work and that this postexilic redaction is also Deuteronomic in that characteristic Deuteronomic language is found in some additions in the MT.

If the Deuteronomic school's redactional work spanned both the exilic and postexilic periods (as the evidence suggests), then a new understanding of the Deuteronomic school's social setting is necessary. The Deuteronomic school is generally understood to have redacted its literature during the Babylonian exile and nothing in this study disputes this. In fact, I argued that the Deuteronomic school has its roots in the scribal institutions of the exiled Jerusalem bureaucracy. With the Persian defeat of the Babylonians, the Persians began the return of exiled peoples to their homelands and the reestablishment of local religious cults. When the Persians returned members of the exiled leadership in Babylon to Jerusalem, it seems likely that scribes would have been included among the returnees. It is in this setting that I place the return of the Deuteronomic school—that is, the Deuteronomic school returned to Jerusalem, probably under Zerubbabel, to support the rebuilding of the temple and the reestablishment of the temple cult with its scribal skills. Certainly, this hopeful return to the promised land would have generated a heightened interest in Israel's literature, probably including the revision of earlier texts and the composition of new texts. The Deuteronomic school certainly would have been active in this period.

As time went on, the hopes of the returnees went unfulfilled; Zerubbabel did not become king and Judah did not become politically autonomous. The hope associated with the Persian-supported policy of returning the exiles to Jerusalem and reestablishing the temple cult began to diminish as the Deuteronomic school increasingly understood how Persian support meant Persian control. This diminished hope became disillusionment, leading to growing conflict between the Deuteronomic school and other groups in the Jerusalem administration. This conflict probably led to a more eschatological perspective within the Deuteronomic school that depended even less on historical, human institutions. This disillusionment and conflict probably affected the fate of the Deuteronomic school. The mission of Ezra, who brought "the law of the God of Heaven," might suggest that by 458 B.C.E. the Deuteronomic school had lost favor with the administration in Jerusalem and the Persian authorities. The lack of the necessary support of the Jerusalem administration led to the Deuteronomic school's demise.

Comparative evidence of scribal schools in the ancient Near East helps to reconstruct how the Deuteronomic school may have functioned in the Jerusalem administration and how it may have structured itself organizationally. Scribal guilds in the ancient Near East were often associated with the palace or temple, where the scribes performed administrative duties such as keeping economic and legal records. However, scribes did not limit their work to such administrative duties as is evident in the literary, historical, and scientific documents found in libraries and archives associated with some palaces and temples. Moreover, some scribes were not merely copyists but were redactors and composers of new literary works. Persian administrative practices certainly included the use of non-Persian scribal guilds commissioned to work in association with specific local religious cults (for example, Udjahoresnet in Sais and Ezra in Jerusalem). Therefore, the proposed reconstruction of the Deuteronomic school returning to Jerusalem with Zerubbabel to provide scribal support for the rebuilding of the temple and the reestablishment of the temple cult is consistent with what we know about Persian administration.

The variety of literature preserved and redacted by the Deuteronomic school also has analogies in the ancient Near East. The Deuteronomic school appears to have preserved some of the sources it used in its compositions for it refers readers to these sources (for example, "the Book of the Annals of the Kings of Judah"). The Deuteronomic compositions are also varied, including law (Deuteronomy), historiography (Joshua–Kings), and prophecy (for example, Jeremiah). The Deuteronomic school may have also preserved early works that it did not originally compose, but may have later redacted (possibly the book of Amos). Such a collection of diverse literature within a particular theological tradition is certainly evident in the Dead Sea Scrolls found at Qumran.

The hierarchical organization of scribal guilds implicit in the missions of Udjahoresnet and Ezra and evident at Qumran suggests that the Deuteronomic school was also organized hierarchically. The Deuteronomic school probably trained its own scribes by the repeated study and copying of its authoritative literature. Lower ranked Deuteronomic scribes probably spent most of their time serving the administrative needs of the Jerusalem administration. The few higher ranked scribes were probably given more freedom to produce new redactions of Deuteronomic literature and new compositions. With such an organization, the Deuteronomic school would have preserved its own theology by passing on its characteristic language and theology in the training of its scribes and the transmission of Deuteronomic literature, while at the same time providing opportunities for new, creative interpretations of authoritative literature and new compositions to meet its changing historical circumstances.

As members of a primarily oral society, all Deuteronomic scribes would have undertaken their scribal tasks (that is, literate activities) with a perspective significantly influenced by an oral mentality. The hierarchical structure suggests that the lower ranked scribes would have been held more accountable for the careful and precise reproduction of their *Vorlagen*; however, the very definitions of "careful" and "precise" in a primarily oral society would be broader than in our own modern, literate society. That is, although these scribes would have been held to the more literate standards for reproducing their *Vorlagen* according to their own cultural standards, these same standards would have allowed what from a modern perspective would be considered variants, such as synonymous readings and additions of certain phrases. In this way, Deuteronomic literature could have evolved gradually over a long period of time, even if no systematic, intentional revisions were made. Although the change from one *Vorlage* to its copy may have been minor, a long series of copies over time may have produced what we might consider as a significantly different text. Moreover, even when higher ranked Deuteronomic scribes produced revisions that most likely were intentional and systematic, thereby constituting new redactions, their results may not have been understood as "new" redactions of "earlier" works as long as the redactions were judged to be well within the limits of what the tradition understood as acceptable according to characteristic Deuteronomic language and theology.

If the Deuteronomic school continued its redactional activity into the postexilic period, then Deuteronomic literature must have had some meaningful relationships to the circumstances of the postexilic period; therefore, Deuteronomic literature should be analyzed with this perspective in mind. The reinterpretations above for selected passages during the administration of Zerubbabel (Chapter 5) and after his administration (Chapter 6) suggest that such reinterpretations are not only possible, but in many cases they come easily. These reinterpretations suggest that the Deuteronomic school cautiously placed its hope in the rebuilding of the Jerusalem temple and the reestablishment of the temple cult as the beginning of a divinely initiated process moving towards the restoration of the Davidic monarchy and the political independence of Israel. The Deuteronomic school advocated strict obedience to the law, while at the same time realizing that absolute obedience to the law can only come from the Lord's transformation of human nature, something that will occur as a part of the divinely initiated process of restoration. This process will lead to a permanent peace and security for a fully restored Israel.

The end of Zerubbabel's governorship and, therefore, the end of Davidic leadership in Judah required an evaluation of the Deuteronomic school's cautious hope in the restoration of the temple and the Davidic monarchy. The Deuteronomic school's cautious hope undergirded its theological rationale for participating in the Persian-supported Jerusalem administration. With this hope undermined, the Deuteronomic school became disillusioned with its involvement in the Jerusalem administration and, therefore, became increasingly eschatological in its outlook. That is, the Deuteronomic school now placed less hope in the human institutions of palace and temple, relying more on divine intervention. Although the Deuteronomic school became increasingly disillusioned with the Jerusalem administration, it nevertheless remained realistic in relationship to armed rebellion against the mighty Persian empire. Its increasingly critical stance toward the administration, however, would have been understood as increasingly defiant by the Jerusalem administration and other Persian authorities. This defiance led to the Deuteronomic school's demise probably in the form of Ezra's mission, in which Ezra brought "the law of the God of Heaven" as the true law, replacing the law in use since the time of Zerubbabel.

In sum, Deuteronomic literature has its roots in written sources most likely produced by the administrative bureaucracy of the monarchy. The Deuteronomic school probably formed in Babylon among exiled scribes, who formerly served in the Jerusalem temple and palace and carried various texts into exile with them. During the Babylonian exile, the Deuteronomic school produced the first redaction of the Deuteronomic History, telling the story of Israel and Judah from Moses to the exile. When the Persians defeated the Babylonians, they began a process of returning the exiles to Jerusalem. The Deuteronomic school probably returned to Jerusalem under Zerubbabel, providing scribal support for the rebuilding of the temple and the restoration of its cult. This hopeful time probably saw a great deal of literary activity for such a short period of time. With the end of Zerubbabel's governorship, the Deuteronomic school became disillusioned with the Persian-supported Jerusalem administration and increasingly eschatological in its hope for the future. This disillusionment probably led to its demise, one of the results of Ezra's mission to impose a new law in Jerusalem.

BIBLIOGRAPHY

Albertz, Rainer. "Wer waren die Deuteronomisten? Das historische Rätsel einer literarischen Hypothese." *Evangelische Theologie* 57 (1997): 319–38.

Alexander, Elizabeth Shanks. "The Fixing of the Oral Mishnah and the Displacement of Meaning." *Oral Tradition* 14 (1999): 100–39.

Auld, A. Graeme. "The Deuteronomists and the Former Prophets, Or What Makes the Former Prophets Deuteronomistic?" Pages 116–26 in *Those Elusive Deuteronomists: The Phenomenon of Pan-Deuteronomism.* Edited by S. L. McKenzie and L. S. Schearing. Journal for the Study of the Old Testament: Supplement Series 268. Sheffield: Sheffield Academic Press, 1999.

———. *Joshua, Judges, and Ruth.* Philadelphia: Westminster Press, 1984.

———. "Judges 1 and History: A Reconsideration." *Vetus Testamentum* 25 (1975): 261–85.

———. *Kings without Privilege: David and Moses in the Story of the Bible's Kings.* Edinburgh: T. & T. Clark, 1994.

———. "The 'Levitical Cities': Text and History." *Zeitschrift für die alttestamentliche Wissenschaft* 91 (1979): 194–206.

———. "Prophets through the Looking Glass: A Response to Robert Carroll and Hugh Williamson." *Journal for the Study of the Old Testament* 27 (1983): 41–44.

———. "Prophets through the Looking Glass: Between Writings and Moses." *Journal for the Study of the Old Testament* 27 (1983): 3–23.

———. "Reading Joshua after Kings." Pages 167–81 in *Words Remembered, Texts Renewed: Essays in Honour of John F. A. Sawyer.* Edited by J. Davies, G. Harvey, and W. G. E. Watson. Journal for the Study of the Old Testament: Supplement Series 195. Sheffield: Sheffield Academic Press, 1995.

———. "Textual and Literary Studies in the Book of Joshua." *Zeitschrift für die alttestamentliche Wissenschaft* 90 (1978): 412–417.

———. "Trois niveaux d'analyse." Pages 5–18 in *The Story of David and Goliath: Textual and Literary Criticism*. Edited by D. Barthélemy, et al. Orbis biblicus et orientalis 73. Fribourg: Éditions Universitaires Fribourg; Göttingen: Vandenhoeck und Ruprecht, 1986.

Barthélemy, Dominique, David W. Gooding, Johan Lust, and Emanuel Tov, eds. *The Story of David and Goliath: Textual and Literary Criticism*. Orbis biblicus et orientalis 73. Fribourg: Éditions Universitaires Fribourg; Göttingen: Vandenhoeck und Ruprecht, 1986.

Becking, Bob. "Jehojachin's Amnesty, Salvation for Israel? Notes on 2 Kings 25, 27–30." Pages 283–93 in *Pentateuchal and Deuteronomic Studies*. Edited by C. Brekelmans and J. Lust. Bibiotheca ephemeridum theologicarum lovaniensium 44. Leuven: Leuven University Press, 1990.

Begg, Christopher T. "A Bible Mystery: The Absence of Jeremiah in the Deuteronomic History." *Irish Biblical Studies* 7 (1985): 139–64.

———. "The Death of Josiah in Chronicles: Another View." *Vetus Testamentum* 37 (1987): 1–8.

———. "The Significance of Jehoiachin's Release: A New Proposal." *Journal for the Study of the Old Testament* 36 (1986): 49–56.

———. "The Table (Deut x) and the Lawbook (Deut xxxi)." *Vetus Testamentum* 33 (1983): 96–97.

Ben Zvi, Ehud. "A Deuteronomistic Redaction in/among 'The Twelve'? A Contribution from the Standpoint of the Books of Micah, Zephaniah, and Obadiah." Pages 232–61 in *Those Elusive Deuteronomists: The Phenomenon of Pan-Deuteronomism*. Edited by S. L. McKenzie and L. S. Schearing. Journal for the Study of the Old Testament: Supplement Series 268. Sheffield: Sheffield Academic Press, 1999.

———. "Looking at the Primary (Hi)Story and the Prophetic Books as Literary/Theological Units within the Frame of the Early Second Temple: Some Considerations." *Journal for the Study of the Old Testament* 12 (1998): 26–43.

———. "The Urban Center of Jerusalem and the Development of the Literature of the Hebrew Bible." Pages 194–209 in *Urbanism in Antiquity*. Sheffield: Sheffield Academic Press, 1997.

Beuken, W. A. *Haggai-Sacharja 1–8*. Assen, Netherlands: Van Gorcum, 1967.

Blenkinsopp, Joseph. *A History of Prophecy in Israel: From the Settlement in the Land to the Hellenistic Period*. Philadelphia: Westminster, 1983.

———. "The Mission of Udjahorresnet and Those of Ezra and Nehemiah." *Journal of Biblical Literature* 106 (1987): 409–21.

———. *Prophecy and Canon*. Center for the Study of Judaism and Christianity in Antiquity 3. Notre Dame: University of Notre Dame Press, 1977.

———. "The Sage, the Scribe, and the Scribalism in the Chronicler's Work." Pages 307–15 in *The Sage in Israel and the Ancient Near East*. Edited by J. G. Gammie and L. G. Perdue. Winona Lake: Eisenbrauns, 1990.

————. "Was the Pentateuch the Civic and Religious Constitution of the Jewish Ethnos in the Persian Period?" Pages 41–62 in *Persia and Torah: The Theory of Imperial Authorization of the Pentateuch*. Edited by J. W. Watts. Symposium 17. Atlanta: Society of Biblical Literature, 2001.

Boecker, Hans Jochen. *Die Beurteilung der Anfänge des Königstums in den deuteronomischen Abschnitten des I. Samuelbuches: Ein Beitrag zum Problem des deuteronomistischen Geschichtswerkes*. Wissenschaftliche Monographien zum Alten und Neuen Testament 31. Neukichen-Vluyn: Neukirchener Verlag, 1969.

Bogaert, Pierre M. "Les trios rédactions conserves et la forme originale de l'envoi du Cantique de Moïse (Dt 32, 43)." Pages 329–40 in *Das Deuteronomium: Entstellung, Gestalt und Botschaft*. Edited by N. Lohfink. Bibiotheca ephemeridum theologicarum Iovaniensium 68. Leuven: Leuven University Press, 1985.

Bolin, Thomas M. "When the End is the Beginning. The Persian Period and the Origins of the Biblical Tradition." *Scandinavian Journal of the Old Testament* 10 (1996): 3–15.

Boling, Robert. G. "In Those Days There Was No King in Israel." Pages 33–48 in *A Light Unto My Path*. Edited by H. Bream, R. Heim, and C. Moore. Philadelphia: Temple University Press, 1974.

————. *Joshua*. Anchor Bible. Garden City: Doubleday, 1982.

————. *Judges*. Anchor Bible. Garden City: Doubleday, 1975.

Brettler, Marc. "Interpretation and Prayer: Notes on the Composition of 1 Kings 8.15–53." Pages 17–35 in *Minhah le-Nahum*. Edited by M. Brettler and M. Fishbane. Journal for the Study of the Old Testament: Supplement Series 154. Sheffield: Sheffield Academic Press, 1993.

Bright, John. *Jeremiah*. Anchor Bible 21. Garden City: Doubleday, 1965.

Brueggeman, Walter. *A Commentary on Jeremiah: Exile and Homecoming*. Grand Rapids: Eerdemans, 1998.

————. *First and Second Samuel*. Interpretation: A Bible Commentary for Teaching and Preaching. Louisville: John Knox Press, 1990.

————. "The Keryma of the Deuteronomistic Historian." *Interpretation* 22 (1968): 387–402.

————. "The Social Significance of Solomon as a Patron of Wisdom." Pages 117–32 in *The Sage in Israel and the Ancient Near East*. Edited by J. G. Gammie and L. G. Perdue. Winona Lake: Eisenbrauns, 1990.

Burrows, Millar, ed. *The Dead Sea Scrolls of St. Mark's Monoastery, Vol. 1: The Isaiah Manuscript and the Habukkuk Commentary*. Cambridge: American Schools of Oriental Research, 1950.

————. "Variant Readings in the Isaiah Manuscript." *Bulletin of the American Schools of Oriental Research* 111 (1948): 16–24; 113 (1949): 24–32.

Campbell, Antony F. "From Philistine to Throne (1 Samuel 16:14–18:16)." *Australian Biblical Review* 34 (1986): 35–41.

Campbell, Antony F. and Mark A. O'Brien. *Unfolding the Deuteronomic History: Origins, Upgrades, Present Text*. Minneapolis: Fortress Press, 2000.

Carroll, Robert P. *Jeremiah: A Commentary.* Old Testament Library. Philadelphia: Westminster Press, 1986.

Carter, Charles E. *Emergence of Yehud in the Persian Period: A Social and Demographic Study.* Journal for the Study of the Old Testament: Supplement Series 294. Sheffield: Sheffield Academic Press, 1999.

———. "The Province of Yehud in the Post-Exilic Period: Soundings in Site Distribution and Demography [graphs, maps, tables]." Pages 106–45 in *Second Temple Studies.* 2 vols. Sheffield: Journal for the Study of the Old Testament Press, 1994.

Clanchy, M. T. *From Memory to Written Record: England, 1066–1307.* Cambridge: Harvard University Press, 1979.

Clements, Ronald E. "The Isaiah Narrative of 2 Kings 20:12–19 and the Date of the Deuteronomic History." Pages 209–20 in Volume 3 of Isac Seeligmann's *Essays on the Bible and the Ancient World.* Edited by A. Rofé and Y. Zakovitch. Jerusalem: E. Rubinstein's Publishing House, 1983.

———. *Jeremiah.* Interpretation: A Bible Commentary for Teaching and Preaching. Altanta: John Knox, 1988.

———. *Prophecy and Tradition.* Atlanta: John Knox, 1975.

Cogan, Mordechai. "'For We, Like You, Worship Your God': Three Biblical Portrayals of Samaritan Origins." *Vetus Testamentum* 36 (1988): 286–92.

Coggins, Richard. "Prophecy—True and False." Pages 80–94 in *Of Prophets' Visions and the Wisdom of Sages.* Sheffield: Journal for the Study of the Old Testament Press, 1993.

———. "What Does 'Deuteronomistic Mean?'" Pages 135–48 in *Words Remembered, Texts Renewed: Essays in Honour of John F. A. Sawyer.* Edited by J. Davies, G. Harvey, and W. G. E. Watson. Journal for the Study of the Old Testament: Supplement Series 195. Sheffield: Sheffield Academic Press, 1995.

Craige, Peter C. *The Book of Deuteronomy.* New International Commentary on the Old Testament. Grand Rapids: Eerdmans, 1976.

Crawford, Sidnie White. "The Rewritten Bible at Qumran." Pages 173–95 in *The Hebrew Bible and Qumran.* Edited by J. H. Charlesworth. N. Richland Hills: BIBAL Press, 2000.

Crenshaw, James L. "The Deuteronomist and the Writings." Pages 145–58 in *Those Elusive Deuteronomists: The Phenomenon of Pan-Deuteronomism.* Edited by S. L. McKenzie and L. S. Schearing. Journal for the Study of the Old Testament: Supplement Series 268. Sheffield: Sheffield Academic Press, 1999.

———. "Education in Ancient Israel." *Journal of Biblical Literature* 104 (1985): 601–15.

———. *Education in Ancient Israel: Across the Deadening Silence.* Anchor Bible Reference Library. New York: Doubleday, 1998.

Cross, Frank M. "The Themes of the Book of Kings and the Structure of the Deuteronomic History." Pages 274–89 in *Canaanite Myth and Hebrew Epic: Essays in History of the Religion of Israel.* Cambridge: Harvard University Press, 1973.

Cross, Frank M. and Shemaryahu Talmon, eds. *Qumran and the History of the Biblical Text*. Cambridge: Harvard University Press, 1975.

Culley, Robert C. "Oral Tradition and Biblical Studies." *Oral Tradition* 1 (1986): 30–65.

Davies, Graham I. "Were There Schools in Ancient Israel?" Pages 199–211 in *Wisdom in Ancient Israel: Essays in Honor of J. A. Emerton*. Edited by J. Day, R. P. Gordon, and H. G. M. Williamson. Cambridge: Cambridge University Press, 1995.

Davies, Philip R. *In Search of "Ancient Israel."* Journal for the Study of the Old Testament: Supplement Series 148. Sheffield: Sheffield Academic Press, 1992.

———. *Scribes and Schools: The Canonization of the Hebrew Scriptures*. Louisville: Westminster. John Knox Press, 1998.

De Vries, Simon J. *1 Kings*. Word Biblical Commentary 12. Waco: Word Books, 1985.

———. "David's Victory over the Philistine as Saga and Legend." *Journal of Biblical Literature* 92 (1973): 23–26.

———. "The Three Comparisons in 1 Kings XXII 4b and Its Parallel and 2 Kings III 7b." *Vetus Testamentum* 39 (1989): 283–306.

Dietrich, Walter. *David, Saul und die Propheten: Das Verhaltnis von Religion und Politik nach den prophetischen Uberlieferung vom fruhesten Konigtum*. Beiträge zur Wissenschaft vom Alten (und Neuen) Testament 72. Stuttgart: W. Kohlhammer, 1987.

———. *Prophetie und Geschichte*. Forschungen zur Religion und Literatur des Alten und Neuen Testaments 108. Göttingen: Vandenhoech und Ruprecht, 1972.

Doane, Alger N. "The Ethnography of Scribal Writing and Anglo-Saxon Poetry: Scribe as Performer." *Oral Tradition* 9 (1994): 420–39.

Driver, S. R. *A Critical and Exegetical Commentary on Deuteronomy*. International Critical Commentary. Edinburgh: T & T Clark, 1965.

Dumbrell, William J. "'In Those Days There Was No King in Israel; Every Man Did What Was Right in His Own Eyes.' The Purpose of the Book of Judges Reconsidered." *Journal for the Study of the Old Testament* 25 (1983): 23–33.

Dutcher-Walls, Patricia. "The Social Location of the Deuteronomists: A Sociological Study of Factional Politics in Late Pre-Exilic Judah." *Journal for the Study of the Old Testament* 52 (1991): 77–94.

Elayi, Josette, J. Edward Crowly, and Jean Sapin. *Beyond the River: New Perspectives on Transeuphratene*. Journal for the Study of the Old Testament: Supplement Series 250. Sheffield: Sheffield Academic Press, 1998.

Elman, Yaakov. "Orality and the Redaction of the Babylonian Talmud." *Oral Tradition* 14 (1999): 52–99.

Eslinger, Lyle. *House of God or House of David: The Rhetoric of 2 Samuel 7*. Journal for the Study of the Old Testament: Supplement Series 164. Sheffield: Sheffield Academic Press, 1994.

Fischer, Georg. "Jeremia 52—ein Schlüssel zum Jeremiabuch." *Biblica* 79 (1998): 333–59.

———. "Les Deux Faces de Jérémie 52." *Etudes théologiques et religieuses* 74 (1999): 481–89.

Fishbane, Michael. *Biblical Interpretation in Ancient Israel*. Oxford: Oxford University Press, 1985.

Foley, John Miles. "Editing Oral Epic Texts: Theory and Practice." *Text* 1 (1981): 77–78.

———. *Homer's Traditional Art*. University Park: Pennsylvania State University Press, 1999.

———. *Immanent Art: From Structure to Meaning*. Bloomington: Indiana University Press, 1991.

——. "Oral Theory in Context." Pages 27–122 in *Oral Traditional Literature: A Festscrift for Albert Bates Lord*. Edited by J. M. Foley. Columbus: Slavica Publishers, 1981.

———. *The Singer of Tales in Performance*. Bloomington: Indiana University Press, 1995.

———. *The Theory of Oral Composition: History and Methodology*. Bloomington: Indiana University Press, 1988.

———. *Traditional Oral Epic: The Odyssey, Beowulf, and the Serbo-Croatian Return Song*. Berkeley: University of Californa Press, 1990.

Fraade, Steven D. "Literary Composition and Oral Performance in Early Midrashim." *Oral Tradition* 14 (1999): 33–51.

Freedman, David N. "The Law and the Prophets." Pages 250-65 in *Congress Volume: Bonn 1962*. Vetus Testamentum Supplements 9. Leiden: E. J. Brill, 1963.

Friedman, Richard E. *The Exile and the Biblical Narrative: The Formation of the Deuteronomistic and Priestly Works*. Harvard Semitic Monographs 22. Chico: Scholars Press, 1981.

———. "From Egypt to Egypt: Dtr 1 and Dtr 2." Pages 167–92 in *Traditions in Transformation: Turning Points in Biblical Faith*. Edited by B. Halpern and J. D. Levensen. Winona Lake: Eisenbrauns, 1981.

Gammie, John G. and Leo G. Perdue, eds. *The Sage in Israel and the Ancient Near East*. Winona Lake: Eisenbrauns, 1990.

Gerhards, Meik. "Die Begnadigung Jojachins-Überlegungen zu 2 Kön 25,27–30 (mit einem Anhang zu den Nennungen Jojachins auf Zuteilungslisten aus Babylon)." *Biblische Notizen* 94 (1998): 52–67.

Goldman, Yohanan. *Prophétie et royauté au retour de l'exil*. Orbis biblicus et orientalis 118. Freiburg: Universitätsverlag Freiburg, 1992.

Gooding, David W. "An Approach to the Literary and Textual Problems in the David-Goliath Story." Pages 55–86 in *The Story of David and Goliath: Textual and Literary Criticism*. Orbis biblicus et orientalis 73. Fribourg: Éditions Universitaires Fribourg; Göttingen: Vandenhoeck und Ruprecht, 1986.

Gosse, Bernard. "Isa 59,21 et 2 Sam 23,1–7, l'opposition entre les lignées sacredotales et royales à l'époche post-exilique." *Biblische Notizen* 68 (1993): 10–12.

———. "La menace qui vient du nord, les retournements d'oracles contre Babylone et Jérémie 30–31." *Estudios biblicos* 56 (1998): 289–314.

Grabbe, Lester L. "What was Ezra's Mission?" Pages 286–99 in *Second Ttemple Studies: 2. Temple and Community in the Persian Period*. Edited by T. C. Eskenazi and K.

H. Richards. Journal for the Study of the Old Testament: Supplement Series 175. Sheffield Academic Press, 1994.

Granowski, Jan Jaynes. "Jehoichin at the King's Table: A Reading of the Ending of the Second Book of Kings." Pages 173–88 in *Reading between Texts: Intertextuality and the Hebrew Bible*. Edited by D. N. Fewell. Louisville: Westminster/John Knox Press, 1992.

Gray, John. *I & II Kings: A Commentary*. Old Testament Library. Philadelphia: Westminster, 1970.

———. *Joshua, Judges and Ruth*. New Century Bible. London: Nelson, 1967.

Greenspoon, Leonard J. *Textual Studies in the Book of Joshua*. Harvard Semitic Monographs 28. Chico: Scholars Press, 1983.

Haines-Eitzen, Kim. *Guardians of Letters: Literary, Power, and the Transmitters of Early Christian Literature*. Oxford: Oxford University Press, 2000.

Halpern, Baruch. *The First Historians: The Hebrew Bible and History*. San Francisco: Harper & Row, 1988.

Haran, Menahem. "On the Diffusion of Literacy and Schools in Ancient Israel." Pages 81–95 in *Congress Volume: Jerusalem 1986*. Edited by J. A. Emerton. Vetus Testamentum Supplements 40. Leiden: E. J. Brill, 1988.

Harris, Rivkah. "The Female 'Sage'in Mesopotamian Literature (with an Appendix on Egypt)." Pages 3–17 in *The Sage in Israel and the Ancient Near East*. Edited by J. G. Gammie and L. G. Perdue. Winona Lake: Eisenbrauns, 1990.

Heaton, Eric. *The School Tradition of the Old Testament*. Oxford: Clarendon Press, 1994.

Herrmann, Siegfried. *Die prophetischen Heilserwartungen in Alten Testament*. Beihefte zur Zeitschrift für die alttestamentliche Wissenschaft 5.5. Stuttgart: W. Kohlhammer, 1965.

———. *Prophetie und Wirklichkeit in der Epoche des babylonischen Exils*. Stuttgart: Calwer, 1967.

Hobbs, T. R. *2 Kings*. Word Biblical Commentary 18. Waco: Word Books, 1985.

Hoffmann, Hans Detlef. *Reform und Reformen. Untersuchungen zu einem Grundthema der deuteronomistischen Geschichtsschreibung*. Abhandlungen zur Theologie des Alten und Neuen Testaments 66. Zürich: Theologischer Verlag, 1980.

Hoglund, Kenneth G. *Achaemenid Imperial Adminstration in Syria-Palestine and the Missions of Ezra and Nehemiah*. Society of Biblical Literature Dissertation Series 125. Atlanta: Scholar Press, 1992.

Holladay, William L. *Jeremiah*. 2 vols. Hermeneia. Philadelphia: Fortress Press, 1986, 1989.

Hurwitz, Avi. "The Historical Quest for 'Ancient Israel' and the Linguistic Evidence of the Hebrew Bible: Some Methodological Observations." *Vetus Testamentum* 47 (1997): 301–15.

Hyatt, J. Philip. "The Book of Jeremiah." Pages 777-1142 in *Interpreter's Bible*, vol. 5. Edited by G. Buttrick et al. Nashville: Abingdon Press, 1956.

————. "Jeremiah and Deuteronomy." Pages 113–27 in *A Prophet to the Nations: Essays in Jeremiah Studies*. Edited by L. G. Perdue and B. W. Kovacs. Winona Lake: Eisenbrauns, 1984.

Jaffee, Martin S. "Oral Tradition in the Writings of Rabbinic Oral Torah: On Theorizing Rabbinic Orality." *Oral Tradition* 14 (1999): 3–32.

Jamieson-Drake, David W. *Scribes and Schools in Monarchic Judah: A Socio-Archeological Approach*. Journal for the Study of the Old Testament: Supplement Series 109. Sheffield: Almond Press, 1991.

Janzen, David. "The 'Mission' of Ezra and the Persian-Period Temple Community." *Journal of Biblical Literature* 119 (2000): 619–43.

Jones, Gwilyn H. *1 and 2 Kings*. 2 vols. New Century Bible. Grand Rapids: Eerdmans, 1984.

Kelber, Werner. "Scripture and Logos: The Hermeneutics of Communication." Paper presented at the annual meeting of the SBL, Kansas City, November 1991.

Kessler, John. "Reconstructing Haggai's Jerusalem: Demographic and Sociological Considerations and the Quest for an Adequate Methodological Point of Departure." Pages 137–58 in *Every City Shall Be Forsaken: Urbanism and Prophecy in Ancient Israel and the Near East*. Edited by L. Grabbe and R. Haak. Journal for the Study of the Old Testament: Supplement Series 330. Sheffield: Sheffield Academic Press, 2001.

Knauf, Ernst A. "Does 'Deuteronomistic Historiography' (DtrH) Exist?" Pages 388–98 in *Israel Constructs Its History: Deuteronomistic Historiography in Recent Research*. Edited by A. de Pury, T. Römer, and J.-D. Macchi. Journal for the Study of the Old Testament: Supplement Series 306. Sheffield: Sheffield Academic Press, 2000.

Knoppers, Gary N. "Prayer and Propaganda: Solomon's Dedication of the Temple and the Deuteronomist's Program." *Catholic Biblical Quarterly* 57 (1995): 229–54.

————. *Two Nations Under God: The Deuteronomistic History of Solomon and the Dual Monarchies*. 2 vols. Harvard Semitic Monographs 52–53. Atlanta: Scholars Press, 1993, 1994.

Kramer, Samuel N. "The Sage in Sumerian Literature: A Composite Portrait." Pages 31–44 in *The Sage in Israel and the Ancient Near East*. Edited by J. G. Gammie and L. G. Perdue. Winona Lake: Eisenbrauns, 1990.

Kugler, Robert A. "The Deuteronomists and the Latter Prophets." Pages 127–44 in *Those Elusive Deuteronomists: The Phenomenon of Pan-Deuteronomism*. Edited by S. L. McKenzie and L. S. Schearing. Journal for the Study of the Old Testament: Supplement Series 268. Sheffield: Sheffield Academic Press, 1999.

Lemaire, André. "The Sage in School and Temple." Pages 165–81 in *The Sage in Israel and the Ancient Near East*. Edited by J. G. Gammie and L. G. Perdue. Winona Lake: Eisenbrauns, 1990.

Lemke, Niels P. "The Old Testament: A Hellenistic Book?" *Scandinavian Journal of the Old Testament* 7 (1993): 163–93.

Lemke, Werner E. "The Synoptic Problem in the Chronicler's History." *Harvard Theological Review* 58 (1965): 349–63.

Levensen, Jon D. "From Temple to Synagogue: 1 Kings 8." Pages 143–63 in *Traditions in Transformation: Turning Points in Biblical Faith*. Edited by B. Halpern. Winona Lake: Eisenbrauns, 1981.

———. "The Last Four Verses in Kings." *Journal of Biblical Literature* 103 (1983): 353–61.

Linville, James R. *Israel in the Book of Kings: The Past as a Project of Social Identity*. Journal for the Study of the Old Testament: Supplement Series 272. Sheffield: Sheffield Academic Press, 1998.

Lloyd, A. B. "The Inscription of Udjahorresnet: A Collaborator's Testament." *Journal of Egyptian Achaeology* 68 (1982): 166–80.

Lohfink, Norbert, ed. *Das Deuteronomium: Enstellung, Gestalt und Botschaft*. Bibliotheca ephemeridum theologicarum lovaniensium 68. Leuven: Leuven University Press, 1985.

———. "Was There a Deuteronomistic Movement?" Pages 36–66 in *Those Elusive Deuteronomists: The Phenomenon of Pan-Deuteronomism*. Edited by S. L. McKenzie and L. S. Schearing. Journal for the Study of the Old Testament: Supplement Series 268. Sheffield: Sheffield Academic Press, 1999.

Long, Burke O. *1 Kings with an Introduction to Historical Literature*. Forms of the Old Testament Literature 9. Grand Rapids: Eerdmans, 1984.

———. *2 Kings*. Forms of the Old Testament Literature 10. Grand Rapids: Eerdmans, 1991.

Lord, Albert B. *Singer of Tales*. Cambridge: Harvard University Press, 1960.

Lundbom, Jack R. *Jeremiah 1–20*. Anchor Bible 21A. New York: Doubleday, 1999.

Lust, Johan. "Second Thoughts on David and Goliath." Pages 87–91 in *The Story of David and Goliath: Textual and Literary Criticism*. Edited by D. Barthélemy, et al. Orbis biblicus et orientalis 73. Fribourg: Éditions Universitaires Fribourg/Göttingen: Vandenhoeck und Ruprecht, 1986.

———. "The Story of David and Goliath in Hebrew and Greek." Pages 5–18 in *The Story of David and Goliath: Textual and Literary Criticism*. Edited by D. Barthélemy, et al. Orbis biblicus et orientalis 73. Fribourg: Éditions Universitaires Fribourg; Göttingen: Vandenhoeck und Ruprecht, 1986.

Luyten, Jos. "Primeval and Eschatological Overtones in the Song of Moses (Dt 32, 1–43)." Pages 341–47 in *Das Deuteronomium: Entstellung, Gestalt und Botschaft*. Edited by N. Lohfink. Bibliotheca ephemeridum theologicarum lovaniensium 68. Leuven: Leuven University Press, 1985.

Mack-Fisher, Loren R. "The Scribe (and Sage) in the Royal Court at Ugarit." Pages 109–15 in *The Sage in Israel and the Ancient Near East*. Edited by J. G. Gammie and L. G. Perdue. Winona Lake: Eisenbrauns, 1990.

———. "A Survey and Reading Guide to the Didactic Literature of Ugarit Prolegomenon to a Study on the Sage." Pages 67–80 in *The Sage in Israel and the Ancient Near East*. Edited by J. G. Gammie and L. G. Perdue. Winona Lake: Eisenbrauns, 1990.

Martin, James D. *The Book of Judges*. Cambridge Bible Commentary. Cambridge: Cambridge University Press, 1975.

Margalith, Othniel. "The Political Background of Zerubbabel's Mission and the Samaritan Schism." *Vetus Testamentum* 41 (1991): 312–23.

Mason, Rex A. "The Purpose of the 'Editorial Framework' of the Book of Haggai." *Vetus Testamentum* 27 (1977): 413–21.

Mayes, A. D. H. *Deuteronomy*. New Century Bible. Grand Rapids: Eerdmans, 1979.

———. *The Story of Israel between Settlement and Exile: A Redactional Study of the Deuteronomic History*. London: SCM Press, 1983.

McCarter, P. Kyle. *I Samuel*. Anchor Bible 8. Garden City: Doubleday, 1980.

———. *II Samuel*. Anchor Bible 9. Garden City: Doubleday, 1984.

McConville, J. Gordon. "1 Kings VIII 46–53 and the Deuteronomic Hope." *Vetus Testamentum* 42 (1992): 67–79.

———. "Narrative and Meaning in the Books of Kings." *Biblica* 70 (1989): 31–49.

McKane, William. *A Critical and Exegetical Commentary on Jeremiah*. Vol. 1. International Critical Commentary. Edinburgh: T. & T. Clark, 1986.

McKenzie, Steven L. "1 Kings 8: A Sample Study into the Texts of Kings Used by the Chronicler and Translated by the Old Greek." *Bulletin of the International Organization for Septuagint and Cognate Studies* 19 (1986):15–34.

———. *The Chronicler's Use of the Deuteronomic History*. Harvard Semitic Monographs 33. Atlanta: Scholars Press, 1985.

———. "The Prophetic History and the Redaction of Kings." *Hebrew Annual Review* 9 (1985): 203–20.

———. *The Trouble with Kings*. Vetus Testamentum Supplements 42. Leiden: E. J. Brill, 1991.

McKenzie, Steven L. and M. Patrick Graham, eds. *The History of Israel's Traditions: The Heritage of Marin Noth*. Journal for the Study of the Old Testament: Supplement Series 182. Sheffield: Sheffield Academic Press, 1994.

McKenzie, Steven L. and Linda S. Schearing, eds. Pages 116–26 in *Those Elusive Deuteronomists: The Phenomenon of Pan-Deuteronomism*. Journal for the Study of the Old Testament: Supplement Series 268. Sheffield: Sheffield Academic Press, 1996.

Mendecki, Norbert. "Dtn 30, 3–4—nachexilisch?." *Biblische Zeitschrift* 29 (1985): 267–71.

Mettinger, Tryggve N. D. "'The Last Words of David': A Study of Structure and Meaning in II Samuel 23:1–7." *Svensk exegetisk årsbok* 41–42 (1977): 147–56.

Meyers, Carol L. and Eric M. Meyers. *Haggai–Zechariah 1–8*. Anchor Bible 25B. Garden City: Doubleday, 1987.

Miller, J. Maxwell, and Gene M. Tucker. *The Book of Joshua*. Cambridge: Cambridge University Press, 1974.

Mowinckel, Sigmund. *Zur Komposition des Buches Jeremia*. Kristiania: Jacob Dybwad, 1914.

Murray, Donald F. "Of All the Year of Hopes—or Fears? Jehoichin in Babylon (2 Kings 25:27–30)." *Journal of Biblical Literature* 120 (2001): 245–65.

Na'aman, Nadav. "The Contribution of Royal Inscriptions for a Re-Evaluation of the Book of Kings as a Historical Source." *Journal for the Study of the Old Testament* 82 (1999): 13–17.

Naéh, Shlomo. "A New Suggestion regarding 2 Samuel XXIII 7," *Vetus Testamentum* 46 (1996): 260–65.

Nelson, Richard D. *The Double Redaction of the Deuteronomistic History*. Journal for the Study of the Old Testament: Supplement Series 18. Sheffield: Sheffield Academic Press, 1981.

———. *First and Second Kings*. Interpretation: A Bible Commentary for Teaching and Preaching. Atlanta: John Knox, 1987.

Newsom, Carol A. "The Sage in the Literature of Qumran: The Functions of the *Maskil*." Pages 373–82 in *The Sage in Israel and the Ancient Near East*. Edited by J. G. Gammie and L. G. Perdue. Winona Lake: Eisenbrauns, 1990.

Nicholson, Ernest. *The Book of the Prophet Jeremiah. Chapters 1–25*. Cambridge Bible Commentary. Cambridge: Cambridge University Press, 1973.

———. *Preaching to the Exiles: A Study of the Prose Tradition in the Book of Jeremiah*. New York: Schocken Books, 1970.

Niditch, Susan. *Oral World and Written Word: Ancient Israelite Literature*. Louisville: Westminster/John Knox Press, 1996.

Nogalski, James. *Literary Precursors to the Book of the Twelve*. Beihefte zur Zeitschrift für die alttestamentliche Wissenschaft 217. Berlin: Walter de Gruyter, 1993.

Noth, Martin. *The Deuteronomistic History*. Journal for the Study of the Old Testament: Supplement Series 15. Sheffield: Journal for the Study of the Old Testament Press, 1981.

———. *Überlieferungsgeschichtliche Studien*. Tübingen: Niemeyer, 1943.

O'Brien, Mark A. *The Deuteronomistic History Hypothesis: A Reassessment*. Orbis biblicus et orientalis 92. Freiburg: Universitätsverlag Freiburg, 1989.

O'Keefe, Katherine O. *Visible Song: Transitional Literacy in Old English Verse*. Cambridge: Cambridge University Press, 1990.

del Olmo Lete, G. "David's Farewell Oracle (2 Samuel XXIII 1–7): A Literary Analysis." *Vetus Testamentum* 34 (1984): 414–38.

Parker, Simon B. "Did the Authors of the Books of Kings Make Use of the Royal Inscriptions?" *Vetus Testamentum* 50 (2000): 357–78.

Parry, Milman. "A Comparative Study of Diction as One of the Elements of Style in Early Greek Epic Poetry." Pages 421–36 in *The Making of Homeric Verse: The Collected Papers of Milman Parry*. Edited by A. Parry. Oxford: Oxford University Press, 1971.

Person, Raymond F., Jr. *The Kings–Isaiah and Kings–Jeremiah Recensions*. Beihefte zur Zeitschrift für die alttestamentliche Wissenschaft 252. Berlin: Walter de Gruyter, 1997.

————. "A Rolling Corpus and Oral Tradition: A Not-So-Literate Solution to a Highly Literate Problem." Pages 263–71 in *Troubling Jeremiah*. Edited by A. R. P. Diamond, K. M. O'Connor, and L. Stulman. Journal for the Study of the Old Testament: Supplement Series 260. Sheffield: Sheffield Academic Press, 1999.

————. "II Kings 24, 18–25, 30 and Jeremiah 52: A Text-Critical Case Study in the Redaction History of the Deuteronomic History." *Zeitschrift für die alttestamentliche Wissenschaft* 105 (1993): 174–205.

————. *Second Zechariah and the Deuteronomic School*. Journal for the Study of the Old Testament: Supplement Series 167. Sheffield: Sheffield Academic Press, 1993.

Petersen, David L. *Haggai and Zechariah 1–8*. Old Testament Library. Philadelphia: Westminster, 1984.

————. *Late Israelite Prophecy: Studies in Deutero-Prophetic Literature and in Chronicles*. Society of Biblical Literature Monograph Series 23. Missoula: Scholar Press, 1977.

Petersén, Olof. *Archives and Libraries in the Anient Near East 1500–300 B.C.* Bethesda: CDL Press, 1998.

Phillips, Anthony. *Deuteronomy*. Cambridge Bible Commentary. Cambridge: Cambridge University Press, 1973.

Pisano, Stephen. "2 Samuel 5–8 and the Deuteronomist: Textual Criticism or Literary Criticism?" Pages 258–83 in *Israel Constructs Its History: Deuteronomistic Historiography in Recent Research*. Edited by A. de Pury, T. Römer, and J.-D. Macchi. Journal for the Study of the Old Testament: Supplement Series 306. Sheffield: Sheffield Academic Press, 2000.

Polzin, Robert. *David and the Deuteronomist: A Literary Study of the Deuteronomic History*. Bloomington: Indiana University Press, 1993.

————. *Late Biblical Hebrew: Toward an Historial Typology of Biblical Hebrew Prose*. Harvard Semitic Monographs 12. Missoula: Scholars Press, 1976.

————. *Moses and the Deuteronomist*. New York: Seabury, 1980.

————. *Samuel and the Deuteronomist: A Literary Study of the Deuteronomic History*. San Franciso: Harper & Row, 1989.

Provan, Iain W. *Hezekiah and the Book of Kings*. Beihefte zur Zeitschrift für die alttestamentliche Wissenschaft 172. Berlin: Walter de Gruyter, 1988.

Puech, Emile "Les écoles dans l'Israël preexilique: données épigraphiques." Pages 189–203 in *Congress Volume: Jerusalem 1986*. Edited by J. A. Emerton. Vetus Testamentum Supplements 40. Leiden: E. J. Brill, 1988.

von Rad, Gerhard. *Deuteronomy: A Commentary*. Old Testament Library. Philadelphia: Westminster, 1966.

————. *Old Testament Theology, I: The Theology of Israel's Historical Traditions*. Translated by D. M. G. Stalker. New York: Harper & Row, 1962.

————. "The Promised Land and Yahweh's Land in the Hexateuch." Pages 79–93 in *The Problem of the Hexateuch and Other Essays*. Translated by E. W. Trueman Dicken. New York: McGraw-Hill, 1966.

————. *Studies in Deuteronomy*. Studies in Biblical Theology 9. London, SCM Press, 1953.

Richardson, H. Neil. "The Last Words of David: Some Notes on II Samuel 23:1–7." *Journal of Biblical Literature* 90 (1971): 257–66.

Rofé, Alexander. "The Battle of David and Goliath: Folklore, Theology, Eschatology." Pages 117–51 in *Judaic Perspectives on Ancient Israel*. Edited by J. Neusner, A. Levine, and E. S. Frerichs. Philadelphia: Fortress Press, 1987.

————. "The End of the Book of Joshua according to the Septuagint." *Henoch* 4 (1982): 17–32.

————. "The History of the Cities of Refuge in Biblical Law." Pages 205–39 in *Studies in Bible*. Edited by S. Japhet. Scripta hierosolmitana 31. Jerusalem: Magnes Press, 1988.

————. "Joshua 20: Historico-Literary Criticism Illustrated." Pages 131–47 in *Empirical Models for Biblical Criticism*. Edited by J. H. Tigay. Philadelpia: University of Pennsylvania Press, 1985.

————. "The Monotheistic Argumentation in Deuteronomy 4:32–40: Content, Composition, and Text." *Vetus Testamentum* 35 (1985): 434–45.

————. "The Vineyard of Naboth: The Origin and Message of the Story." *Vetus Testamentum* 38 (1988): 89–104.

Römer, Thomas C. "How Did Jeremiah Become a Convert to Deuteronomic Ideology?" Pages 189–99 in *Those Elusive Deuteronomists: The Phenomenon of Pan-Deuteronomism*. Edited by L. S. Schearing and S. L. McKenzie. Journal for the Study of the Old Testament: Supplement Series 268. Sheffield: Sheffield Academic Press, 1999.

————. "Transformations in Deuteronomistic and Biblical Historiography: On 'Book-Finding' and other Literary Strategies." *Zeitschrift für alttestamentliche Wissenschaft* 109 (1997): 10–11.

Russell, James R. "Sages and Scribes at the Courts of Ancient Iran." Pages 141–146 in *The Sage in Israel and the Ancient Near East*. Edited by J. G. Gammie and L. G. Perdue. Winona Lake: Eisenbrauns, 1990.

Schams, Christine. *Jewish Scribes in the Second Temple Period*. Journal for the Study of the Old Testament: Supplement Series 291. Sheffield: Sheffield Academic Press, 1998.

Schenker, Adrian. "Jeroboam and the Division of the Kingdom in the Ancient Septuagint: LXX 3 Kingdoms 12:24a–z, MT 1 Kings 11–12; 14 and the Deuteronomistic History." Pages 214–57 in *Israel Constructs Its History: Deuteronomistic Historiography in Recent Research*. Edited by A. de Pury, T. Römer, and J.-D. Macchi. Journal for the Study of the Old Testament: Supplement Series 306. Sheffield: Sheffield Academic Press, 2000.

Schmidt, Werner H. "Die deuteronomische Redaktion des Amosbuches: Zu den theologischen Unterschieden zwischen dem Prophetenwort und seinem Sammler." *Zeitschrift für die alttestamentliche Wissenschaft* 77 (1965): 168–93.

Schniedewind, William M. "History and interpretation: The Religion of Ahab and Manasseh in the Book of Kings." *Catholic Biblical Quarterly* 55 (1993): 649–61.

———. "The Problem with Kings: Study of the Deuteronomistic History." *Religious Studies Review* 22 (1996): 25.

Shenkel, James D. *Chronology and Recensional Development in the Greek Text of Kings.* Harvard Semitic Monographs 1. Cambridge: Harvard University Press, 1968.

Sjöberg, Å. W. "The Old Babylonian Edubba." Pages 159–79 in *Sumeriological Studies in Honor of Thorkild Jacobsen on His Seventieth Birthday.* Edited by S. Lieberman. Assyriological Studies 20. Chicago: University of Chicago Press, 1975.

Smend, Rudolf. *Die Entstehung des Alten Testaments.* Stuttgart: Verlag W. Kohlhammer, 1981.

Soggin, J. Alberto. *Joshua: A Commentary.* Old Testament Library. Philadelphia: Westminster Press, 1972.

Spieckermann, Hermann. *Juda unter Assur in der Sargonidenzeit.* Forschungen zur Religion und Literatur des Alten und Neuen Testaments 129. Göttingen: Vandenhoeck und Ruprecht, 1982.

Steiner, Richard C. "The *MBQR* at Qumran, the *EPISKOPOS* in the Athenian Empire, and the Meaning of *LBQR'* in Ezra 7:14: On the Relation of Ezra's Mission to the Persian Legal Project." *Journal of Biblical Literature* 120 (2001): 623–646.

Stock, Brian. *The Implications of Literacy: Written Language and Models of Interpretation in the Eleventh and Twelfth Centuries.* Princeton: Princeton University Press, 1983.

———. *Listening for the Text: On the Uses of the Past.* Baltimore: John Hopkins University Press, 1990.

Stoebe, Hans J. "Die Goliathperikope 1 Sam 17, 1–18, 5 und die Text-Form der Septuaginta." *Vetus Testamentum* 6 (1956): 397–413.

Stulman, Louis. *The Prose Sermons of the Book of Jeremiah: A Redescription of the Correspondence with Deuteronomistic Literature in Light of Recent Text-Critical Research.* Society of Biblical Literature Dissertation Series 83. Atlanta: Scholars Press, 1986.

Swanson, Steven R. "Zechariach 1–8 and the Deuteronomistic Stream of Tradition." Paper Presented at the annual meeting of the SBL. Chicago, Ill., November 1988.

Sweeney, Marvin A. "Davidic Polemics in the Book of Judges." *Vetus Testamentum* 46 (1997): 517–29.

Sweet, Ronald F. G. "The Sage in Mesopotamian Palace and Royal Courts." Pages 99–107 in *The Sage in Israel and the Ancient Near East.* Edited by J. G. Gammie and L. G. Perdue. Winona Lake: Eisenbrauns, 1990.

Talmon, Shemaryahu. "Aspects of the Textual Transmission of the Bible in the Light of the Qumran Manuscripts." Pages 226–63 in *Qumran and the History of the Biblical Text.* Edited by F. M. Cross and S. Talmon. Cambridge: Harvard University Press, 1975.

———. "The Community of the Renewed Covenant: Between Judaism and Christianity." Pages 3–24 in *The Community of the Renewed Covenant: The Notre*

Dame Symposium of the Dead Sea Scrolls. Edited by E. Ulrich and J. VanderKam. Notre Dame: University of Notre Dame, 1994.

⸻. "Observations on Variant Readings in the Isaiah Scroll (1QIsaª)." Pages 117–30 in *The World of Qumran from Within: Collected Studies*. Jerusalem: Magnes Press, 1989.

⸻. "Polemic and Apology in Biblical Historiography—2 Kings 17:24–41." Pages 57–68 in *The Creation of Sacred Literature: Composition and Redaction of the Biblical Text*. Edited by R. E. Friedman. Berkeley: University of California Press, 1981.

⸻. "Synonymous Readings in the Textual Traditions of the Old Testament." *Scripta hierosolymitana* 8 (1961): 335–83.

Talshir, Zipora. *The Alternative Story of the Division of the Kingdom. 2 Kingdoms 12:24a–z*. Jerusalem Biblical Studies 6. Jerusalem: Simor, 1993.

Thiel, Winfried. *Die deuteronomische Redaktion von Jeremia 1–25*. Wissenschaftliche Monographien zum Alten und Neuen Testament 41. Neukirchen: Neukirchener Verlag, 1973.

⸻. *Die deuteronomische Redaktion von Jeremia 26–45*. Wissenschaftliche Monographien zum Alten und Neuen Testament 52. Neukirchen: Neukirchener Verlag, 1981.

Thomas, Rosalind. *Oral Tradition and Written Records in Classical Athens*. Cambridge: Cambridge University Press, 1989.

Tov, Emanuel. "Biblical Texts as Reworked in Some Qumran Manuscripts with Special Attention to 4QRP and 4QParaGen–Exod." Pages 111–34 in *The Community of the Renewed Covenant: The Notre Dame Symposium of the Dead Sea Scrolls*. Edited by E. Ulrich and J. VanderKam. Notre Dame: University of Notre Dame, 1994.

⸻. "The Composition of I Samuel 16–18 in the Light of the Septuagint Version." Pages 97–130 in *Empirical Models for Biblical Criticism*. Edited by J. Tigay. Philadelphia: University of Pennsylvania Press, 1985.

⸻. "The Growth of the Book of Joshua in the Light of the Evidence of the LXX Translation." Pages 321–39 in *Studies of the Bible*. Edited by S. Japhet. Scripta hierosolymitana 31. Jerusalem: Magnes Press, 1986.

⸻. "L'incidence de la critique textuelle sur la critique littéraire dans la livre de Jérémie."*Revue biblique* 79 (1972): 189–99.

⸻. "The Literary History of the Book of Jeremiah in the Light of its Textual History." Pages 211–37 in *Empirical Models for Biblical Criticism*. Edited by J. H. Tigay. Philadelphia: University of Pennsylvania Press, 1985.

⸻. "The Nature of the Difference between MT and LXX." Pages 19–46 in *The Story of David and Goliath: Textual and Literary Criticism*. Edited by D. Barthélemy, et al. Orbis biblicus et orientalis 73. Fribourg: Éditions Universitaires Fribourg; Göttingen: Vandenhoeck und Ruprecht, 1986.

⸻. "Scribal Practices Reflected in the Documents from the Judean Desert and in the Rabbinic Literature: A Comparative Study." Pages 383–403 in *Texts, Temples, and Traditions: A Tribute to Menahem Haran.* Edited by M. V. Fox. Winona Lake: Eisenbrauns, 1996.

———. "Some Aspects of the Textual and Literary History of the Book of Jeremiah." Pages 145–67 in *Le livre de Jérémie: le prophete et son milieu. Les oracles et leur transmission.* Edited by P.-M. Bogaert. Bibliotheca ephemeridum theologicarum lovaniensium 54. Leuven: Leuven University Press, 1981.

———. "The Textual Base of the Corrections in the Biblical Texts Found at Qumran." Pages 299–314 in *The Dead Sea Scrolls: Forty Years of Research.* Edited by D. Dimant and U. Rappaport. Studies on the Texts of the Desert of Judah 10; Leiden: E. J. Brill, 1992.

———. *Textual Criticism of the Hebrew Bible.* Minneapolis: Fortress Press, 1992.

Trebolle Barrera, Julio C. "Old Latin, Old Greek and Old Hebrew in the Book of Kings (1 Ki. 18:25 and 2 Ki. 20:11)." *Textus* 13 (1986): 85–94.

———. "Redaction, Recension, and Midrash in the Books of Kings." *Bulletin of the International Organization for Septuagint and Cognate Studies* 15 (1982): 12–35.

———. *Salomón y Jeroboán. Historia de la recensión y redacción de 1 Reyes, 2–12, 14.* Salmanca and Jerusalem: Institute Español Biblica Arqueologico/Universidad Pontificia, 1980.

———. "The Story of David and Goliath (1 Sam 17–18): Textual Variants and Literary Composition." *Bulletin of the International Organization for Septuagint and Cognate Studies* 23 (1990): 16–30.

———. "The Text-Critical Use of the Septuagint in the Books of Kings." Pages 285–99 in *VII Congress of the International Organization for Septuagint and Cognate Studies, Leuven, 1989.* Edited by C. E. Cox. Society of Biblical Literature Septuagint and Cognate Studies 31. Atlanta: Scholars Press, 1991.

Ulrich, Eugene. *The Dead Sea Scrolls and the Origins of the Bible.* Grand Rapids: Eerdemans, 1999.

———. *The Qumran Text of Samuel and Josephus.* Harvard Semitic Monographs 19. Missoula: Scholars Press, 1978.

van der Kooij, Arie. "Zum Verhältnis von Textkritik und Literarkritik: Überlegungen anhand einiger Beispiele." Pages 185–202 in *Congress Volume.* Vetus Testamentum Supplements. Leiden: E. J. Brill, 1997.

Van Seters, John. "Histories and Historians of the Ancient Near East: The Israelites'." *Orientalia* 50 (1981): 137–85.

Van Seters, John. *In Search of History.* New Haven: Yale University Press, 1983.

Vanderhooft, David. "New Evidence Pertaining to the Transition from Neo-Babylonian to Achaemenid Administration in Palestine." In *Yahwism after the Exile.* Edited by R. Albertz and B. Becking. Studies in Theology and Religion. Assen-Maastricht: Van Gorcum, forthcoming 2002.

VanderKam, James. *The Dead Sea Scrolls Today.* Grand Rapids: Eerdemans, 1994.

———. "Ezra–Nehemiah or Ezra and Nehemiah?" Pages 55–75 in *Priests, Prophets and Scribes: Essays on the Formation and Heritage of Second Temple Judaism in Honour of Joseph Blenkinsopp.* Edited by E. Ulrich, et al. Journal for the Study of the Old Testament: Supplement Series 149. Sheffield: Sheffield Academic Press, 1992.

Vanoni, Gottfried. "Beobachtungen zur deuteronomistischen Terminologie in 2 Kön 23, 25–25, 30." Pages 357–62 in *Das Deuteronomium*. Edited by N. Lohfink. Bibliotheca ephemeridum theologicarum lovaniensium 68. Leuven: Leuven University Press, 1985.

Veijola, Timo. *Die ewige Dynastie: David und die Entstehung seiner Dynastie nach der deuteronomistischen Darstellung*. Annales Academiae scientiarum fennicae 193. Helsinki: Suomaleinen Tiedeakatemia, 1975.

Vermes, Geza. *The Dead Sea Scrolls in English*. Sheffield: Sheffield Academic Press, 1987.

Viviano, Pauline A. "2 Kings 17: Rhetorical and Form-Critical Analysis." *Catholic Biblical Quarterly* 49 (1987): 548–59.

Weinfeld, Moshe. *Deuteronomy and the Deuteronomic School*. Oxford: Clarendon Press, 1972.

Weippert, Helga. "Die 'deuteronomistischen' Beurteilungen der Könige von Israel und Jusa und das Problem der Redaktion der Königsbücher." *Biblica* 53 (1972): 301–39.

———. *Die Prosareden des Jeremiasbuches*. Beihefte zur Zeitschrift für die alttestamentliche Wissenschaft 132. Berlin: Walter de Gruyter, 1973.

Whybray, Roger N. "The Sage in the Israelite Royal Court." Pages 133–39 in *The Sage in Israel and the Ancient Near East*. Edited by J. G. Gammie and L. G. Perdue. Winona Lake: Eisenbrauns, 1990.

Williams, Ronald J. "The Sage in Egyptian Literature." Pages 19–30 in *The Sage in Israel and the Ancient Near East*. Edited by J. G. Gammie and L. G. Perdue. Winona Lake: Eisenbrauns, 1990.

———. "Scribal Training in Ancient Egypt." *Journal of the American Oriental Society* 92 (1972): 214–21.

Williamson, Hugh G. M. "The Death of Josiah and the Continuing Development of the Deuteronomic History." *Vetus Testamentum* 32 (1982): 242–48.

———. "Reliving the Death of Josiah: A Reply to C. T. Begg." *Vetus Testamentum* 37 (1987): 9–15.

Wilson, Robert R. "Who Was the Deuteronomist?" Pages 67–82 in *Those Elusive Deuteronomists: The Phenomenon of Pan-Deuteronomism*. Edited by S. L. McKenzie and L. S. Schearing. Journal for the Study of the Old Testament: Supplement Series 268. Sheffield: Sheffield Academic Press, 1999.

Wolff, Hans Walter. *Haggai: A Commentary*. Minneapolis: Augsburg, 1988.

———. *Hosea*. Hermeneia. Translated by G. Stansell. Philadelphia: Fortress, Press, 1974.

———. "The Kerygma of the Deuteronomic Historical Work." Pages 83–100 in *The Vitality of Old Testament Traditions*. Edited by W. Brueggemann and H. W. Wolff. Translated by F. C. Prussner. Atlanta: John Knox, 1975.

Woudstra, Marten H. *The Book of Joshua*. Grand Rapids: Eerdmans, 1981.

Würthwein, Ernst. *Die Bücher der Könige*, 2 vols. Das Alte Testament Deutsch 11,1–2. Göttingen: Vandenhoeck und Ruprecht, 1977, 1984.

―――. *Studien zum deuteronomistischen Geschichtswerk*. Beihefte zur Zeitschrift für die alttestamentliche Wissenschaft 227. Berlin: Walter de Gruyter, 1994.

Zenger, E. "Die deuteronomistische Interpretation der Rahabilitierung Jojachins." *Biblische Zeitschrift* 12 (1968): 16–30.

AUTHOR INDEX

171